Words Aptly Spoken
SHORT STORIES

an introduction to short story classics

SECOND EDITION

compiled and edited by Jen Greenholt

Jen Greenholt, *Words Aptly Spoken* Series
An Introduction to Short Story Classics
First edition published 2005. Second edition published 2011.

©2011 Classical Conversations® MultiMedia. All rights reserved.

Published by Classical Conversations, Inc.
P.O. Box 909
West End, NC 27376
www.ClassicalConversations.com | www.ClassicalConversationsBooks.com

Cover design by Classical Conversations. Image: Hand-colored lithograph by Serge Goursat, *Caricature of man with hands tucked in his pants standing outside theatrer* (sic), 1893. Courtesy Library of Congress, reproduction number LC-USZC4-1268.

Printed in the United States of America.
All rights reserved. No part of this publication may be reproduced, stored in a retrieval system, or transmitted in any form by any means, electronic, mechanical, photocopy, recording, or otherwise, without prior permission of the author, except as provided by USA copyright law.

ISBN: 978-0-9829845-3-6

Acknowledgments

Many thanks to the editors at Classical Conversations:

The opportunity to read and ponder the great stories in this collection has been a privilege. Your input and advice have been gifts throughout the process.

Foreword

When you read a good story, what does it make you feel? What sets a classic tale apart from the rest? Is it a vague, happy feeling that you get when you reach, "The End"? Or is it, perhaps, a more concrete reaction—the story had an important message that made you think? Whatever the reason, there is something special about a story that can both provide enjoyment and entertainment for its readers and help them to see or understand a deeper message.

Many authors have the priceless gift of being able to combine these two aspects in their work. In the pages that follow, you will have a chance to enjoy the works of writers like Nathaniel Hawthorne, Hans Christian Andersen, O. Henry, and more. This short story collection provides an introduction to classic literature in a slightly less threatening form—the short story.

Being able to read works of classic literature and understand what makes them classics is an invaluable skill that can carry you from the classroom to educated society and beyond. However, in order to develop that skill, you need to begin at the beginning. Sometimes the best way to do that is to think like a writer as well as a reader. For this reason, *Words Aptly Spoken: Short Stories* focuses on the basic elements that make up a story. Through reading and writing exercises, this guide will help you understand what features make up a polished short story.

As with other collections in the *Words Aptly Spoken* series, *Short Stories* contains a series of questions about each work being studied. Review Questions help you identify the basic plot, characters, setting, and message of the book. Thought Questions take the themes and ideas raised by each author and help you apply them to other, more familiar situations.

Sometimes it is easier to learn by doing, and *Short Stories* gives you tools to practice your own creativity. Writing Practices at the end of each section will give you the opportunity to imitate good writing skills. Thinking about a story from a writer's perspective will help you recognize strong and weak elements in other authors' works, but it also makes reading and writing about classic literature a more fulfilling experience.

All this being said, take a deep breath, and get ready to plunge into some great short stories.

Table of Contents

A Note for Parents: Tools for the Journey 9
 Story Comprehension Questions 11

STUDY GUIDES

Where Did That Come From? Plot Twists and Surprise Endings 13
 "A Man and the Snake," Ambrose Bierce 15
 "The Notorious Jumping Frog of Calaveras County," Mark Twain ... 21
 "The Cop and the Anthem," O. Henry 27

Can You Please Focus? Story Focus 33
 "Little Girls Wiser than Men," Leo Tolstoy 35

What Happened to Kansas? Settings 39
 "The Mansion," Henry Van Dyke 41

Have We Met? Character Development 59
 "The Hiltons' Holiday," Sarah Orne Jewett 61
 "The Schoolboy's Story," Charles Dickens 73

What's Cooking? Plot 83
 "The Celestial Railroad," Nathaniel Hawthorne 85
 "The Necklace," Henri Guy de Maupassant 97

Do I Sense a Connection? Theme 105
 "God Lives," Hans Christian Andersen 107
 "The Teapot," Hans Christian Andersen 109
 "Father Zossima's Brother," Fyodor Dostoevsky 111
 "The Startling Painting," Fyodor Dostoevsky 115

Was it a Dark and Stormy Night? Mood 119
 "The Casket Scenes" from *The Merchant of Venice*,
  William Shakespeare 121
 "Iago's intentions" from *Othello*, William Shakespeare 133
 "The Pardoner's Tale," Geoffrey Chaucer 141
 Paradise Lost, Book 1, John Milton 155
 "Christmas Bells," Henry Wadsworth Longfellow 175

May I Ask Who is Speaking? Point of View 179
 "The Hammer of God," G.K. Chesterton 181
 "The Tell-Tale Heart," Edgar Allan Poe 193

What Does It Have To Do With Me? Moral Application 199
    "Stolen Fruit," Saint Augustine 201
    "Alypius and the Gladiators," Saint Augustine 203

Looking Back, Looking Forward 207

Bibliography 209
Photo Credits 211

A Note for Parents: Tools for the Journey

If you have ever heard Shakespeare performed before a live audience and marveled at the ease with which the words flowed from the actors' lips; if you have ever envied people who can call on Milton, Dickens, Joyce, and Lewis to lend eloquence to their argument; if you have skimmed a list of the hundred greatest novels of all time and winced as you remembered struggling to finish *The Grapes of Wrath* in high school—you may think that the great conversations of literature are forever closed to you.

The good news is, they're not! Whether you are a student, an adult, a parent, a child, or all of the above, you have the capability to train yourself not only to read great literature, but also to share its beauty, truth, and joy with others.

Although most people learn to read as children, the art of deliberately engaging with the content and ideas of a novel or short story requires ongoing practice.

The *Words Aptly Spoken* series is based on the classical model of education,[1] which breaks learning into three natural stages: grammar, dialectic, and rhetoric. In the grammar stage, you learn the vocabulary of a subject. In the dialectic stage, you learn to develop logical arguments and analyze others' ideas. In the rhetoric stage, you explore the consequences of ideas as you form and express your own. This guide will help you as you begin to apply the classical model to the study of literature.

Why Short Stories?

As a parent or adult, you might be asking, "But why short stories? Aren't they inferior to novels? How hard can it be to read a short story, or write one? How much can you really say in a thousand words?" The short answer? A lot.

As a developing reader and writer, however, short stories have a very specific advantage over longer books: they are short. It sounds obvious, but it's actually important. Because the stories in this collection are short in length, you can easily read them multiple times. Whereas you might need a week to complete a four hundred-page novel, you might be able to read a four-page story twice in a single hour. As a result, you can pick out different pieces of the story each time and focus on the details.

For short stories as well as long novels, one of the characteristics of a classic is that you can read it over and over again. The first time, you read to find out what happens. The second time, you might notice what events move the plot forward. The third time, you might see how the characters grow and change. The fourth time, you might pick out individual descriptive words that create a specific mood in a scene. The fifth time might reveal similarities between this story and others you have read.

How to Use This Book

Despite popular belief, reading is not wholly instinctive. Because comprehension, analysis, and critical thinking require practice, each story in this collection comes with a set of questions designed to give structure and guidance to your reading. Treat these questions

---

[1] See Dorothy Sayers' essay, "The Lost Tools of Learning."

as tools not only for reading, but also for writing, leading discussion, and sharing your ideas with others.

Review Questions pull out the **grammar** for each selection: Who is it about? (Characters) What happens? (Plot) Where does it take place? (Setting) What is the message? (Theme) What is the scope or time frame? (Focus), and so on. For readers of all ages, repeatedly asking these questions will generate good reading habits; eventually, as you read, your brain will automatically take note of this information and store it for future use.

Thought Questions are an exercise in **dialectic**, taking the basic elements from the Review Questions and encouraging you to analyze that information in light of other knowledge. As you become more familiar with the building blocks of a story, you should begin to ask questions of your own. What does this mean for me? How should I respond to this argument? You can use the Thought Questions as a jump-start for your own thinking process, as training tools for leading discussion, or as topics for essays and book reports.

You may not be able to answer the questions after just one reading, and because these stories are short, you should take time to read each story at least twice. The first time should be for general enjoyment and to get a feel for the author's writing style. The next reading should look a little deeper at the underlying issues the author confronts.

A word of caution: don't merely "look up" the answers to the questions and skim the rest of the story. Once established, this habit will make it harder for you to read and understand more difficult books. After all, self-respecting Olympic runners know that they would be at a severe disadvantage in the actual games if they secretly completed only half of their daily training regimen. In the same way, the results you achieve as a reader will reflect the quality and consistency of your training.

Another important part of your training as a reader is learning to think about literature from the perspective of a writer. For this reason, *Short Stories* is divided into sections dealing with different elements of a good story: plot, characters, point of view, and so on. Each section begins with a short overview of the topic and suggested questions to keep in mind as you read one or more stories that demonstrate different approaches to that topic.

Each section ends with a writing practice that will help you to develop your creativity and begin to think like a short story writer. Although a particular exercise is suggested for each story studied, if you would rather practice a different skill or work on several at once, feel free to do so.

The Journey in Perspective

One of the most important things to remember as you start—or resume—this journey is that it doesn't happen overnight. The art of leading and sharing in conversations about classical literature takes a lifetime to refine. You must begin with the fundamentals: learning to read closely, taking notes, and developing the vocabulary to structure your ideas and explain them to others (**grammar**). You must practice: adding new techniques, revising old ones, and comparing the results (**dialectic**). And then you will be ready to start all over again as you share the joy of the journey with others around you (**rhetoric**). Let's get started!

Story Comprehension Questions

Although every story is different, all authors must consider certain common elements. A good reader thinks like a writer and vice versa, so whether reading or writing, you will benefit from thinking about the parts of a story (**grammar**).

In the nineteenth century, a German writer named Gustav Freytag developed a model he used to analyze plays. Here is a modified version that may help you visualize the relationship between the different elements of a story:

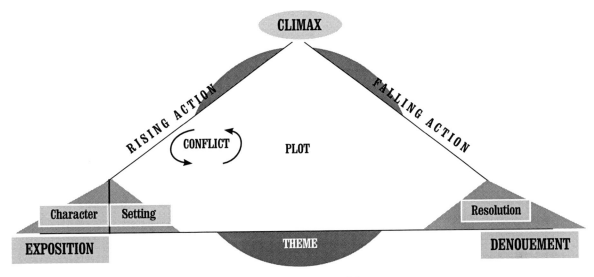

Freytag's Pyramid

As you read, you should keep certain questions in the back of your mind to ensure that you understand what's going on and can pick out the different features of a story. Each section in this book will focus on one set of questions, but to develop good reading habits, refer back to this page frequently to make sure you can answer all the questions for each story you read.

Focus

- What is the time span of the story?
- Does the author give background information on the characters? The setting? The plot?
- How is background information given (flashbacks, references by characters or narrator)?
- Is the author able to wrap up all loose ends satisfactorily by the conclusion of the story?

Setting

- Where does the story take place? How do you know?

- How does the author describe the setting? What does the setting look like?
- What kind of emotions does the setting evoke? Spooky? Normal? Funny? Why?
- Is the setting important to the story? Why?
- Does the author assume you are familiar with the place, or does he or she provide that information?

Characters

- How many characters are in the story?
- What are their names?
- What does each character look like?
- Does the author make you like or dislike any of the characters? How? Why?
- What is the major character trait of each person? How does the author reveal that to you?
- Are the characters believable? Do they act the way you expect or are they complicated?
- Do any of the characters change in the course of the story? How and why?

Plot

- Outline the specific chain of events.
- How is the story introduced?
- Is there a rising action?
- Is there a climax or turning point?
- Is there a falling action?
- How does the story conclude?
- How is the plot revealed (through action, conversation, or the author's descriptions)?
- Does everything happen in sequence, or are there flashbacks?
- Does the author lay out the plot clearly, or are there events you must guess at?

Theme/Moral

- What is the theme of the story? Love? Greed? Sacrifice?
- What is the moral of the story?
- What is the author trying to reveal about human nature?
- What is the worldview of each of the characters?
- What do you think might be the author's worldview? What makes you think so?

Your Perspective

- Did you like the story?
- What would have made it more interesting?
- How would you have changed any of the characters? Why?
- Which character did you like best? Least?
- Could you relate to any aspect of the story? How?

Where Did That Come From?
PLOT TWISTS and SURPRISE ENDINGS

Have you ever heard someone say, "That movie (or book) was way too predictable"? If you have, then you have heard a very common complaint. Think about it: people have been writing books for centuries. Writing a story with a completely original plot is highly unlikely. So what keeps an author's work from becoming "just another Cinderella story"?

For some authors, the answer lies in plot twists and surprise endings, which lead you to expect one type of ending and then at the last moment go a different direction. These devices keep the reader off balance and interested in what happens next. The following three stories are written by authors who excelled at using plot twists. As you read each story, remind yourself of the following questions about plots:

- How is the story introduced?
- Is there a rising action?
- Is there a climax or turning point?
- Is there a falling action?
- How does the story conclude?
- How is the plot revealed (through action, conversation, or the author's descriptions)?
- Does everything happen in sequence, or are there flashbacks?
- Does the author lay out the plot clearly, or are there events you must guess at?

Some stories with unexpected endings—like the ones in this section—invite you to be a detective, especially as you read them a second time and look for the hints you might have missed the first time. Sometimes, though, the author deliberately avoids giving clues to his or her ending. As you read, also consider the relationship between an author and a reader. As a reader, is it more satisfying to be able to predict the ending of a story or to be surprised? Put yourself in the author's position, and think through what your own approach to the element of surprise would be.

"A Man and the Snake"
Ambrose Bierce

Ambrose Bierce (1842-1914) was an American newspaper columnist, novelist, and short story writer. He was known as a very cynical writer, who, in the tradition of Edgar Allan Poe, took a very dark position on the nature of man. "A Man and the Snake," first published in 1891, is one of his earlier stories. One theme of this story is the distinction between reality and the things that the mind creates, especially as a result of outside influences.

I.

It is of veritabyll report, and attested of so many that there be nowe of wyse and learned none to gaynsaye it, that ye serpente hys eye hath a magnetick propertie that whosoe falleth into its svasion is drawn forwards in despyte of his wille, and perisheth miserabyll by ye creature hys byte.

Stretched at ease upon a sofa, in gown and slippers, Harker Brayton smiled as he read the foregoing sentence in old Morryster's *Marvells of Science*. "The only marvel in the matter," he said to himself, "is that the wise and learned in Morryster's day should have believed such nonsense as is rejected by most of even the ignorant in ours."

A train of reflections followed—for Brayton was a man of thought—and he unconsciously lowered his book without altering the direction of his eyes. As soon as the volume had gone below the line of sight, something in an obscure corner of the room recalled his attention to his surroundings. What he saw, in the shadow under his bed, were two small points of light, apparently about an inch apart. They might have been reflections of the gas jet above him, in metal nail heads; he gave them but little thought and resumed his reading.

A moment later something—some impulse which it did not occur to him to analyze—impelled him to lower the book again and seek for what he saw before. The points of light were still there. They seemed to have become brighter than before, shining with a greenish luster which he had not at first observed. He thought, too, that they might have moved a trifle—were somewhat nearer. They were still too much in the shadow, however, to reveal their nature and origin to an indolent attention, and he resumed his reading. Suddenly something in the text suggested a thought which made him start and drop the book for the third time to the side of the sofa, whence, escaping from his hand, it fell sprawling to the floor, back upward.

Brayton, half-risen, was staring intently into the obscurity beneath the bed, where the points of light shone with, it seemed to him, an added fire. His attention was now fully aroused, his gaze eager and imperative. It disclosed, almost directly beneath the foot rail of the bed, the coils of a large serpent—the points of light were its eyes! Its horrible head, thrust flatly forth from the innermost coil and resting upon the outermost, was directed straight toward him, the definition of the wide, brutal jaw and the idiot-like forehead serving to show the direction of its malevolent gaze. The eyes were no longer merely luminous points; they looked into his own with a meaning, a malign significance.

II.

A snake in a bedroom of a modern city dwelling of the better sort is, happily, not so common a phenomenon as to make explanation altogether needless. Harker Brayton, a bachelor of thirty-five, a scholar, idler, and something of an athlete, rich, popular, and of sound health, had returned to San Francisco from all manner of remote and unfamiliar countries. His tastes, always a trifle luxurious, had taken on an added exuberance from long privation; and the resources of even the Castle Hotel being inadequate for their perfect gratification, he had gladly accepted the hospitality of his friend, Dr. Druring, the distinguished scientist.

Dr. Druring's house, a large, old-fashioned one in what was now an obscure quarter of the city, had an outer and visible aspect of reserve. It plainly would not associate with the contiguous elements of its altered environment, and appeared to have developed some of the eccentricities which come of isolation. One of these was a "wing," conspicuously irrelevant in point of architecture and no less rebellious in the matter of purpose; for it was a combination of laboratory, menagerie, and museum. It was here that the doctor indulged the scientific side of his nature in the study of such forms of animal life as engaged his interest and comforted his taste—which, it must be confessed, ran rather to the lower forms. For one of the higher types nimbly and sweetly to recommend itself unto his gentle senses, it had at least to retain certain rudimentary characteristics allying it to such "dragons of the prime" as toads and snakes. His scientific sympathies were distinctly reptilian; he loved nature's vulgarians and described himself as the Zola of zoology.

His wife and daughters, not having the advantage to share his enlightened curiosity regarding the works and ways of our ill-starred fellow-creatures, were, with needless austerity, excluded from what he called the Snakery, and doomed to companionship with their own kind; though, to soften the rigors of their lot, he had permitted them, out of his great wealth, to outdo the reptiles in the gorgeousness of their surroundings and to shine with a superior splendor.

Architecturally, and in point of "furnishing," the Snakery had a severe simplicity befitting the humble circumstances of its occupants, many of whom, indeed, could not safely have been entrusted with the liberty which is necessary to the full enjoyment of luxury, for they had the troublesome peculiarity of being alive. In their own apartments, however, they were under as little personal restraint as was compatible with their protection from the baneful habit of swallowing one another; and, as Brayton had thoughtfully been apprised, it was more than a tradition that some of them had at divers times been found in parts of the premises where it would have embarrassed them to explain their presence. Despite the Snakery and its uncanny associations—to which, indeed, he gave little attention—Brayton found life at the Druring mansion very much to his mind.

III.

Beyond a smart shock of surprise and a shudder of mere loathing, Mr. Brayton was not greatly affected. His first thought was to ring the call bell and bring a servant; but, although the bell cord dangled within easy reach, he made no movement toward it; it had occurred to his mind that the act might subject him to the suspicion of fear, which he certainly did not feel. He was more keenly conscious of the incongruous nature of the situation than affected by its perils; it was revolting, but absurd.

The reptile was of a species with which Brayton was unfamiliar. Its length he could only conjecture; the body at the largest visible part seemed about as thick as his forearm. In what way was it dangerous, if in any way? Was it venomous? Was it a constrictor? His knowledge of nature's danger signals did not enable him to say; he had never deciphered the code.

If not dangerous, the creature was at least offensive. It was *de trop*—"matter out of place"— an impertinence. The gem was unworthy of the setting. Even the barbarous taste of our time and country, which had loaded the walls of the room with pictures, the floor with furniture, and the furniture with bric-a-brac, had not quite fitted the place for this bit of the savage life of the jungle. Besides—insupportable thought!—the exhalations of its breath mingled with the atmosphere which he himself was breathing!

These thoughts shaped themselves with greater or less definition in Brayton's mind, and begot action. The process is what we call consideration and decision. It is thus that we are wise and unwise. It is thus that the withered leaf in an autumn breeze shows greater or less intelligence than its fellows, falling upon the land or upon the lake. The secret of human action is an open one—something contracts our muscles. Does it matter if we give to the preparatory molecular changes the name of will?

Brayton rose to his feet and prepared to back softly away from the snake, without disturbing it, if possible, and through the door. People retire so from the presence of the great, for greatness is power, and power is a menace. He knew that he could walk backward without obstruction, and find the door without error. Should the monster follow, the taste which had plastered the walls with paintings had consistently supplied a rack of murderous Oriental weapons from which he could snatch one to suit the occasion. In the meantime the snake's eyes burned with a more pitiless malevolence than ever.

Brayton lifted his right foot free of the floor to step backward. That moment he felt a strong aversion to doing so. "I am accounted brave," he murmured; "is bravery, then, no more than pride? Because there are none to witness the shame shall I retreat?"

He was steadying himself with his right hand upon the back of a chair, his foot suspended. "Nonsense!" he said aloud; "I am not so great a coward as to fear to seem to myself afraid."

He lifted the foot a little higher by slightly bending the knee, and thrust it sharply to the floor—an inch in front of the other! He could not think how that occurred. A trial with the left foot had the same result; it was again in advance of the right. The hand upon the chair back was grasping it; the arm was straight, reaching somewhat backward. One might have seen that he was reluctant to lose his hold. The snake's malignant head was still thrust forth from the inner coil as before, the neck level. It had not moved, but its eyes were now electric sparks, radiating an infinity of luminous needles.

The man had an ashy pallor. Again he took a step forward, and another, partly dragging the chair, which, when finally released, fell upon the floor with a crash. The man groaned; the snake made neither sound nor motion, but its eyes were two dazzling suns. The reptile itself was wholly concealed by them. They gave off enlarging rings of rich and vivid colors, which at their greatest expansion successively vanished like soap bubbles; they seemed to approach his very face, and anon were an immeasurable distance away. He heard, somewhere, the continual throbbing of a great drum, with desultory bursts of far music, inconceivably sweet, like the tones of an aeolian harp. He knew it for the sunrise melody of Memnon's statue, and thought he stood in the Nileside reeds, hearing, with exalted sense, that immortal anthem through the silence of the centuries.

The music ceased; rather, it became by insensible degrees the distant roll of a retreating thunderstorm. A landscape, glittering with sun and rain, stretched before him, arched with a vivid rainbow, framing in its giant curve a hundred visible cities. In the middle distance a vast serpent, wearing a crown, reared its head out of its voluminous convolutions and looked at him with his dead mother's eyes. Suddenly this enchanting landscape seemed to rise swiftly upward, like the drop scene at a theater, and vanished in a blank. Something struck him a hard blow upon the face and breast. He had fallen to the floor; the blood ran from his broken nose and his bruised lips. For a moment he was dazed and stunned, and lay with closed eyes, his face against the door. In a few moments he had recovered, and then realized that his fall, by withdrawing his eyes, had broken the spell which held him. He felt that now, by keeping his gaze averted, he would be able to retreat. But the thought of the serpent within a few feet of his head, yet unseen—perhaps in the very act of springing upon him and throwing its coils about his throat—was too horrible. He lifted his head, stared again into those baleful eyes, and was again in bondage.

The snake had not moved, and appeared somewhat to have lost its power upon the imagination; the gorgeous illusions of a few moments before were not repeated. Beneath that flat and brainless brow its black, beady eyes simply glittered, as at first, with an expression unspeakably malignant. It was as if the creature, knowing its triumph assured, had determined to practice no more alluring wiles.

Now ensued a fearful scene. The man, prone upon the floor, within a yard of his enemy, raised the upper part of his body upon his elbows, his head thrown back, his legs extended to their full length. His face was white between its gouts of blood; his eyes were strained open to their uttermost expansion. There was froth upon his lips; it dropped off in flakes. Strong convulsions ran through his body, making almost serpentine undulations. He bent himself at the waist, shifting his legs from side to side. And every movement left him a little nearer to the snake. He thrust his hands forward to brace himself back, yet constantly advanced upon his elbows.

IV.

Dr. Druring and his wife sat in the library. The scientist was in rare good humor. "I have just obtained, by exchange with another collector," he said, "a splendid specimen of the *Ophiophagus*."

"And what may that be?" the lady inquired with a somewhat languid interest.

"Why, bless my soul, what profound ignorance! My dear, a man who ascertains after marriage that his wife does not know Greek, is entitled to a divorce. The *Ophiophagus* is a snake which eats other snakes."

"I hope it will eat all yours," she said, absently shifting the lamp. "But how does it get the other snakes? By charming them, I suppose."

"That is just like you, dear," said the doctor, with an affectation of petulance. "You know how irritating to me is any allusion to that vulgar superstition about the snake's power of fascination."

The conversation was interrupted by a mighty cry which rang through the silent house like the voice of a demon shouting in a tomb. Again and yet again it sounded, with terrible distinctness. They sprang to their feet, the man confused, the lady pale and speechless with fright. Almost before the echoes of the last cry had died away the doctor was out of the room, springing up the staircase two steps at a time. In the corridor, in front of Brayton's chamber, he met some servants who had come from the upper floor. Together they rushed at the door without knocking. It was unfastened, and gave way. Brayton lay upon his stomach on the floor, dead. His head and arms were partly concealed under the foot rail of the bed. They pulled the body away, turning it upon the back. The face was daubed with blood and froth, the eyes were wide open, staring—a dreadful sight!

"Died in a fit," said the scientist, bending his knee and placing his hand upon the heart. While in that position he happened to glance under the bed. "Good God!" he added; "how did this thing get in here?"

He reached under the bed, pulled out the snake, and flung it, still coiled, to the center of the room, whence, with a harsh, shuffling sound, it slid across the polished floor till stopped by the wall, where it lay without motion. It was a stuffed snake; its eyes were two shoe buttons.

Review Questions
1. What first brought the snake to Brayton's attention?
2. Why did he not call for help when he saw the snake?
3. What special power did Brayton think the snake had? Why did he think so?
4. What statement of the doctor's wife always irritated the doctor? (See Section IV). Why did it irritate him?
5. How did Brayton die?

Thought Questions
1. Did the snake really have power over Brayton? If so, how did it get this power?
2. In Section III, the narrator talks about "what we call consideration and decision." What does the story suggest about free will and humans' ability to make decisions? (Use quotations from the story to support your answer.) Do you agree? Discuss.
3. Brayton said it is cowardly to be unable to show fear. Do you agree? Does a person always have to act bravely in order to be brave? Why or why not?
4. Do you think Brayton would have been affected the same way by the snake if he had not been reading the book about the snake's power of fascination? How can what you read and watch influence your perceptions? How do you decide what media is appropriate to view?
5. How did you expect the story to end? What events or phrases led you to think so? Were there any clues that gave away the actual ending?

"The Notorious Jumping Frog of Calaveras County"

Mark Twain

Samuel L. Clemens (1835-1910), one of America's most renowned authors, is better known by his pen name, Mark Twain. What set him apart from the other notable authors of the nineteenth century was the easy way in which he combined realistic dialogue and characters of a most ordinary nature with deeper critiques of social issues like poverty and addiction. "The Notorious Jumping Frog of Calaveras County" was Twain's first published story. It was published in 1865, and, is a humor-tinged account of a man's addiction to gambling.

In compliance with the request of a friend of mine, who wrote me from the East, I called on good-natured, garrulous old Simon Wheeler, and inquired after my friend's friend, Leonidas W. Smiley, as requested to do, and I hereunto append the result. I have a lurking suspicion that Leonidas W. Smiley is a myth; that my friend never knew such a personage; and that he only conjectured that if I asked old Wheeler about him, it would remind him of his infamous Jim Smiley, and he would go to work and bore me to death with some exasperating reminiscence of him as long and as tedious as it should be useless to me. If that was the design, it succeeded.

I found Simon Wheeler dozing comfortably by the bar-room stove of the dilapidated tavern in the decayed mining camp of Angel's, and I noticed that he was fat and bald-headed, and had an expression of winning gentleness and simplicity upon his tranquil countenance. He roused up, and gave me good day. I told him that a friend of mine had commissioned me to make some inquiries about a cherished companion of his boyhood named Leonidas W. Smiley—Rev. Leonidas W. Smiley, a young minister of the Gospel, who he had heard was at one time a resident of Angel's Camp. I added that if Mr. Wheeler could tell me anything about this Rev. Leonidas W. Smiley, I would feel under many obligations to him.

Simon Wheeler backed me into a corner and blockaded me there with his chair, and then sat down and reeled off the monotonous narrative which follows this paragraph. He never smiled, he never frowned, he never changed his voice from the gentle-flowing key to which he tuned his initial sentence, he never betrayed the slightest suspicion of enthusiasm; but all through the interminable narrative there ran a vein of impressive earnestness and sincerity, which showed me plainly that, so far from his imagining that there was anything ridiculous or funny about his story, he regarded it as a really important matter, and admired its two heroes as men of transcendent genius in finesse. I let him go on in his own way, and never interrupted him once.

"Rev. Leonidas W. H'm, Reverend Le—well, there was a feller here once by the name of Jim Smiley, in the winter of '49—or maybe it was the spring of '50—I don't recollect exactly, somehow though what makes me think it was one or the other is because I remember the big flume warn't finished when he first come to the camp; but anyway, he was the curiousest man about always betting on anything that turned up you ever see, if he could get anybody to bet on the other side; and if he couldn't he'd change sides. Any way that suited the other man would suit him—any way just so's he got a bet, he was satisfied. But still he was lucky, uncommon lucky; he most always come out winner. He was always ready and laying for a chance; there couldn't be no solit'ry thing mentioned but that feller'd offer to bet on it, and take ary side you please, as I was just telling you. If there was a horse-race, you'd find him flush or you'd find him busted at the end of it; if there was a dog-fight, he'd bet on it; if there was a cat-fight, he'd bet on it; if there was a chicken-fight, he'd bet on it; why, if there was two birds setting on a fence, he would bet you which one would fly first; or if there was a camp-meeting, he would be there reg'lar to bet on Parson Walker, which he judged to be the best exhorter about here, and so he was too, and a good man. If he even see a straddle-bug start to go anywheres, he would bet you how long it would take him to get to—to wherever he was going to, and if you took him up, he would foller that straddle-bug to Mexico but what he would find out where he was bound for and how long he was on the road. Lots of the boys here has seen that Smiley, and can tell you about him. Why, it never made no difference to him—he'd bet on arly thing—the dangdest feller. Parson Walker's wife laid very sick once, for a good while, and it seemed as if they warn't going to save her; but one morning he come in, and Smiley up and asked him how she was, and he said she was considerable better—thank the Lord for his inf'nite mercy—and coming on so smart that with the blessing of Prov'dence she'd get well yet; and Smiley, before he thought, says, 'Well, I'll resk two-and-a-half she don't anyway.'

"Thish-yer Smiley had a mare—the boys called her the fifteen-minute nag, but that was only in fun, you know, because of course she was faster than that—and he used to win money on that horse, for all she was so slow and always had the asthma, or the distemper, or the consumption, or something of that kind. They used to give her two or three hundred yards' start, and then pass her under way; but always at the fag end of the race she'd get excited and desperate like, and come cavorting and straddling up, and scattering her legs around limber, sometimes in the air, and sometimes out to one side among the fences, and kicking up m-o-r-e dust and raising m-o-r-e racket with her coughing and sneezing and blowing her nose—and always fetch up at the stand just about a neck ahead, as near as you could cipher it down.

"And he had a little small bull-pup, that to look at him you'd think he warn't worth a cent but to set around and look ornery and lay for a chance to steal something. But as soon as money was up on him he was a different dog; his under-jaw'd begin to stick out like the fo'castle of a steamboat, and his teeth would uncover and shine like the furnaces. And a dog might tackle him and bully-rag him, and bite him, and throw him over his shoulder two or three times, and Andrew Jackson —which was the name of the pup—Andrew Jackson would never let on but what he was satisfied, and hadn't expected nothing else—and the bets being doubled and doubled on the other side all the time, till the money was all up; and then all of a sudden he would grab that other dog jest by the j'int of his hind leg and freeze to it—not chaw, you understand, but only just grip and hang on till they threw up the sponge, if it was a year. Smiley always come out winner on that pup, til he harnessed a dog once that didn't have no hind legs, because they'd been sawed off in a circular saw, and when the thing had gone along far enough, and the money was all up, and he come to make a snatch for his pet holt, he see in a minute how he'd been imposed on and how the other dog had him in the door, so to speak, and he 'peared surprised, and then he looked sorter discouraged-like, and didn't try no more to win the fight, and so he got shucked out bad. He give Smiley a look, as much as to say his heart was broke, and it was his fault, for putting up a dog that hadn't no hind legs for him to take holt of, which was his main dependence in a fight, and then he limped off a piece and laid down and died. It was a good pup, was that Andrew Jackson, and would have made a name for hisself if he'd lived, for the stuff was in him and he had genius—I know it, because he hadn't no opportunities to speak of, and it don't stand to reason that a dog could make such a fight as he could under them circumstances if he hadn't no talent. It always makes me feel sorry when I think of that last fight of his'n, and the way it turned out.

"Well, thish-yer Smiley had rat-tarriers, and chicken cocks, and tomcats and all them kind of things, till you couldn't rest, and you couldn't fetch nothing for him to bet on but he'd match you. He ketched a frog one day, and took him home, and said he cal'lated to educate him; and so he never done nothing for three months but set in his back yard and learn that frog to jump. And you bet you he did learn him, too. He'd give him a little punch behind, and the next minute you'd see that frog whirling in the air like a doughnut—see him turn one summerset, or maybe a couple, if he got a good start, and come down flat-footed and all right, like a cat. He got him up so in the matter of ketching flies, and kep' him in practice so constant, that he'd nail a fly every time as fur as he could see him. Smiley said all a frog wanted was education, and he could do 'most anything—and I believe him. Why, I've seen him set Dan'l Webster down here on this floor—Dan'l Webster was the name of the frog—and sing out, 'Flies, Dan'l, flies!' and quicker'n you could wink he'd spring straight up and snake a fly off'n the counter there, and flop down on the floor ag'in as solid as a gob of mud, and fall to scratching the side of his head with his hind foot as indifferent as if he hadn't no idea he'd been doin' any more'n any frog might do. You never see a frog so modest

and straightfor'ard as he was, for all he was so gifted. And when it come to fair and square jumping on a dead level, he could get over more ground at one straddle than any animal of his breed you ever see. Jumping on a dead level was his strong suit, you understand; and when it come to that, Smiley would ante up money on him as long as he had a red. Smiley was monstrous proud of his frog, and well he might be, for fellers that had traveled and been everywheres all said he laid over any frog that ever they see.

"Well, Smiley kep' the beast in a little lattice box, and he used to fetch him down-town sometimes and lay for a bet. One day a feller—a stranger in the camp, he was—come acrost him with his box, and says: 'What might it be that you've got in the box?'

"And Smiley says, sorter indifferent-like, 'It might be a parrot, or it might be a canary, maybe, but it ain't—it's only just a frog.'

"And the feller took it, and looked at it careful, and turned it round this way and that, and says, 'H'm—so 'tis. Well, what's he good for?'

"'Well,' Smiley says, easy and careless, 'he's good enough for one thing, I should judge—he can outjump any frog in Calaveras County.'

"The feller took the box again, and took another long, particular look, and give it back to Smiley, and says, very deliberate, 'Well,' he says, 'I don't see no p'ints about that frog that's any better'n any other frog.'

"'Maybe you don't,' Smiley says. 'Maybe you understand frogs and maybe you don't understand 'em; maybe you've had experience, and maybe you ain't only a amature, as it were. Anyways, I've got my opinion, and I'll resk forty dollars that he can outjump any frog in Calaveras County.'

"And the feller studied a minute, and then says, kinder sadlike, 'Well, I'm only a stranger here, and I ain't got no frog; but if I had a frog, I'd bet you.'

"And then Smiley says, 'That's all right—that's all right—if you'll hold my box a minute, I'll go and get you a frog.' And so the feller took the box, and put up his forty dollars along with Smiley's, and set down to wait.

"So he set there a good while thinking and thinking to himself, and then he got the frog out and prized his mouth open and took a teaspoon and filled him full of quail-shot—filled him pretty near up to his chin—and set him on the floor. Smiley he went to the swamp and slopped around in the mud for a long time, and finally he ketched a frog, and fetched him in, and give him to this feller, and says: 'Now, if you're ready, set him alongside of Dan'l, with his fore paws just even with Dan'l's, and I'll give the word.'

"Then he says, 'One—two—three-git' and him and the feller touched up the frogs from behind, and the new frog hopped off lively, but Dan'l give a heave, and hysted up his shoulders—so—like a Frenchman, but it warn't no use—he couldn't budge; he was planted as solid as a church, and he couldn't no more stir than if he was anchored out. Smiley was a good deal surprised, and he was disgusted too, but he didn't have no idea what the matter was, of course.

"The feller took the money and started away; and when he was going out at the door, he sorter jerked his thumb over his shoulder—so—at Dan'l, and says again, very deliberate,

'Well,' he says, 'I don't see no p'ints about that frog that's any better'n any other frog.'

"Smiley he stood scratching his head and looking down at Dan'l a long time, and at last he says, 'I do wonder what in the nation that frog throw'd off for—I wonder if there ain't something the matter with him—he 'pears to look mighty baggy, somehow.' And he ketched Dan'l by the nap of the neck, and hefted him, and says, 'Why blame my cats if he don't weigh five pound!' and turned him upside down and he belched out a double handful of shot. And then he see how it was, and he was the maddest man—he set the frog down and took out after that feller, but he never ketched him. And—"

[Here Simon Wheeler heard his name called from the front yard, and got up to see what was wanted.] And turning to me as he moved away, he said: "Just set where you are, stranger, and rest easy — I ain't going to be gone a second."

But, by your leave, I did not think that a continuation of the history of the enterprising vagabond Jim Smiley would be likely to afford me much information concerning the Rev. Leonidas W. Smiley, and so I started away.

At the door I met the sociable Wheeler returning, and he buttonholed me and recommenced: "Well, thish-yer Smiley had a yaller one-eyed cow that didn't have no tail, only just a short stump like a bannanner, and—" However, lacking both time and inclination, I did not wait to hear about the afflicted cow, but took my leave.

Review Questions
1. Who was Leonidas W. Smiley? Why did the narrator want to find him?
2. For what habit was Jim Smiley widely known?
3. How did Smiley's dog win so many fights? Why did the dog eventually lose?
4. Why did Jim Smiley's frog lose the contest?
5. What happened to Jim Smiley after the jumping contest? To the stranger?

Thought Questions
1. Is there a deeper moral to this story? What does it suggest about gambling? Cheating?
2. What kind of person was Jim Smiley? Did you like him? Why or why not?
3. Does honesty always prevail?
4. Have you ever been in a situation where someone was telling you a story that you were not interested in hearing? How did you react? Are there limitations on being polite?
5. How did you think the story would end? Were you surprised? Why do you think Twain ended the story the way he did? How would you have ended it?

"The Cop and the Anthem"
O. Henry

William S. Porter (1862-1910), an American writer, was imprisoned in 1898 for alleged embezzlement and spent three years in a federal prison. When he was freed in 1901, he turned over a new leaf and took a new name as well. He is remembered by this name: O. Henry. He had a gift for finding extraordinary occurrences in the lives of ordinary people. Most of his subjects lived in the poorer sections of New York City. "The Cop and the Anthem," first published in 1904, presents the life of a man who finds prison preferable to another winter out in the cold.

On his bench in Madison Square Soapy moved uneasily. When wild geese honk high of nights, and when women without sealskin coats grow kind to their husbands, and when Soapy moves uneasily on his bench in the park, you may know that winter is near at hand.

A dead leaf fell in Soapy's lap. That was Jack Frost's card. Jack is kind to the regular denizens of Madison Square, and gives fair warning of his annual call. At the corners of four streets he hands his pasteboard to the North Wind, footman of the mansion of All Outdoors, so that the inhabitants thereof may make ready.

Soapy's mind became cognisant of the fact that the time had come for him to resolve himself into a singular Committee of Ways and Means to provide against the coming rigour. And therefore he moved uneasily on his bench.

The hibernatorial ambitions of Soapy were not of the highest. In them there were no considerations of Mediterranean cruises, of soporific Southern skies drifting in the Vesuvian Bay. Three months on the Island was what his soul craved. Three months of assured board and bed and congenial company, safe from Boreas and bluecoats, seemed to Soapy the essence of things desirable.

For years the hospitable Blackwell's had been his winter quarters. Just as his more fortunate fellow New Yorkers had bought their tickets to Palm Beach and the Riviera each winter, so Soapy had made his humble arrangements for his annual hegira to the Island. And now the time was come. On the previous night three Sabbath newspapers, distributed beneath his coat, about his ankles and over his lap, had failed to repulse the cold as he slept on his bench near the spurting fountain in the ancient square. So the Island loomed big and timely in Soapy's mind. He scorned the provisions made in the name of charity for the city's dependents. In Soapy's opinion the Law was more benign than Philanthropy. There was an endless round of institutions, municipal and eleemosynary, on which he might set out and receive lodging and food accordant with the simple life. But to one of Soapy's proud spirit the gifts of charity are encumbered. If not in coin you must pay in humiliation of spirit for every benefit received at the hands of philanthropy. As Caesar had his Brutus, every bed of charity must have its toll of a bath, every loaf of bread its compensation of a private and personal inquisition. Wherefore it is better to be a guest of the law, which though conducted by rules, does not meddle unduly with a gentleman's private affairs.

Soapy, having decided to go to the Island, at once set about accomplishing his desire. There were many easy ways of doing this. The pleasantest was to dine luxuriously at some expensive restaurant; and then, after declaring insolvency, be handed over quietly and without uproar to a policeman. An accommodating magistrate would do the rest.

Soapy left his bench and strolled out of the square and across the level sea of asphalt, where Broadway and Fifth Avenue flow together. Up Broadway he turned, and halted at a glittering cafe, where are gathered together nightly the choicest products of the grape, the silkworm and the protoplasm.

Soapy had confidence in himself from the lowest button of his vest upward. He was shaven, and his coat was decent and his neat black, ready-tied four-in-hand had been presented to him by a lady missionary on Thanksgiving Day. If he could reach a table in the restaurant unsuspected success would be his. The portion of him that would show above the table would raise no doubt in the waiter's mind. A roasted mallard duck, thought Soapy, would be about the thing—with a bottle of Chablis, and then Camembert, a demi-tasse and a cigar. One dollar for the cigar would be enough. The total would not be so high as to call forth any supreme manifestation of revenge from the cafe management; and yet the meat would leave him filled and happy for the journey to his winter refuge.

But as Soapy set foot inside the restaurant door the head waiter's eye fell upon his frayed trousers and decadent shoes. Strong and ready hands turned him about and conveyed him in silence and haste to the sidewalk and averted the ignoble fate of the menaced mallard.

Soapy turned off Broadway. It seemed that his route to the coveted island was not to be an epicurean one. Some other way of entering limbo must be thought of.

At a corner of Sixth Avenue electric lights and cunningly displayed wares behind plate-glass made a shop window conspicuous. Soapy took a cobblestone and dashed it through the glass. People came running around the corner, a policeman in the lead. Soapy stood still, with his hands in his pockets, and smiled at the sight of brass buttons.

"Where's the man that done that?" inquired the officer excitedly.

"Don't you figure out that I might have had something to do with it?" said Soapy, not without sarcasm, but friendly, as one greets good fortune.

The policeman's mind refused to accept Soapy even as a clue. Men who smash windows do not remain to parley with the law's minions. They take to their heels. The policeman saw a man half way down the block running to catch a car. With drawn club he joined in the pursuit. Soapy, with disgust in his heart, loafed along, twice unsuccessful.

On the opposite side of the street was a restaurant of no great pretensions. It catered to large appetites and modest purses. Its crockery and atmosphere were thick; its soup and napery thin. Into this place Soapy took his accusive shoes and telltale trousers without challenge. At a table he sat and consumed beefsteak, flapjacks, doughnuts and pie. And then to the waiter he betrayed the fact that the minutest coin and himself were strangers.

"Now, get busy and call a cop," said Soapy. "And don't keep a gentleman waiting."

"No cop for youse," said the waiter, with a voice like butter cakes and an eye like the cherry in a Manhattan cocktail. "Hey, Con!"

Neatly upon his left ear on the callous pavement two waiters pitched Soapy. He arose, joint by joint, as a carpenter's rule opens, and beat the dust from his clothes. Arrest seemed but a rosy dream. The Island seemed very far away. A policeman who stood before a drug store two doors away laughed and walked down the street.

Five blocks Soapy travelled before his courage permitted him to woo capture again. This time the opportunity presented what he fatuously termed to himself a "cinch." A young woman of a modest and pleasing guise was standing before a show window gazing with sprightly interest at its display of shaving mugs and inkstands, and two yards from the window a large policeman of severe demeanour leaned against a water plug.

It was Soapy's design to assume the role of the despicable and execrated "masher." The refined and elegant appearance of his victim and the contiguity of the conscientious cop encouraged him to believe that he would soon feel the pleasant official clutch upon his arm that would insure his winter quarters on the right little, tight little isle.

Soapy straightened the lady missionary's readymade tie, dragged his shrinking cuffs into the open, set his hat at a killing cant and sidled toward the young woman. He made eyes at her, was taken with sudden coughs and "hems," smiled, smirked and went brazenly through the impudent and contemptible litany of the "masher." With half an eye Soapy saw that the policeman was watching him fixedly. The young woman moved away a few steps, and again bestowed her absorbed attention upon the shaving mugs. Soapy followed, boldly stepping to her side, raised his hat and said:

"Ah there, Bedelia! Don't you want to come and play in my yard?"

The policeman was still looking. The persecuted young woman had but to beckon a finger and Soapy would be practically en route for his insular haven. Already he imagined he could feel the cozy warmth of the station-house. The young woman faced him and, stretching out a hand, caught Soapy's coat sleeve.

"Sure, Mike," she said joyfully, "if you'll blow me to a pail of suds. I'd have spoke to you sooner, but the cop was watching."

With the young woman playing the clinging ivy to his oak Soapy walked past the policeman overcome with gloom. He seemed doomed to liberty.

At the next corner he shook off his companion and ran. He halted in the district where by night are found the lightest streets, hearts, vows and librettos. Women in furs and men in greatcoats moved gaily in the wintry air. A sudden fear seized Soapy that some dreadful enchantment had rendered him immune to arrest. The thought brought a little of panic upon it, and when he came upon another policeman lounging grandly in front of a transplendent theatre he caught at the immediate straw of "disorderly conduct."

On the sidewalk Soapy began to yell drunken gibberish at the top of his harsh voice. He danced, howled, raved and otherwise disturbed the welkin.

The policeman twirled his club, turned his back to Soapy and remarked to a citizen. "'Tis one of them Yale lads celebratin' the goose egg they give to the Hartford College. Noisy; but no harm. We've instructions to lave them be."

Disconsolate, Soapy ceased his unavailing racket. Would never a policeman lay hands on him? In his fancy the Island seemed an unattainable Arcadia. He buttoned his thin coat against the chilling wind.

In a cigar store he saw a well-dressed man lighting a cigar at a swinging light. His silk umbrella he had set by the door on entering. Soapy stepped inside, secured the umbrella and sauntered off with it slowly. The man at the cigar light followed hastily. "My umbrella," he said, sternly.

"Oh, is it?" sneered Soapy, adding insult to petit larceny. "Well, why don't you call a policeman? I took it. Your umbrella! Why don't you call a cop? There stands one on the corner."

The umbrella owner slowed his steps. Soapy did likewise, with a presentiment that luck would again run against him. The policeman looked at the two curiously.

"Of course," said the umbrella man—"that is—well, you know how these mistakes occur—I—if it's your umbrella I hope you'll excuse me—I picked it up this morning in a restaurant—If you recognise it as yours, why—I hope you'll—"

"Of course it's mine," said Soapy, viciously.

The ex-umbrella man retreated. The policeman hurried to assist a tall blonde in an opera cloak across the street in front of a street car that was approaching two blocks away.

Soapy walked eastward through a street damaged by improvements. He hurled the umbrella wrathfully into an excavation. He muttered against the men who wear helmets and carry clubs. Because he wanted to fall into their clutches, they seemed to regard him as a king who could do no wrong.

At length Soapy reached one of the avenues to the east where the glitter and turmoil was but faint. He set his face down this toward Madison Square, for the homing instinct survives even when the home is a park bench.

But on an unusually quiet corner Soapy came to a standstill. Here was an old church, quaint and rambling and gabled. Through one violet-stained window a soft light glowed, where, no doubt, the organist loitered over the keys, making sure of his mastery of the coming Sabbath anthem. For there drifted out to Soapy's ears sweet music that caught and held him transfixed against the convolutions of the iron fence.

The moon was above, lustrous and serene; vehicles and pedestrians were few; sparrows twittered sleepily in the eaves—for a little while the scene might have been a country church-yard. And the anthem that the organist played cemented Soapy to the iron fence, for he had known it well in the days when his life contained such things as mothers and roses and ambitions and friends and immaculate thoughts and collars.

The conjunction of Soapy's receptive state of mind and the influences about the old church wrought a sudden and wonderful change in his soul. He viewed with swift horror the pit into which he had tumbled, the degraded days, unworthy desires, dead hopes, wrecked faculties and base motives that made up his existence.

And also in a moment his heart responded thrillingly to this novel mood. An instantaneous and strong impulse moved him to battle with his desperate fate. He would pull himself out of the mire; he would make a man of himself again; he would conquer the evil that had taken possession of him. There was time; he was comparatively young yet; he would resurrect his old eager ambitions and pursue them without faltering. Those solemn but sweet organ notes had set up a revolution in him. To-morrow he would go into the roaring downtown district and find work. A fur importer had once offered him a place as driver. He would find him to-morrow and ask for the position. He would be somebody in the world. He would—

Soapy felt a hand laid on his arm. He looked quickly around into the broad face of a policeman.

"What are you doin' here?" asked the officer.

"Nothin'," said Soapy.

"Then come along," said the policeman.

"Three months on the Island," said the Magistrate in the Police Court the next morning.

Review Questions
1. Where did Soapy usually go for the winter months? How did he get there?
2. How did Soapy first attempt to get arrested? Why did his strategy fail?
3. Why did the man with the umbrella choose not to have Soapy arrested?
4. What brought about Soapy's change of heart?
5. For what crime was Soapy finally arrested?

Thought Questions
1. Imagine what it would be like to have no home or even shelter during the winter. Do you think a prison cell would be preferable to taking charity? Why or why not?
2. Should prison be harsh and unpleasant, or is the loss of freedom punishment enough? What is the purpose of imprisoning criminals? Discuss.
3. Do you think Soapy would still want to change when he got off the Island again? Is it harder to make promises to reform in tough times or when things are going well? Why?
4. Do you think O. Henry's portrayal of the law and its relation to society still applies today?
5. Is it "fair" for an author to surprise readers without giving them clues to how a story will end? Why or why not? Does an author owe his or her readers anything?

PLOT TWISTS and SURPRISE ENDINGS

Writing Practice

Ambrose Bierce, Mark Twain, and O. Henry were all masters of the surprise endings and unexpected plot twists that keep readers' attention. The introduction, stage-setting, and climax of the story lead toward a seemingly straightforward conclusion. At the last minute, the story does a 180-degree turn and ends up in a completely different location than you might have guessed.

Now that you have seen examples of these authors' writing, ask yourself what characteristics of the stories made you think the stories were going to end in a predictable way. Think about the structure of the stories, who narrates them, how they begin, in what order the events occur, the way the characters are introduced, and how the plot twists are revealed. After reading each story a second time, do you notice any clues that point toward the surprise ending?

Now it's your turn. Think about each of the following familiar stories:

Cinderella

Beauty and the Beast

The Three Little Pigs

Rudolph the Red-Nosed Reindeer

The Frog Prince

Hansel and Gretel

Your goal is to re-imagine the stories to produce the "shock effect" that Bierce, Twain, and O. Henry produced. Using some of the techniques you have seen, come up with a way to end each classic story with a twist. Be as specific as you can, and don't forget to decide if you will give your reader "clues" to the new ending, and if so, how you will do it.

Can You Please Focus? STORY FOCUS

Short stories have one characteristic that immediately sets them apart from novels. They are short. While this observation may seem obvious, it is an important one to remember. Novels can have three plots, five subplots, and fifteen characters and deal with all of them thoroughly by the end. Short stories do not generally have this ability. Within the scope of most short stories, it is very difficult to deal with multiple plots or numerous characters. The author has to choose a focus for their story.

In a short story, often the entire plot will be focused on one small event. This event may be the last straw on an already loaded-down camel, but the author does not have to include all the other straws. While some background information may be needed, it is usually kept as brief as possible. Pay particular attention to these questions as you read the following short story:

- What is the time span of the story?
- Does the author give background information on the characters? The setting? The plot?
- How is background information given (flashbacks, references by the characters or narrator)?
- Is the author able to wrap up all of the loose ends by the conclusion of the story?

A short story author is a little bit like the writer of a history book. All of human history would never fit into a single book, so historians have to choose which events and people to include. When you write a short story, you have to do the same thing. The good news is that even if you're telling a story that has been told a million times before, it is possible to make it fresh by changing the focus.

"Little Girls Wiser Than Men"
Leo Tolstoy

Leo Tolstoy (1828-1910) was one of the most prominent Russian authors of the nineteenth century. His works are characterized by a concern for the inner thoughts and feelings of his characters. Tolstoy also believed strongly in the need for truth in literature. This belief is reflected in the moral teachings of his later works. "Little Girls Wiser than Men," written in 1885, is a good example of Tolstoy's later works. It is a brief but thought-provoking story about the wisdom of young people, which can sometimes allow them to see things more clearly than their elders can.

It was an early Easter. Sledging was only just over; snow still lay in the yards; and water ran in streams down the village street.

Two little girls from different houses happened to meet in a lane between two homesteads, where the dirty water after running through the farmyards had formed a large puddle. One girl was very small, the other a little bigger. Their mothers had dressed them both in new frocks. The little one wore a blue frock, the other a yellow print, and both had red kerchiefs on their heads. They had just come from church when they met, and first they showed each other their finery, and then they began to play. Soon the fancy took them to splash about in the water, and the smaller one was going to step into the puddle, shoes and all, when the elder checked her:

"Don't go in so, Malasha," said she, "your mother will scold you. I will take off my shoes and stockings, and you take off yours."

They did so, and then, picking up their skirts, began walking toward each other through the puddle. The water came up to Malasha's ankles, and she said: "It is deep, Akoulya, I'm afraid!"

"Come on," replied the other. "Don't be frightened. It won't get any deeper."

When they got near one another, Akoulya said: "Mind, Malasha, don't splash. Walk carefully!"

She had hardly said this, when Malasha plumped down her foot so that the water splashed right on to Akoulya's frock. The frock was splashed, and so were Akoulya's eyes and nose. When she saw the stains on her frock, she was angry and ran after Malasha to strike her. Malasha was frightened, and seeing that she had got herself into trouble, she scrambled out of the puddle, and prepared to run home. Just then Akoulya's mother happened to be passing, and seeing that her daughter's skirt was splashed, and her sleeves dirty, she said: "You naughty, dirty girl, what have you been doing?"

"Malasha did it on purpose," replied the girl.

At this Akoulya's mother seized Malasha, and struck her on the back of her neck. Malasha began to howl so that she could be heard all down the street.

Her mother came out. "What are you beating my girl for?" said she; and began scolding her neighbor. One word led to another and they had an angry quarrel. The men came out and a crowd collected in the street, every one shouting and no one listening. They all went on quarrelling, till one gave another a push, and the affair had very nearly come to blows, when Akoulya's old grandmother, stepping in among them, tried to calm them.

"What are you thinking of, friends? Is it right to behave so? On a day like this, too! It is a time for rejoicing, and not for such folly as this."

They would not listen to the old woman and nearly knocked her off her feet. And she would not have been able to quiet the crowd if it had not been for Akoulya and Malasha themselves. While the women were abusing each other, Akoulya had wiped the mud off her frock, and gone back to the puddle. She took a stone and began scraping away the earth in front of the puddle to make a channel through which the water could run out into the street. Presently Malasha joined her, and with a chip of wood helped her dig the channel. Just as the men were beginning to fight, the water from the little girls' channel ran streaming into the street toward the very place where the old woman was trying to pacify the men. The girls followed it; one running along each side of the little stream.

"Catch it, Malasha! Catch it!" shouted Akoulya; while Malasha could not speak for laughing.

Highly delighted, and watching the chip float along on their stream, the little girls ran straight into the group of men; and the old woman, seeing them, said to the men: "Are you not ashamed of yourselves? To go fighting on account of these lassies, when they themselves have forgotten all about it, and are playing happily together. Dear little souls! They are wiser than you!"

The men looked at the little girls and were ashamed, and, laughing at themselves, went back each to his own home.

"Except ye turn, and become as little children, ye shall in no wise enter into the kingdom of heaven."

Review Questions
1. What caused the little girls' fight to begin?
2. How did the adults become involved?
3. What did the little girls do while the adults were fighting?
4. What stopped the fight?
5. What wisdom did the old grandmother draw from this event?

Thought Questions
1. How do children and adults fight differently?
2. Which version of fighting is more productive? Explain.
3. Is it good to be able to lose interest in a fight without resolving it? Why or why not?
4. Does wisdom always depend on age? Think of an example to support your answer.
5. Is it harder to be mature or to be childlike? Does the answer depend on whom you ask?

STORY FOCUS

Writing Practice

Think about writing with focus as taking a picture of the Grand Canyon with a small, disposable camera. You can't possibly fit the whole scene into the viewfinder. If you try, you'll end up with a picture that contains little bits of everything but a complete picture of nothing. Instead, you have to pick the part of the scene that is the most important to you.

In the example of the Grand Canyon, your focus could be a particularly steep drop-off, or a raft floating down the river, or a rock shaped like a mountain goat. These narrower subjects allow you to capture a scene that is complete in itself. (Hint: pulling focus from a larger work is also a valuable skill that you will use when you write essays about literature.)

"Little Girls Wiser than Men" is a very short, focused story. As you re-read it, look at the ways Tolstoy maintains his focus. What can you tell about the characters of the townspeople? The girls? Does Tolstoy say anything directly about their personalities? How does he imply this information?

Pretend you were going to write a short story based on one of the following novels (if you haven't read some of them, you can substitute other books that you have read):

The Lion, the Witch and the Wardrobe
The Bronze Bow
Black Beauty
The Hobbit
The Secret Garden

Pick a focus for your short story. It could be a particular scene or event from the book, a character, or a certain setting, or even an object. Go back to the questions at the beginning of this section, and think about how you would answer them in relation to your chosen story focus. Try to make these familiar stories new and interesting by changing the focus.

What Happened to Kansas?
SETTING

Imagine a movie where the actors perform in front of a completely blank, white background. There are no landscapes, no furnishings, and no props. Only the actors are visible. Think about how much harder it would be to follow the story or have a clear sense of what was happening. Just like in screenplays, the setting in a short story is vital. It defines the context of the story, makes the characters come alive, and determines the boundaries of the plot.

As you read the following short story, focus on the settings the author created. Pay attention to the ways the author helps you picture each scene. Focus on these questions:

- Where does the story take place? How do you know?
- How does the author describe the setting?
- What kind of emotions does the setting evoke? Spooky? Normal? Funny? Why?
- Is the setting important to the story? Why?
- Does the author assume you are familiar with the place, or does he or she provide that information?

As an author, your goal may be to make an imaginary place come to life or simply to give the reader a vivid picture of a real place. It's up to you to choose words that employ all five of the reader's senses: sight, hearing, touch or texture, smell, and taste. Sometimes the setting is simply a stage on which the events of the story take place, but sometimes the setting is essential to the plot. As you read the next story, try to brainstorm ways you could use setting in a story of your own.

"The Mansion"
Henry Van Dyke

Henry Van Dyke (1852-1933) was the son of a Christian minister and was himself a pastor as well as an American author. His religious upbringing is evident in his writing, which focuses on finding the redeeming qualities in humanity and restoring goodness and right thinking to people who have gone astray. "The Mansion" was written in 1911 as half of a two-part book (the other half being "The Story of the Other Wise Man"). This story relates to the passage in Matthew 6:1-4 that says not to seek earthly rewards for good deeds but to wait for the heavenly reward God is preparing.

There was an air of calm and reserved opulence about the Weightman mansion that spoke not of money squandered, but of wealth prudently applied. Standing on a corner of the Avenue no longer fashionable for residence, it looked upon the swelling tide of business with an expression of complacency and half-disdain.

The house was not beautiful. There was nothing in its straight front of chocolate-colored stone, its heavy cornices, its broad, staring windows of plate glass, its carved and bronze-bedecked mahogany doors at the top of the wide stoop, to charm the eye or fascinate the imagination. But it was eminently respectable, and in its way imposing. It seemed to say that the glittering shops of the jewelers, the milliners, the confectioners, the florists, the picture-dealers, the furriers, the makers of rare and costly antiquities, retail traders in luxuries of life, were beneath the notice of a house that had its foundations in the high finance, and was built literally and figuratively in the shadow of St. Petronius' Church.

At the same time there was something self-pleased and congratulatory in the way in which the mansion held its own amid the changing neighborhood. It almost seemed to be lifted up a little, among the tall buildings near at hand, as if it felt the rising value of the land on which it stood.

John Weightman was like the house into which he had built himself thirty years ago and in which his ideals and ambitions were incrusted. He was a self-made man. But in making himself he had chosen a highly esteemed pattern and worked according to the approved rules. There was nothing irregular, questionable, flamboyant about him. He was solid, correct, and justly successful.

His minor tastes, of course, had been carefully kept up to date. At the proper time, pictures by the Barbizon masters, old English plate and portraits, bronzes by Barye and marbles by Rodin, Persian carpets and Chinese porcelains, had been introduced to the mansion. It contained a Louis Quinze reception-room, an Empire drawing-room, a Jacobean dining-room, and various apartments dimly reminiscent of the styles of furniture affected by deceased monarchs. That the hallways were too short for the historic perspective did not make much difference. American decorative art is *capable de tout*, it absorbs all periods. Of each period Mr. Weightman wished to have something of the best. He understood its value, present as a certificate, and prospective as an investment.

It was only in the architecture of his town house that he remained conservative, immovable, one might almost say Early-Victorian-Christian. His country house at Dulwich-on-the-Sound was a palace of the Italian Renaissance. But in town he adhered to an architecture which had moral associations, the Nineteenth-Century-Brownstone epoch. It was a symbol of his social position, his religious doctrine, and even, in a way, of his business creed.

"A man of fixed principles," he would say, "should express them in the looks of his house. New York changes its domestic architecture too rapidly. It is like divorce. It is not dignified. I don't like it. Extravagance and fickleness are advertised in most of these new houses. I wish to be known for different qualities. Dignity and prudence are the things that people trust. Every one knows that I can afford to live in the house that suits me. It is a guarantee to the public. It inspires confidence. It helps my influence. There is a text in the Bible about 'a house that hath foundations.' That is the proper kind of a mansion for a solid man."

Harold Weightman had often listened to his father discoursing in this fashion on the fundamental principles of life, and always with a divided mind. He admired immensely his father's talents and the single-minded energy with which he improved them. But in the paternal philosophy there was something that disquieted and oppressed the young man, and made him gasp inwardly for fresh air and free action.

At times, during his college course and his years at the law school, he had yielded to this impulse and broken away—now toward extravagance and dissipation, and then, when the reaction came, toward a romantic devotion to work among the poor. He had felt his father's disapproval for both of these forms of imprudence; but it was never expressed in a harsh or violent way, always with a certain tolerant patience, such as one might show for the mistakes and vagaries of the very young. John Weightman was not hasty, impulsive, inconsiderate, even toward his own children. With them, as with the rest of the world, he felt that he had a reputation to maintain, a theory to vindicate. He could afford to give them time to see that he was absolutely right.

One of his favorite Scripture quotations was, "Wait on the Lord." He had applied it to real estate and to people, with profitable results.

But to human persons the sensation of being waited for is not always agreeable. Sometimes, especially with the young, it produces a vague restlessness, a dumb resentment, which is increased by the fact that one can hardly explain or justify it. Of this John Weightman was not conscious. It lay beyond his horizon. He did not take it into account in the plan of life which he had made for himself and for his family as the sharers and inheritors of his success.

"Father plays us," said Harold, in a moment of irritation, to his mother, "like pieces in a game of chess."

"My dear," said that lady, whose faith in her husband was religious, "you ought not to speak so impatiently. At least he wins the game. He is one of the most respected men in New York. And he is very generous, too."

"I wish he would be more generous in letting us be ourselves," said the young man. "He always has something in view for us and expects to move us up to it."

"But isn't it always for our benefit?" replied his mother. "Look what a position we have. No one can say there is any taint on our money. There are no rumors about your father. He has kept the laws of God and of man. He has never made any mistakes."

Harold got up from his chair and poked the fire. Then he came back to the ample, well-gowned, firm-looking lady, and sat beside her on the sofa. He took her hand gently and looked at the two rings—a thin band of yellow gold, and a small solitaire diamond—which kept their place on her third finger in modest dignity, as if not ashamed, but rather justified, by the splendor of the emerald which glittered beside them.

"Mother," he said, "you have a wonderful hand. And father made no mistake when he won you. But are you sure he has always been so inerrant?"

"Harold," she exclaimed, a little stiffly, "what do you mean? His life is an open book."

"Oh," he answered, "I don't mean anything bad, mother dear. I know the governor's life is an open book—a ledger, if you like, kept in the best bookkeeping hand, and always ready for inspection—every page correct, and showing a handsome balance. But isn't it a mistake not to allow us to make our own mistakes, to learn for ourselves, to live our own lives? Must we be always working for 'the balance,' in one thing or another? I want to be myself—to get outside of this everlasting, profitable 'plan'—to let myself go, and lose myself for awhile at least—to do the things that I want to do, just because I want to do them."

"My boy," said his mother, anxiously, "you are not going to do anything wrong or foolish? You know the falsehood of that old proverb about wild oats."

He threw back his head and laughed. "Yes, mother," he answered, "I know it well enough. But in California, you know, the wild oats are one of the most valuable crops. They grow all over the hillsides and keep the cattle and the horses alive. But that wasn't what I meant—to sow wild oats. Say to pick wild flowers, if you like, or even to chase wild geese—to do something that seems good to me just for its own sake, not for the sake of wages of one kind or another. I feel like a hired man, in the service of this magnificent mansion—say in training

for father's place as majordomo. I'd like to get out some way, to feel free—perhaps to do something for others."

The young man's voice hesitated a little. "Yes, it sounds like cant, I know, but sometimes I feel as if I'd like to do some good in the world, if father only wouldn't insist upon God's putting it into the ledger."

His mother moved uneasily, and a slight look of bewilderment came into her face. "Isn't that almost irreverent?" she asked. "Surely the righteous must have their reward. And your father is good. See how much he gives to all the established charities, how many things he has founded. He's always thinking of others, and planning for them. And surely, for us, he does everything. How well he has planned this trip to Europe for me and the girls—the court-presentation at Berlin, the season on the Riviera, the visits in England with the Plumptons and the Halverstones. He says Lord Halverstone has the finest old house in Sussex, pure Elizabethan, and all the old customs are kept up, too—family prayers every morning for all the domestics. By-the-way, you know his son Bertie, I believe."

Harold smiled a little to himself as he answered: "Yes, I fished at Catalina Island last June with the Honorable Ethelbert; he's rather a decent chap, in spite of his in-growing mind. But you?—mother, you are simply magnificent! You are father's masterpiece." The young man leaned over to kiss her, and went up to the Riding Club for his afternoon canter in the Park.

So it came to pass, early in December, that Mrs. Weightman and her two daughters sailed for Europe, on their serious pleasure trip, even as it had been written in the book of Providence; and John Weightman, who had made the entry, was left to pass the rest of the winter with his son and heir in the brownstone mansion.

They were comfortable enough. The machinery of the massive establishment ran as smoothly as a great electric dynamo. They were busy enough, too. John Weightman's plans and enterprises were complicated, though his principle of action was always simple—to get good value for every expenditure and effort. The banking-house of which he was the chief, the brain, the will, the absolutely controlling hand, was so admirably organized that the details of its direction took but little time. But the scores of other interests that radiated from it and were dependent upon it—or perhaps it would be more accurate to say that contributed to its solidity and success—the many investments, industrial, political, benevolent, reformatory, ecclesiastical, that had made the name of Weightman well known and potent in city, church, and state, demanded much attention and careful steering, in order that each might produce the desired result. There were board meetings of corporations and hospitals, conferences in Wall Street and at Albany, consultations and committee meetings in the brownstone mansion.

For a share in all this business and its adjuncts John Weightman had his son in training in one of the famous law firms of the city; for he held that banking itself is a simple affair, the only real difficulties of finance are on its legal side. Meantime he wished the young man to meet and know the men with whom he would have to deal when he became a partner in the house. So a couple of dinners were given in the mansion during December, after which the father called the son's attention to the fact that over a hundred million dollars had sat around the board.

But on Christmas Eve father and son were dining together without guests, and their talk across the broad table, glittering with silver and cut glass, and softly lit by shaded candles, was intimate, though a little slow at times. The elder man was in rather a rare mood, more expansive and confidential than usual; and, when the coffee was brought in and they were left alone, he talked more freely of his personal plans and hopes than he had ever done before.

"I feel very grateful to-night," said he, at last; "it must be something in the air of Christmas that gives me this feeling of thankfulness for the many divine mercies that have been bestowed upon me. All the principles by which I have tried to guide my life have been justified. I have never made the value of this salted almond by anything that the courts would not uphold, at least in the long run, and yet—or wouldn't it be truer to say and therefore?—my affairs have been wonderfully prospered. There's a great deal in that text 'Honesty is the best'— but no, that's not from the Bible, after all, is it? Wait a moment; there is something of that kind, I know."

"May I light a cigar, father," said Harold, turning away to hide a smile, "while you are remembering the text?"

"Yes, certainly," answered the elder man, rather shortly; "you know I don't dislike the smell. But it is a wasteful, useless habit, and therefore I have never practised it. Nothing useless is worth while, that's my motto—nothing that does not bring the reward. Oh, now I recall the text, 'Verily I say unto you they have their reward.' I shall ask Doctor Snodgrass to preach a sermon on that verse some day."

"Using you as an illustration?"

"Well, not exactly that; but I could give him some good material from my own experience to prove the truth of Scripture. I can honestly say that there is not one of my charities that has not brought me in a good return, either in the increase of influence, the building-up of credit, or the association with substantial people. Of course you have to be careful how you give, in order to secure the best results—no indiscriminate giving—no pennies in beggars' hats! It has been one of my principles always to use the same kind of judgment in charities that I use in my other affairs, and they have not disappointed me."

"Even the check that you put in the plate when you take the offertory up the aisle on Sunday morning?"

"Certainly; though there the influence is less direct; and I must confess that I have my doubts in regard to the collection for Foreign Missions. That always seems to me romantic and wasteful. You never hear from it in any definite way. They say the missionaries have done a good deal to open the way for trade; perhaps—but they have also gotten us into commercial and political difficulties. Yet I give to them—a little—it is a matter of conscience with me to identify myself with all the enterprises of the Church; it is the mainstay of social order and a prosperous civilization. But the best forms of benevolence are the well-established, organized ones here at home, where people can see them and know what they are doing."

"You mean the ones that have a local habitation and a name."

"Yes; they offer by far the safest return, though of course there is something gained by contributing to general funds. A public man can't afford to be without public spirit. But on the whole I prefer a building, or an endowment. There is a mutual advantage to a good name and a good institution in their connection in the public mind. It helps them both. Remember that, my boy. Of course at the beginning you will have to practise it in a small way; later, you will have larger opportunities. But try to put your gifts where they can be identified and do good all around. You'll see the wisdom of it in the long run."

"I can see it already, sir, and the way you describe it looks amazingly wise and prudent. In other words, we must cast our bread on the waters in large loaves, carried by sound ships marked with the owner's name, so that the return freight will be sure to come back to us."

The father laughed, but his eyes were frowning a little as if he suspected something irreverent under the respectful reply. "You put it humorously, but there's sense in what you say. Why not? God rules the sea; but He expects us to follow the laws of navigation and commerce. Why not take good care of your bread, even when you give it away?"

"It's not for me to say why not—and yet I can think of cases—" The young man hesitated for a moment. His half-finished cigar had gone out. He rose and tossed it into the fire, in front of which he remained standing—a slender, eager, restless young figure, with a touch of hunger in the fine face, strangely like and unlike the father, at whom he looked with half-wistful curiosity.

"The fact is, sir," he continued, "there is such a case in my mind now, and it is a good deal on my heart, too. So I thought of speaking to you about it to-night. You remember Tom Rollins, the Junior who was so good to me when I entered college?"

The father nodded. He remembered very well indeed the annoying incidents of his son's first escapade, and how Rollins had stood by him and helped to avoid a public disgrace, and how a close friendship had grown between the two boys, so different in their fortunes. "Yes," he said, "I remember him. He was a promising young man. Has he succeeded?"

"Not exactly—that is, not yet. His business has been going rather badly. He has a wife and little baby, you know. And now he has broken down,—something wrong with his lungs. The doctor says his only chance is a year or eighteen months in Colorado. I wish we could help him."

"How much would it cost?"

"Three or four thousand perhaps, as a loan."

"Does the doctor say he will get well?"

"A fighting chance—the doctor says."

The face of the older man changed subtly. Not a line was altered, but it seemed to have a different substance, as if it were carved out of some firm, imperishable stuff. "A fighting chance," he said, "may do for a speculation, but it is not a good investment. You owe something to young Rollins. Your grateful feeling does you credit. But don't overwork it. Send him three or four hundred, if you like. You'll never hear from it again, except in the letter of thanks. But for Heaven's sake don't be sentimental. Religion is not a matter of sentiment; it's a matter of principle."

The face of the younger man changed now. But instead of becoming fixed and graven, it seemed to melt into life by the heat of an inward fire. His nostrils quivered with quick breath, his lips were curled. "Principle!" he said, "You mean principal—and interest too. Well, sir, you know best whether that is religion or not. But if it is, count me out, please. Tom saved me from a going to the devil, six years ago; and I'll be d— if I don't help him to the best of my ability now."

John Weightman looked at his son steadily. "Harold," he said at last, "you know I dislike violent language, and it never has any influence with me. If I could honestly approve of this proposition of yours, I'd let you have the money; but I can't; it's extravagant and useless. But you have your Christmas check for a thousand dollars coming to you to-morrow. You can use it as you please. I never interfere with your private affairs."

"Thank you," said Harold. "Thank you very much! But there's another private affair. I want to get away from this life, this town, this house. It stifles me. You refused last summer when I asked you to let me go up to Grenfell's Mission on the Labrador. I could go now, at least as far as the Newfoundland Station. Have you changed your mind?"

"Not at all. I think it is an exceedingly foolish enterprise. It would interrupt the career that I have marked out for you."

"Well, then, here's a cheaper proposition. Algy Vanderhoof wants me to join him on his yacht with—well, with a little party—to cruise in the West Indies. Would you prefer that?"

"Certainly not! The Vanderhoof set is wild and godless—I do not wish to see you keeping company with fools who walk in the broad and easy way that leads to perdition."

"It is rather a hard choice," said the young man, with a short laugh, turning toward the door. "According to you there's very little difference—a fool's paradise or a fool's hell! Well, it's one or the other for me, and I'll toss up for it to-night: heads, I lose; tails, the devil wins. Anyway, I'm sick of this, and I'm out of it."

"Harold," said the older man (and there was a slight tremor in his voice), "don't let us quarrel on Christmas Eve. All I want is to persuade you to think seriously of the duties and responsibilities to which God has called you—don't speak lightly of heaven and hell—remember, there is another life."

The young man came back and laid his hand upon his father's shoulder. "Father," he said, "I want to remember it. I try to believe in it. But somehow or other, in this house, it all seems unreal to me. No doubt all you say is perfectly right and wise. I don't venture to argue against it, but I can't feel it—that's all. If I'm to have a soul, either to lose or to save, I must really live. Just now neither the present nor the future means anything to me. But surely we won't quarrel. I'm very grateful to you, and we'll part friends. Good-night, sir."

The father held out his hand in silence. The heavy portière dropped noiselessly behind the son, and he went up the wide, curving stairway to his own room.

Meantime John Weightman sat in his carved chair in the Jacobean dining-room. He felt strangely old and dull. The portraits of beautiful women by Lawrence and Reynolds and Raeburn, which had often seemed like real company to him, looked remote and uninteresting. He fancied something cold and almost unfriendly in their expression, as if they were staring through him or beyond him. They cared nothing for his principles, his hopes, his disappointments, his successes; they belonged to another world, in which he had no place. At this he felt a vague resentment, a sense of discomfort that he could not have defined or explained. He was used to being considered, respected, appreciated at his full value in every region, even in that of his own dreams.

Presently he rang for the butler, telling him to close the house and not to sit up, and walked with lagging steps into the long library, where the shaded lamps were burning. His eye fell upon the low shelves full of costly books, but he had no desire to open them. Even the carefully chosen pictures that hung above them seemed to have lost their attraction. He paused for a moment before an idyll of Corot—a dance of nymphs around some forgotten altar in a vaporous glade—and looked at it curiously. There was something rapturous and serene about the picture, a breath of spring-time in the misty trees, a harmony of joy in the dancing figures, that wakened in him a feeling of half-pleasure and half-envy. It represented something that he had never known in his calculated, orderly life. He was dimly mistrustful of it.

"It is certainly very beautiful," he thought, "but it is distinctly pagan; that altar is built to some heathen god. It does not fit into the scheme of a Christian life. I doubt whether it is consistent with the tone of my house. I will sell it this winter. It will bring three or four times what I paid for it. That was a good purchase, a very good bargain."

He dropped into the revolving chair before his big library table. It was covered with pamphlets, and reports of the various enterprises in which he was interested. There was a pile of newspaper clippings in which his name was mentioned with praise for his sustaining power as a pillar of finance, for his judicious benevolence, for his support of wise and prudent reform movements, for his discretion in making permanent public gifts—"the Weightman Charities," one very complaisant editor called them, as if they deserved classification as a distinct species.

He turned the papers over listlessly. There was a description and a picture of the "Weightman Wing of the Hospital for Cripples," of which he was president; and an article on the new professor in the "Weightman Chair of Political Jurisprudence" in Jackson University, of which he was a trustee; and an illustrated account of the opening of the "Weightman Grammar School" at Dulwich-on-the-Sound, where he had his legal residence for purposes of taxation.

This last was perhaps the most carefully planned of all the Weightman Charities. He desired to win the confidence and support of his rural neighbors. It had pleased him much when the local newspaper had spoken of him as an ideal citizen and the logical candidate for the Governorship of the State; but upon the whole it seemed to him wiser to keep out of active politics. It would be easier and better to put Harold into the running, to have him sent to the Legislature from the Dulwich district, then to the national House, then to the Senate. Why not? The Weightman interests were large enough to need a direct representative and guardian at Washington.

But to-night all these plans came back to him with dust upon them. They were dry and crumbling like forsaken habitations: The son upon whom his complacent ambition had rested had turned his back upon the mansion of his father's hopes. The break might not be final; and in any event there would be much to live for; the fortunes of the family would be secure. But the zest of it all would be gone if John Weightman had to give up the assurance of perpetuating his name and his principles in his son. It was a bitter disappointment, and he felt that he had not deserved it.

He rose from the chair and paced the room with leaden feet. For the first time in his life his age was visibly upon him. His head was heavy and hot, and the thoughts that roiled in it were confused and depressing. Could it be that he had made a mistake in the principles of his existence? There was no argument in what Harold had said—it was almost childish—and yet it had shaken the elder man more deeply than he cared to show. It held a silent attack which touched him more than open criticism.

Suppose the end of his life were nearer than he thought—the end must come some time—what if it were now? Had he not founded his house upon a rock? Had he not kept the commandments? Was he not, "touching the law, blameless"? And beyond this, even if there were some faults in his character—and all men are sinners—yet he surely believed in the saving doctrines of religion—the forgiveness of sins, the resurrection of the body, the life everlasting. Yes, that was the true source of comfort, after all. He would read a bit in the Bible, as he did every night, and go to bed and to sleep.

He went back to his chair at the library table. A strange weight of weariness rested upon him, but he opened the book at a familiar place, and his eyes fell upon the verse at the bottom of the page. "Lay not up for yourselves treasures upon earth." That had been the text of the sermon a few weeks before. Sleepily, heavily, he tried to fix his mind upon it and recall it. What was it that Doctor Snodgrass had said? Ah, yes—that it was a mistake to pause here in reading the verse. We must read on without a pause—Lay not up treasures upon earth where moth and rust do corrupt and where thieves break through and steal—that was the true doctrine. We may have treasures upon earth but they must not be put into unsafe places, but into safe places. A most comforting doctrine! He had always followed it. Moths and rust and thieves had done no harm to his investments.

John Weightman's drooping eyes turned to the next verse, at the top of the second column. "But lay up for yourselves treasures in heaven." Now what had the Doctor said about that? How was it to be understood—in what sense—treasures—in heaven?

The book seemed to float away from him. The light vanished, he wondered dimly if this could be Death, coming so suddenly, so quietly, so irresistibly. He struggled for a moment to hold himself up, and then sank slowly forward upon the table. His head rested upon his folded hands. He slipped into the unknown.

How long afterward conscious life returned to him he did not know. The blank might have been an hour or a century. He knew only that something had happened in the interval. What it was he could not tell. He found great difficulty in catching the thread of his identity again. He felt that he was himself; but the trouble was to make his connections, to verify and place himself, to know who and where he was.

At last it grew clear. John Weightman was sitting on a stone, not far from a road in a strange land.

The road was not a formal highway, fenced and graded. It was more like a great travel-trace, worn by thousands of feet passing across the open country in the same direction. Down in the valley, into which he could look, the road seemed to form itself gradually out of many minor paths; little footways coming across the meadows, winding tracks following along beside the streams, faintly marked trails emerging from the woodlands. But on the hillside the threads were more firmly woven into one clear band of travel, though there were still a few dim paths joining it here and there, as if persons had been climbing up the hill by other ways and had turned at last to seek the road.

From the edge of the hill, where John Weightman sat, he could see the travelers, in little groups or larger companies, gathering from time to time by the different paths, and making the ascent. They were all clothed in white, and the form of their garments was strange to him; it was like some old picture. They passed him, group after group, talking quietly together or singing; not moving in haste, but with a certain air of eagerness and joy as if they were glad to be on their way to an appointed place. They did not stay to speak to him, but they looked at him often and spoke to one another as they looked; and now and then one of them would smile and beckon him a friendly greeting, so that he felt they would like him to be with them.

There was quite an interval between the groups; and he followed each of them with his eyes after it had passed, blanching the long ribbon of the road for a little transient space, rising and receding across the wide, billowy upland, among the rounded hillocks of aerial green and gold and lilac, until it came to the high horizon, and stood outlined for a moment, a tiny cloud of whiteness against the tender blue, before it vanished over the hill.

For a long time he sat there watching and wondering. It was a very different world from that in which his mansion on the Avenue was built; and it looked strange to him, but most real—as real as anything he had ever seen. Presently he felt a strong desire to know what country it was and where the people were going. He had a faint premonition of what it must be, but he wished to be sure. So he rose from the stone where he was sitting, and came down through the short grass and the lavender flowers, toward a passing group of people. One of them turned to meet him, and held out his hand. It was an old man, under whose white beard and brows John Weightman thought he saw a suggestion of the face of the village doctor who had cared for him years ago, when he was a boy in the country.

"Welcome," said the old man. "Will you come with us?"

"Where are you going?"

"To the heavenly city, to see our mansions there."

"And who are these with you?"

"Strangers to me, until a little while ago; I know them better now. But you I have known for a long time, John Weightman. Don't you remember your old doctor?"

"Yes," he cried—"yes; your voice has not changed at all. I'm glad indeed to see you, Doctor McLean, especially now. All this seems very strange to me, almost oppressive. I wonder if—but may I go with you, do you suppose?"

"Surely," answered the doctor, with his familiar smile; "it will do you good. And you also must have a mansion in the city waiting for you—a fine one, too—are you not looking forward to it?"

"Yes," replied the other, hesitating a moment; "yes—I believe it must be so, although I had not expected to see it so soon. But I will go with you, and we can talk by the way."

The two men quickly caught up with the other people, and all went forward together along the road. The doctor had little to tell of his experience, for it had been a plain, hard life, uneventfully spent for others, and the story of the village was very simple. John Weightman's adventures and triumphs would have made a far richer, more imposing history, full of contacts with the great events and personages of the time. But somehow or other he did not care to speak much about it, walking on that wide heavenly moorland, under that tranquil, sunless arch of blue, in that free air of perfect peace, where the light was diffused without a shadow, as if the spirit of life in all things were luminous.

There was only one person besides the doctor in that little company whom John Weightman had known before—an old bookkeeper who had spent his life over a desk, carefully keeping accounts—a rusty, dull little man, patient and narrow, whose wife had been in the insane asylum for twenty years and whose only child was a crippled daughter, for whose comfort and happiness he had toiled and sacrificed himself without stint. It was a surprise to find him here, as care-free and joyful as the rest.

The lives of others in the company were revealed in brief glimpses as they talked together—a mother, early widowed, who had kept her little flock of children together and labored through hard and heavy years to bring them up in purity and knowledge—a Sister of Charity who had devoted herself to the nursing of poor folk who were being eaten to death by cancer—a schoolmaster whose heart and life had been poured into his quiet work of training boys for a clear and thoughtful manhood—a medical missionary who had given up a brilliant career in science to take the charge of a hospital in darkest Africa—a beautiful woman with silver hair who had resigned her dreams of love and marriage to care for an invalid father, and after his death had made her life a long, steady search for ways of doing kindnesses to others—a poet who had walked among the crowded tenements of the great city, bringing cheer and comfort not only by his songs, but by his wise and patient works of practical aid—a paralyzed woman who had lain for thirty years upon her bed, helpless but not hopeless, succeeding by a miracle of courage in her single aim, never to complain, but always to impart a bit of her joy and peace to every one who came near her. All these, and other persons like them, people of little consideration in the world, but now seemingly all full of great contentment and an inward gladness that made their steps light, were in the company that passed along the road, talking together of things past and things to come, and singing now and then with clear voices from which the veil of age and sorrow was lifted.

John Weightman joined in some of the songs—which were familiar to him from their use in the church—at first with a touch of hesitation, and then more confidently. For as they went on his sense of strangeness and fear at his new experience diminished, and his thoughts began to take on their habitual assurance and complacency. Were not these people going to the Celestial City? And was not he in his right place among them? He had always looked forward to this journey. If they were sure, each one, of finding a mansion there, could not he be far more sure? His life had been more fruitful than theirs. He had been a leader, a founder of new enterprises, a pillar of church and state, a prince of the house of Israel. Ten talents had been given him, and he had made them twenty. His reward would be proportionate. He was glad that his companions were going to find fit dwellings prepared for them; but he thought also with a certain pleasure of the surprise that some of them would feel when they saw his appointed mansion.

So they came to the summit of the moorland and looked over into the world beyond. It was a vast, green plain, softly rounded like a shallow vase, and circled with hills of amethyst.

A broad, shining river flowed through it, and many silver threads of water were woven across the green; and there were borders of tall trees on the banks of the river, and orchards full of roses abloom along the little streams, and in the midst of all stood the city, white and wonderful and radiant.

When the travelers saw it they were filled with awe and joy. They passed over the little streams and among the orchards quickly and silently, as if they feared to speak lest the city should vanish.

The wall of the city was very low, a child could see over it, for it was made only of precious stones, which are never large. The gate was not like a gate at all, for it was not barred with iron or wood, but only a single pearl, softly gleaming, marked the place where the wall ended and the entrance lay open.

A person stood there whose face was bright and grave, and whose robe was like the flower of the lily, not a woven fabric, but a living texture. "Come in," he said to the company of travelers; "you are at your journey's end, and your mansions are ready for you."

John Weightman hesitated, for he was troubled by a doubt. Suppose that he was not really, like his companions, at his journey's end, but only transported for a little while out of the regular course of his life into this mysterious experience. Suppose that, after all, he had not really passed through the door of death, like these others, but only through the door of dreams, and was walking in a vision, a living man among the blessed dead. Would it be right for him to go with them into the heavenly city? Would it not be a deception, a desecration, a deep and unforgivable offense? The strange, confusing question had no reason in it, as he very well knew; for if he was dreaming, then it was all a dream; but if his companions were real, then he also was with them in reality, and if they had died then he must have died too. Yet he could not rid his mind of the sense that there was a difference between them and him, and it made him afraid to go on. But, as he paused and turned, the Keeper of the Gate looked straight and deep into his eyes, and beckoned to him. Then he knew that it was not only right but necessary that he should enter.

They passed from street to street among fair and spacious dwellings, set in amaranthine gardens, and adorned with an infinitely varied beauty of divine simplicity. The mansions differed in size, in shape, in charm: each one seemed to have its own personal look of loveliness; yet all were alike in fitness to their place, in harmony with one another, in the addition which each made to the singular and tranquil splendor of the city.

As the little company came, one by one, to the mansions which were prepared for them, and their Guide beckoned to the happy inhabitant to enter in and take possession, there was a soft murmur of joy, half wonder and half recognition; as if the new and immortal dwelling were crowned with the beauty of surprise, lovelier and nobler than all the dreams of it had been; and yet also as if it were touched with the beauty of the familiar, the remembered, the long-loved. One after another the travelers were led to their own mansions, and went in gladly; and from within, through the open doorways, came sweet voices of welcome, and low laughter, and song.

At last there was no one left with the Guide but the two old friends, Doctor McLean and John Weightman. They were standing in front of one of the largest and fairest of the houses, whose garden glowed softly with radiant flowers. The Guide laid his hand upon the doctor's shoulder.

"This is for you," he said. "Go in; there is no more pain here, no more death, nor sorrow, nor tears; for your old enemies are all conquered. But all the good that you have done for others, all the help that you have given, all the comfort that you have brought, all the strength and love that you have bestowed upon the suffering, are here; for we have built them all into this mansion for you."

The good man's face was lighted with a still joy. He clasped his old friend's hand closely, and whispered: "How wonderful it is! Go on, you will come to your mansion next, it is not far away, and we shall see each other again soon, very soon." So he went through the garden, and into the music within.

The Keeper of the Gate turned to John Weightman with level, quiet, searching eyes. Then he asked, gravely: "Where do you wish me to lead you now?"

"To see my own mansion," answered the man, with half-concealed excitement. "Is there not one here for me? You may not let me enter it yet, perhaps, for I must confess to you that I am only—"

"I know," said the Keeper of the Gate—"I know it all. You are John Weightman."

"Yes," said the man, more firmly than he had spoken at first, for it gratified him that his name was known. "Yes, I am John Weightman, Senior Warden of St. Petronius' Church. I wish very much to see my mansion here, if only for a moment. I believe that you have one for me. Will you take me to it?"

The Keeper of the Gate drew a little book from the breast of his robe and turned over the pages. "Certainly," he said, with a curious look at the man, "your name is here; and you shall see your mansion, if you will follow me."

It seemed as if they must have walked miles and miles, through the vast city, passing street after street of houses larger and smaller, of gardens richer and poorer, but all full of beauty and delight. They came into a kind of suburb, where there were many small cottages, with plots of flowers, very lowly but bright and fragrant. Finally they reached an open field, bare and lonely-looking. There were two or three little bushes in it, without flowers, and the grass was sparse and thin. In the center of the field was a tiny hut, hardly big enough for a shepherd's shelter. It looked as if it had been built of discarded things, scraps and fragments of other buildings, put together with care and pains, by some one who had tried to make the most of cast-off material. There was something pitiful and shamefaced about the hut. It shrank and drooped and faded in its barren field, and seemed to cling only by sufferance to the edge of the splendid city.

"This," said the Keeper of the Gate, standing still, and speaking with a low, distinct voice—"this is your mansion, John Weightman."

An almost intolerable shock of grieved wonder and indignation choked the man for a moment so that he could not say a word. Then he turned his face away from the poor little hut and began to remonstrate eagerly with his companion. "Surely, sir," he stammered, "you must be in error about this. There is something wrong—some other John Weightman—a confusion of names—the book must be mistaken."

"There is no mistake," said the Keeper of the Gate, very calmly; "here is your name, the record of your title and your possessions in this place."

"But how could such a house be prepared for me," cried the man, with a resentful tremor in his voice, "for me, after my long and faithful service? Is this a suitable mansion for one so well known and devoted? Why is it so pitifully small and mean? Why have you not built it large and fair, like the others?"

"That is all the material you sent us."

"What!"

"We have used all the material that you sent us," repeated the Keeper of the Gate.

"Now I know that you are mistaken," cried the man, with growing earnestness, "for all my life long I have been doing things that must have supplied you with material. Have you not heard that I have built a school-house; the wing of a hospital; two—yes, three—small churches, and the greater part of a large one, the spire of St. Petro—"

The Keeper of the Gate lifted his hand. "Wait," he said; "we know all these things. They were not ill done. But they were all marked and used as foundation for the name and mansion of John Weightman in the world. Did you not plan them for that?"

"Yes," answered the man, confused and taken aback, "I confess that I thought often of them in that way. Perhaps my heart was set upon that too much. But there are other things—my endowment for the college—my steady and liberal contributions to all the established charities—my support of every respectable—"

"Wait," said the Keeper of the Gate again. "Were not all these carefully recorded on earth where they would add to your credit? They were not foolishly done. Verily, you have had your reward for them. Would you be paid twice?"

"No," cried the man, with deepening dismay, "I dare not claim that. I acknowledge that I considered my own interest too much. But surely not altogether. You have said that these things were not foolishly done. They accomplished some good in the world. Does not that count for something?"

"Yes," answered the Keeper of the Gate, "it counts in the world—where you counted it. But it does not belong to you here. We have saved and used everything that you sent us. This is the mansion prepared for you."

As he spoke, his look grew deeper and more searching, like a flame of fire. John Weightman could not endure it. It seemed to strip him naked and wither him. He sank to the ground under a crushing weight of shame, covering his eyes with his hands and cowering face downward upon the stones. Dimly through the trouble of his mind he felt their hardness and coldness. "Tell me, then," he cried, brokenly, "since my life has been so little worth, how came I here at all?"

"Through the mercy of the King"—the answer was like the soft tolling of a bell.

"And how have I earned it?" he murmured.

"It is never earned; it is only given," came the clear, low reply.

"But how have I failed so wretchedly," he asked, "in all the purpose of my life? What could I have done better? What is it that counts here?"

"Only that which is truly given," answered the bell-like voice. "Only that good which is done for the love of doing it. Only those plans in which the welfare of others is the master thought. Only those labors in which the sacrifice is greater than the reward. Only those gifts in which the giver forgets himself."

The man lay silent. A great weakness, an unspeakable despondency and humiliation were upon him. But the face of the Keeper of the Gate was infinitely tender as he bent over him. "Think again, John Weightman. Has there been nothing like that in your life?"

"Nothing," he sighed. "If there ever were such things it must have been long ago—they were all crowded out—I have forgotten them."

There was an ineffable smile on the face of the Keeper of the Gate, and his hand made the sign of the cross over the bowed head as he spoke gently: "These are the things that the King never forgets; and because there were a few of them in your life, you have a little place here."

The sense of coldness and hardness under John Weightman's hands grew sharper and more distinct. The feeling of bodily weariness and lassitude weighed upon him, but there was a calm, almost a lightness, in his heart as he listened to the fading vibrations of the silvery bell-tones. The chimney clock on the mantel had just ended the last stroke of seven as he lifted his head from the table. Thin, pale strips of the city morning were falling into the room through the narrow partings of the heavy curtains.

What was it that had happened to him? Had he been ill? Had he died and come to life again? Or had he only slept, and had his soul gone visiting in dreams? He sat for some time, motionless, not lost, but finding himself in thought. Then he took a narrow book from the table drawer, wrote a check, and tore it out.

He went slowly up the stairs, knocked very softly at his son's door, and, hearing no answer, entered without noise. Harold was asleep, his bare arm thrown above his head, and his eager face relaxed in peace. His father looked at him a moment with strangely shining eyes, and then tip-toed quietly to the writing-desk, found a pencil and a sheet of paper, and wrote rapidly: "My dear boy, here is what you asked me for; do what you like with it, and ask for more if you need it. If you are still thinking of that work with Grenfell, we'll talk it over to-day after church. I want to know your heart better; and if I have made mistakes—"

A slight noise made him turn his head. Harold was sitting up in bed with wide-open eyes. "Father!" he cried, "is that you?"

"Yes, my son," answered John Weightman; "I've come back—I mean I've come up—no, I mean come in—well, here I am, and God give us a good Christmas together."

Review Questions
1. In John Weightman's eyes, what was the difference between a good and a bad charity?
2. What did Harold mean when he told his father, "According to you there's very little difference—a fool's paradise or a fool's hell"?
3. Why was John unwilling to give money to Harold's friend?
4. How did John interpret the Bible verse "Lay not up for yourselves treasures upon earth"?
5. How did the Keeper of the Gate explain the poor quality of John's mansion?

Thought Questions
1. Van Dyke uses the word "mansion" in several different contexts in this story. What are they? Can you think of some places in the Bible that the word "mansion" is used?
2. John placed emphasis on having a solid foundation for all of his works. (Think about his last name.) Did he really have a secure foundation? Why or why not? How can Christians avoid insisting God put their good works "in the ledger"?
3. With whom do you empathize more, Harold or John Weightman? Can you appreciate the point of view of the other? What were the strengths of each? The weaknesses?
4. Compare the description of John Weightman's house and his mansion in heaven. Are there similarities? What words does Van Dyke use to describe each? How does he use the setting of the story to reveal John Weightman's character?

STORY FOCUS

Writing Practice

In writing, one must be an artist to make settings come alive. A well-described setting is similar to a painting of the scene; the reader can clearly "see" the characters' surroundings. One of the strengths of Van Dyke's stories is the lively settings that he creates. By using specific naming terms and details, Van Dyke allows readers to picture the scene as though they were experiencing it first-hand.

Pick a scene from Van Dyke's "The Mansion" that was particularly vivid to you and re-read it closely. What details or descriptive words made it come alive for you?

Using what you have learned from Van Dyke's story, look at the list of general words on the left, and try to come up with two or three specific words that would paint a clearer picture for a reader. Try to avoid "adverbitis" (using too many words that end in "ly"). Instead, use specific nouns.

Example: Road – cobblestone path, gravel driveway, two-lane highway

Car	Flowers
Blue	Cold
Colorful	Girl/Boy
Dog	Sweet
Food	Pretty
Fence	Clothes

Have We Met? CHARACTERS

Where would a good story be without characters? Certainly it would not be a good story! In both reading and writing literature, characters are central. Character development is one of the most distinguishing features between a well-written story and a poorly-written one.

People are not one-dimensional. Very few humans completely fit the stereotypes "jock," "cheerleader," "hero," or "villain." Characters should mirror the complexity of real people. They should have strengths and weaknesses, good days and bad days, pet peeves and favorite cousins.

Classic literature should be something like spending time with a new acquaintance. By the end of the story, you should be familiar with each character's appearance, personality, and strengths and weaknesses. As you read the next few stories, make sure that you can answer the following questions about the characters' development:

- How many characters are in the story?
- What are their names?
- What does each character look like?
- Does the author make you like or dislike any of the characters? How? Why?
- What is the major character trait of each person? How does the author reveal that to you?
- Are the characters believable? Do they act the way you expect or are they complicated?
- Do any of the characters change in the course of the story? How and why?

Portraying characters in a realistic and engaging way can be difficult. A helpful saying to remember (both in writing and in evaluating someone else's writing) is "show, don't tell." In other words, avoid saying, "Jane is happy today." Instead, show Jane's happiness. Is she walking with a spring in her step? Laughing even when there is nothing funny? Singing in the shower? Descriptions like these allow readers to draw their own conclusions.

One of the most exciting moments in writing a story is when your characters begin to take on a life of their own. You don't have to think about what they will say next, because you know how they would react in that situation. When they come alive in your mind, that's when they come alive for readers.

"The Hiltons' Holiday"
Sarah Orne Jewett

Sarah Orne Jewett (1849-1909) was born in New England. Books were her only means of experiencing the greater world. As a short story writer, her characters reflect this lifestyle, being ordinary residents of an everyday world. Much of Jewett's work has been character-driven rather than plot-driven. For this, her writing has sometimes been criticized. Nonetheless, she remains one of the leading female short story writers of the nineteenth century, in part because her characters are not overshadowed by plot. "The Hiltons' Holiday," a story about relationships within a New England family, follows this style closely.

There was a bright, full moon in the clear sky, and the sunset was still shining faintly in the west. Dark woods stood all about the old Hilton farmhouse, save down the hill, westward, where lay the shadowy fields which John Hilton, and his father before him, had cleared and tilled with much toil the small fields to which they had given the industry and even affection of their honest lives.

John Hilton was sitting on the doorstep of his house. As he moved his head in and out of the shadows, turning now and then to speak to his wife, who sat just within the doorway, one could see his good face, rough and somewhat unkempt, as if he were indeed a creature of the shady woods and brown earth, instead of the noisy town. It was late in the long spring evening, and he had just come from the lower field as cheerful as a boy, proud of having finished the planting of his potatoes.

"I had to do my last row mostly by feelin'," he said to his wife. "I'm proper glad I pushed through, an' went back an' ended off after supper.

'Twould have taken me a good part o' to-morrow mornin', an' broke my day."

"'Tain't no use for ye to work yourself all to pieces, John," answered the woman, quickly. "I declare it does seem harder than ever that we couldn't have kep' our boy; he'd been comin' fourteen years old this fall, most a grown man, and he'd work right 'longside of ye now the whole time."

"'Twas hard to lose him; I—do seem to miss little John," said the father, sadly. "I expect there was reasons why 'twas best. I feel able an' smart to work; my father was a girt strong man, an' a monstrous worker afore me. 'Tain't that; but I was thinkin' myself to-day what a sight o' company the boy would ha' been. You know, small's he was, how I could trust him to leave anywheres with the team, and how he'd beseech to go with me wherever I was goin'; always right in my tracks I used to tell 'em. Poor little John, for all he was so young he had a great deal o' judgment; he'd ha' made a likely man."

The mother sighed heavily as she sat within the shadow.

"But then there's the little girls, a sight o' help an' company," urged the father, eagerly, as if it were wrong to dwell upon sorrow and loss. "Katy, she's most as good as a boy, except that she ain't very rugged. She's a real little farmer, she's helped me a sight this spring; an' you've got Susan Ellen, that makes a complete little housekeeper for ye as far as she's learnt. I don't see but we're better off than most folks, each on us having a workmate."

"That's so, John," acknowledged Mrs. Hilton, wistfully, beginning to rock steadily in her straight splint-bottom chair. It was always a good sign when she rocked.

"Where be the little girls so late?" asked their father. "'Tis getting' long past eight o'clock. I don't know when we've all set up so late, but it's so kind o' summer-like an' pleasant. Why, where be they gone?"

"I've told ye; only over to Becker's folks," answered the mother. "I don't see myself what keeps 'em so late; they beseeched me after supper till I let 'em go. They're all in a dazzle with the new teacher; she asked 'em to come over. They say she's unusual smart with 'rethmetic, but she has a kind of gorpen look to me. She's goin' to give Katy some pieces for her doll, but I told Katy she ought to be ashamed wantin' dolls' pieces, big as she's gittin' to be. I don't know's she ought, though; she ain't but nine this summer."

"Let her take her comfort," said the kind-hearted man. "Them things draws her to the teacher, an' makes them acquainted. Katy's shy with new folks, more so'n Susan Ellen, who's of the business kind. Katy's shy-feelin' and wishful."

"I don't know but she is," agreed the mother slowly. "Ain't it sing'lar how well acquainted you be with that one, an' I with Susan Ellen? 'Twas always so from the first. I'm doubtful sometimes our Katy ain't one that'll be like to get married anyways not about here. She lives right with herself, but Susan Ellen ain't nothin' when she's alone, she's always after company; all the boys is waitin' on her a'ready. I ain't afraid but she'll take her pick when the time comes. I expect to see Susan Ellen well settled; she feels grown up now but Katy don't care one mite 'bout none o' them things. She wants to be rovin' out o' doors. I do believe she'd stand an' hark to a bird the whole forenoon."

"Perhaps she'll grow up to be a teacher," suggested John Hilton. "She takes to her books more'n the other one. I should like one on 'em to be a teacher same's my mother was. They're good girls as anybody's got."

"So they be," said the mother, with unusual gentleness, and the creak of her rocking-chair was heard, regular as the ticking of a clock. The night breeze stirred in the great woods, and the sound of a brook that went falling down the hillside grew louder and louder. Now and then one could hear the plaintive chirp of a bird. The moon glittered with whiteness like a winter moon, and shone upon the low-roofed house until its small window-panes gleamed like silver, and one could almost see the colours of a blooming bush of lilac that grew in a sheltered angle by the kitchen door. There was an incessant sound of frogs in the lowlands.

"Be you sound asleep, John?" asked the wife presently.

"I don't know but what I was a'most," said the tired man, starting a little. "I should laugh if I was to fall sound asleep right here on the step; 'tis the bright night, I expect, makes my eyes feel heavy, an' 'tis so peaceful. I was up an' dressed a little past four an' out to work. Well, well!" and he laughed sleepily and rubbed his eyes. "Where's the little girls? I'd better step along an' meet 'em."

"I wouldn't just yet; they'll get home all right, but 'tis late for 'em certain. I don't want 'em keepin' Mis' Becker's folks up neither. There, le's wait a few minutes," urged Mrs. Hilton.

"I've be'n a-thinkin' all day I'd like to give the child'n some kind of a treat," said the father, wide awake now. "I hurried up my work 'cause I had it so in mind. They don't have the opportunities some do, an' I want 'em to know the world, an' not stay right here on the farm like a couple o' bushes."

"They're a sight better off not to be so full o' notions as some is," protested the mother, suspiciously.

"Certain," answered the farmer; "but they're good, bright child'n, an' commencin' to take a sight o' notice. I want 'em to have all we can give 'em. I want 'em to see how other folks does things."

"Why, so do I"—here the rocking-chair stopped ominously—"but so long's they're contented—"

"Contented ain't all in this world; hopper-toads may have that quality an' spend all their time a-blinkin'. I don't know's bein' contented is all there is to look for in a child. Ambition's somethin' to me."

"Now you've got your mind on to some plot or other." (The rocking-chair began to move again.) "Why can't you talk right out?"

"Tain't nothin' special," answered the good man, a little ruffled; he was never prepared for his wife's mysterious powers of divination. "Well there, you do find things out the master! I only thought perhaps I'd take 'em to-morrow, an' go off somewhere if 'twas a good day. I've been promisin' for a good while I'd take 'em to Topham Corners; they've never been there since they was very small."

"I believe you want a good time yourself. You ain't never got over bein' a boy." Mrs. Hilton seemed much amused. "There, go if you want to an' take 'em; they've got their summer hats an' new dresses. I don't know o' nothin' that stands in the way. I should sense it better if there was a circus or anythin' to go to. Why don't you wait an' let the girls pick 'em some strawberries or nice ros'berries, and then they could take an' sell 'em to the stores?"

John Hilton reflected deeply. "I should like to get me some good yellow-turnip seed to plant late. I ain't more'n satisfied with what I've been getting' o' late years o' Ira Speed. An' I'm goin' to provide me with a good hoe; mine's getting' wore out an' all shackly. I can't seem to fix it good."

"Them's excuses," observed Mrs. Hilton, with friendly tolerance. "You just cover up the hoe with somethin', if you get it—I would. Ira Speed's so jealous he'll remember it of you this twenty year, your goin' an' buyin' a new hoe o' anybody but him."

"I've always thought 'twas a free country," said John Hilton, soberly. "I don't want to vex Ira neither; he favours us all he can in trade. 'Tis difficult for him to spare a cent, but he's as honest as daylight."

At this moment there was a sudden sound of young voices, and a pair of young figures came out from the shadow of the woods into the moonlighted open space. An old cock crowed loudly from his perch in the shed, as if he were a herald of royalty. The little girls were hand in hand, and a brisk young dog capered about them as they came.

"Wa'n't it dark gittin' home through the woods this time o' night?" asked the mother, hastily, and not without reproach.

"I don't love to have you gone so late; mother an' me was timid about ye, and you've kep' Mis' Becker's folks up, I expect," said their father, regretfully. "I don't want to have it said that my little girls ain't got good manners."

"The teacher had a party," chirped Susan Ellen, the elder of the two children. "Goin' home from school she asked the Grover boys, an' Mary an' Sarah Speed. An' Mis' Becker was real pleasant to us: she passed round some cake, an' handed us sap sugar on one of her best plates, an' we played games an' sung some pieces too. Mis' Becker thought we did real well. I can pick out most of a tune on the cabinet organ; teacher says she'll give me lessons."

"I want to know, dear!" exclaimed John Hilton.

"Yes, an' we played Copenhagen, an' took sides spellin', an' Katy beat everybody spellin' there was there."

Katy had not spoken, she was not so strong as her sister, and while Susan Ellen stood a step or two away addressing her eager little audience, Katy had seated herself close to her father on the doorstep. He put his arm around her shoulder, and drew her close to his side, where she stayed.

"Ain't you got nothin' to tell, daughter?" he asked, looking down fondly, and Katy gave a pleased little sigh for answer.

"Tell 'em what's goin' to be the last day o' school, and about our trimmin' the school-house," she said, and Susan Ellen gave the programme in most spirited fashion.

"'Twill be a great time," said the mother, when she had finished. "I don't see why folks want to go trapesin' off to strange places when such things is happenin' right about 'em." But the children did not observe her mysterious air. "Come, you must step yourselves right to bed."

They all went into the dark, warm house, the bright moon shone upon it steadily all night, and the lilac flowers were shaken by no breath of wind until the early dawn.

The Hiltons always waked early. So did their neighbours, the crows and song-sparrows and robins, the light-footed foxes and squirrels in the woods. When John Hilton waked, before five o'clock, an hour later than usual because he had sat up so late, he opened the house door and came out into the yard, crossing the short green turf hurriedly as if the day were too far spent for any loitering. The magnitude of the plan for taking a whole day of pleasure confronted him seriously, but the weather was fair, and his wife, whose disapproval could not have been set aside, had accepted and even smiled upon the great project. It was inevitable now that he and the children should go to Topham Corners. Mrs. Hilton had the pleasure of waking them, and telling the news.

In a few minutes they came frisking out to talk over the great plans. The cattle were already fed, and their father was milking. The only sign of high festivity was the wagon pulled out into the yard, with both seats put in as if it were Sunday; but Mr. Hilton still wore his everyday clothes, and Susan Ellen suffered instantly from disappointment.

"Ain't we goin', father?" she asked, complainingly, but he nodded and smiled at her, even though the cow, impatient to get to pasture, kept whisking her rough tail across his face. He held his head down and spoke cheerfully, in spite of this vexation.

"Yes, sister, we're goin' certain, an' goin' to have a great time, too." Susan Ellen thought that he seemed like a boy at that delightful moment, and felt new sympathy and pleasure at once. "You go an' help mother about breakfast an' them things; we want to get off quick's we can. You coax mother now, both on ye, an' see if she won't go with us."

"She said she wouldn't be hired to," responded Susan Ellen. "She says it's goin' to be hot, an' she's laid out to go over an' see how her aunt Tamsen Brooks is this afternoon."

The father gave a little sigh; then he took heart again. The truth was that his wife made light of the contemplated pleasure, and, much as he usually valued her companionship and approval, it was sure that they should have a better time without her. It was impossible, however, not to feel guilty of disloyalty at the thought. Even though she might be completely unconscious of his best ideals, he only loved her and the ideals the more, and bent his energies to satisfying her indefinite expectations. His wife still kept much of that youthful beauty which Susan Ellen seemed likely to reproduce.

An hour later the best wagon was ready, and the great expedition set forth. The little dog sat apart, and barked as if it fell entirely upon him to voice the general excitement. Both seats were in the wagon, but the empty place testified to Mrs. Hilton's unyielding disposition. She had wondered why one broad seat would not do, but John Hilton meekly suggested that the wagon looked better. The little girls sat on the back seat dressed alike in their Sunday hats of straw with blue ribbons, and their little plaid shawls pinned neatly about their small shoulders. They wore grey thread gloves, and sat very straight. Susan Ellen was half a head the taller, but otherwise, from behind, they looked much alike. As for their father, he was in his Sunday best, a plain black coat, and a winter hat of felt, which was heavy and rusty-looking for that warm early-summer day. He had it in mind to buy a new straw hat at Topham, so that this with the turnip-seed and the hoe made three important reasons for going.

"Remember an' lay off your shawls when you get there, an' carry them over your arms," said the mother, clucking like an excited hen to her chickens. "They'll do to keep the dust off your new dresses goin' and comin'. An' when you eat your dinners don't get spots on you, an' don't point at folks as you ride by, an' stare, or they'll know you came from the country. An' John, you call into Cousin Ad'line Marlow's an' see how they all be, an' tell her I expect her over certain to stop a while before hayin'. It always eases her phthisic to git up here on the highland, an' I've got a new notion about doin' over her best-room carpet sence I see her that'll save rippin' one breadth. An' don't come home all wore out; an', John, don't you go an' buy me no kickshaws to fetch home. I ain't a child, an' you ain't got no money to waste. I expect you'll go, like's not, an' buy you some kind of a foolish boy's hat; do look an' see if it's reasonable good straw, an' won't splinter all off round the edge. An' you mind, John—"

"Yes, yes, hold on!" cried John, impatiently; then he cast a last affectionate, reassuring look at her face, flushed with the hurry and responsibility of starting them off in proper shape. "I wish you was goin' too," he said, smiling. "I do so!" Then the old horse started, and they went out at the bars, and began the careful long descent of the hill. The young dog, tethered to the lilac bush, was frantic with piteous appeals; the little girls piped their eager good-byes again and again, and their father turned many times to look back and wave his hand. As for their mother, she stood alone and watched them out of sight.

There was one place far out on the high road where she could catch a last glimpse of the wagon, and she waited what seemed a very long time until it appeared and then was lost to sight again behind a low hill. "They're nothin' but a pack o' child'n together," she said aloud, and then felt lonelier than she expected. She even stooped and patted the unresigned little dog as she passed him, going into the house.

The occasion was so much more important than anyone had foreseen that both the little girls were speechless. It seemed at first like going to church in new clothes, or to a funeral; they hardly knew how to behave at the beginning of a whole day of pleasure. They made grave bows at such persons of their acquaintance as happened to be straying in the road. Once or twice they stopped before a farmhouse, while their father talked an inconsiderately long time with someone about the crops and the weather and even dwelt upon town business and the doings of the selectmen, which might be talked of at any time. The explanations that he gave of their excursion seemed quite unnecessary. It was made entirely clear that he had a little business to do at Topham Corners, and thought he had better give the little girls a ride; they had been very steady at school, and he had finished planting, and could take the day as well as not. Soon, however, they all felt as if such an excursion were an everyday affair, and Susan Ellen began to ask eager questions, while Katy silently sat apart enjoying herself as she never had done before. She liked to see the strange houses, and the children who belonged to them; it was delightful to find flowers that she knew growing all along the road, no matter how far she went from home. Each small homestead looked its best and pleasantest, and shared the exquisite beauty that early summer made, shared the luxury of greenness and floweriness that decked the rural world. There was an early peony or a late lilac in almost every dooryard.

It was seventeen miles to Topham. After a while they seemed very far from home, having left the hills far behind, and descended to a great level country with fewer tracts of woodland, and wider fields where the crops were much more forward. The houses were all painted, and the roads were smoother and wider. It had been so pleasant driving along that Katy dreaded going into the strange town when she first caught sight of it, though Susan Ellen kept asking with bold fretfulness if they were not almost there. They counted the steeples of four churches, and their father presently showed them the Topham Academy, where their grandmother once went to school, and told them that perhaps some day they would go there too. Katy's heart gave a strange leap; it was such a tremendous thing to think of, but instantly the suggestion was transformed for her into one of the certainties of life. She looked with solemn awe at the tall belfry, and the long rows of windows in the front of the academy, there where it stood high and white among the clustering trees. She hoped that they were going to drive by, but something forbade her taking the responsibility of saying so.

Soon the children found themselves among the crowded village houses. Their father turned to look at them with affectionate solicitude.

"Now sit up straight and appear pretty," he whispered to them. "We're among the best people now, an' I want folks to think well of you."

"I guess we're just as good as they be," remarked Susan Ellen, looking at some innocent passers-by with dark suspicion, but Katy tried indeed to sit straight, and folded her hands prettily in her lap, and wished with all her heart to be pleasing for her father's sake. Just then an elderly woman saw the wagon and the sedate party it carried, and smiled so kindly that it seemed to Katy as if Topham Corners had welcomed and received them. She smiled back again as if this hospitable person were an old friend, and entirely forgot that the eyes of all Topham had been upon her.

"There, now we're coming to an elegant house that I want you to see; you'll never forget it," said John Hilton. "It's where Judge Masterson lives, the great lawyer; the handsomest house in the county, everybody says."

"Do you know him, father?" asked Susan Ellen.

"I do," answered John Hilton, proudly. "Him and my mother went to school together in their young days, and were always called the two best scholars of their time. The judge called to see her once; he stopped to our house to see her when I was a boy. An' then, some years ago you've heard me tell how I was on the jury, an' when he heard my name spoken he looked at me sharp, and asked if I wa'n't the son of Catharine Winn, an' spoke most beautiful of your grandmother, an' how well he remembered their young days together."

"I like to hear about that," said Katy.

"She had it pretty hard, I'm afraid, up on the old farm. She was keepin' school in our district when father married her that's the main reason I backed 'em down when they wanted to tear the old schoolhouse all to pieces," confided John Hilton, turning eagerly. "They all say she lived longer up here on the hill than she could anywhere, but she never had her health. I wa'n't but a boy when she died. Father an' me lived alone afterward till the time your mother come; 'twas a good while, too; I wa'n't married so young as some. 'T was lonesome, I tell you; father was plumb discouraged losin' of his wife, an' her long sickness an' all set him back, an' we'd work all day on the land an' never say a word. I s'pose 'tis bein' so lonesome early in life that makes me so pleased to have some nice girls growin' up around me now."

There was a tone in her father's voice that drew Katy's heart toward him with new affection. She dimly understood, but Susan Ellen was less interested. They had often heard this story before, but to one child it was always new and to the other old. Susan Ellen was apt to think it tiresome to hear about her grandmother, who, being dead, was hardly worth talking about.

"There's Judge Masterson's place," said their father in an everyday manner, as they turned a corner, and came into full view of the beautiful old white house standing behind its green trees and terraces and lawns. The children had never imagined anything so stately and fine, and even Susan Ellen exclaimed with pleasure. At that moment they saw an old gentleman, who carried himself with great dignity, coming slowly down the wide, box-bordered path toward the gate.

"There he is now, there's the judge!" whispered John Hilton, excitedly, reining his horse quickly to the green roadside. "He's goin' downtown to his office; we can wait right here an' see him. I can't expect him to remember me; it's been a good many years. Now you are goin' to see the great Judge Masterson!"

There was a quiver of expectation in their hearts. The judge stopped at his gate, hesitating a moment before he lifted the latch, and glanced up the street at the country wagon with its two prim little girls on the back seat, and the eager man who drove. They seemed to be waiting for something; the old horse was nibbling at the fresh roadside grass. The judge was used to being looked at with interest, and responded now with a smile as he came out to the sidewalk, and unexpectedly turned their way. Then he suddenly lifted his hat with grave politeness, and came directly toward them.

"Good morning, Mr. Hilton," he said. "I am very glad to see you, sir," and Mr. Hilton, the little girls' own father, took off his hat with equal courtesy, and bent forward to shake hands.

Susan Ellen cowered and wished herself away, but little Katy sat straighter than ever, with joy in her father's pride and pleasure shining in her pale, flower-like little face.

"These are your daughters, I am sure," said the old gentleman, kindly, taking Susan Ellen's limp and reluctant hand; but when he looked at Katy, his face brightened. "How she recalls your mother!" he said with great feeling. "I am glad to see this dear child. You must come to see me with your father, my dear," he added, still looking at her. "Bring both little girls, and let them run about the old garden; the cherries will soon be getting ripe," said Judge Masterson, hospitably. "Perhaps you will have time to stop this afternoon as you go home?"

"I should call it a great pleasure if you would come and see us again some time. You may be driving our way, sir," said John Hilton.

"Not very often in these days," answered the old judge. "I thank you for the kind invitation. I should like to see the fine view again from your hill westward. Can I serve you in any way while you are in town? Good-bye, my little friends!"

Then they parted, but not before Katy, the shy Katy, whose hand the judge still held unconsciously while he spoke, had reached forward as he said good-bye, and lifted her face to kiss him. She could not have told why, except that she felt drawn to something in the serious, worn face. For the first time in her life the child had felt the charm of manners; perhaps she owned a kinship between that which made him what he was, and the spark of nobleness and purity in her own simple soul. She turned again and again to look back at him as they drove away.

"Now you have seen one of the first gentlemen in the country," said their father. "It was worth comin' twice as far." But he did not say any more, nor turn as usual to look in the children's faces.

In the chief business street of Topham a great many country wagons like the Hiltons' were fastened to the posts, and there seemed to our holiday-makers to be a great deal of noise and excitement.

"Now I've got to do my errands, and we can let the horse rest and feed," said John Hilton. "I'll slip his headstall right off, an' put on his halter. I'm goin' to buy him a real good treat o' oats. First we'll go an' buy me my straw hat; I feel as if this one looked a little past to wear in Topham. We'll buy the things we want, an' then we'll walk all along the street, so you can look in the windows an' see the han'some things, same's your mother likes to. What was it mother told you about your shawls?"

"To take 'em off an' carry 'em over our arms," piped Susan Ellen, without comment, but in the interest of alighting and finding themselves afoot upon the pavement the shawls were forgotten. The children stood at the doorway of a shop while their father went inside, and they tried to see what the Topham shapes of bonnets were like, as their mother had advised them; but everything was exciting and confusing, and they could arrive at no decision.

When Mr. Hilton came out with a hat in his hand to be seen in a better light, Katy whispered that she wished he would buy a shiny one like Judge Masterson's; but her father only smiled and shook his head, and said that they were plain folks, he and Katy. There were dry-goods for sale in the same shop, and a young clerk who was measuring linen kindly pulled off some pretty labels with gilded edges and gay pictures, and gave them to the little girls, to their exceeding joy. He may have had small sisters at home, this friendly lad, for he took pains to find two pretty blue boxes besides, and was rewarded by their beaming gratitude.

It was a famous day; they even became used to seeing so many people pass. The village was full of its morning activity, and Susan Ellen gained a new respect for her father, and an increased sense of her own consequence, because even in Topham several persons knew him and called him familiarly by name. The meeting with an old man who had once been a neighbour seemed to give Mr. Hilton the greatest pleasure. The old man called to them from a house doorway as they were passing, and they all went in. The children seated themselves wearily on the wooden step, but their father shook his old friend eagerly by the hand, and declared that he was delighted to see him so well and enjoying the fine weather.

"Oh, yes," said the old man, in a feeble, quavering voice, "I'm astonishin' well for my age. I don't complain, John, I don't complain."

They talked long together of people whom they had known in the past, and Katy, being a little tired, was glad to rest, and sat still with her hands folded, looking about the front yard. There were some kinds of flowers that she never had seen before.

"This is the one that looks like my mother," her father said, and touched Katy's shoulder to remind her to stand up and let herself be seen. "Judge Masterson saw the resemblance; we met him at his gate this morning."

"Yes, she certain does look like your mother, John," said the old man, looking pleasantly at Katy, who found that she liked him better than at first. "She does, certain; the best of young folks is, they remind us of the old ones. 'Tis nateral to cling to life, folks say, but for me, I git impatient at times. Most everybody's gone now, an' I want to be goin'. 'Tis somethin' before me, an' I want to have it over with. I want to be there 'long o' the rest o' the folks. I expect to last quite a while though; I may see ye couple o' times more, John."

John Hilton responded cheerfully, and the children were urged to pick some flowers. The old man awed them with his impatience to be gone. There was such a townful of people about him and he seemed as lonely as if he were the last survivor of a former world. Until that moment they had felt as if everything was just beginning.

"Now I want to buy somethin' pretty for your mother," said Mr. Hilton as they went soberly away down the street, the children keeping fast hold of his hands. "By now the old horse will have eat his dinner and had a good rest, so pretty soon we can jog along home. I'm goin' to take you round by the academy, and the old North meeting-house where Dr. Barstow used to preach. Can't you think o' somethin' that your mother 'd want?" he asked suddenly, confronted by a man's difficulty of choice.

"She was talkin' about wantin' a new pepper-box, one day; the top o' the old one won't stay on," suggested Susan Ellen, with delightful readiness. "Can't we have some candy, father?"

"Yes, ma'am," said John Hilton, smiling and swinging her hand to and fro as they walked. "I feel as if some would be good myself. What's all this?" They were passing a photographer's doorway with its enticing array of portraits. "I do declare!" he exclaimed, excitedly, "I'm goin' to have our pictures taken; 'twill please your mother more'n a little."

This was, perhaps, the greatest triumph of the day, except the delightful meeting with the judge; they sat in a row, with the father in the middle, and there was no doubt as to the excellence of the likeness. The best hats had to be taken off because they cast a shadow, but they were not missed, as their owners had feared. Both Susan Ellen and Katy looked their brightest and best; their eager young faces would forever shine there; the joy of the holiday was mirrored in the little picture. They did not know why their father was so pleased with it; they would not know until age had dowered them with the riches of association and remembrance.

Just at nightfall the Hiltons reached home again, tired out and happy. Katy had climbed over into the front seat beside her father, because that was always her place when they went to church on Sundays. It was a cool evening, there was a fresh sea wind that brought a light mist with it, and the sky was fast growing cloudy.

Somehow the children looked different; it seemed to their mother as if they had grown older and taller since they went away in the morning, and as if they belonged to the town now as much as to the country. The greatness of their day's experience had left her far behind, the day had been silent and lonely without them, and she had had their supper ready, and been watching anxiously, ever since five o'clock. As for the children themselves they had little to say at first; they had eaten their luncheon early on the way to Topham. Susan Ellen was childishly cross, but Katy was pathetic and wan. They could hardly wait to show the picture, and their mother was as much pleased as everybody had expected.

"There, what did make you wear your shawls?" she exclaimed a moment afterward, reproachfully. "You ain't been an' wore 'em all day long? I wanted folks to see how pretty your new dresses was, if I did make 'em. Well, well! I wish more'n ever now I'd gone an' seen to ye!"

"An' here's the pepper-box!" said Katy, in a pleased, unconscious tone.

"That really is what I call beautiful," said Mrs. Hilton, after a long and doubtful look. "Our other one was only tin. I never did look so high as a chiny one with flowers, but I can get us another any time for every day. That's a proper hat, as good as you could have got, John. Where's your new hoe?" she asked, as he came toward her from the barn, smiling with satisfaction.

"I declare to Moses if I didn't forget all about it," meekly acknowledged the leader of the great excursion. "That an' my yellow-turnip seed, too; they went clean out o' my head, there was so many other things to think of. But 'tain't no sort o' matter; I can get a hoe just as well to Ira Speed's."

His wife could not help laughing. "You an' the little girls have had a great time. They was full o' wonder to me about everythin', and I expect they'll talk about it for a week. I guess we was right about havin' 'em see somethin' more o' the world."

"Yes," answered John Hilton, with humility, "yes, we did have a beautiful day. I didn't expect so much. They looked as nice as anybody, and appeared so modest an' pretty. The little girls will remember it perhaps by an' by. I guess they won't never forget this day they had 'long o' father."

It was evening again, the frogs were piping in the lower meadows, and in the woods, higher up the great hill, a little owl began to hoot. The sea air, salt and heavy, was blowing in over the country at the end of the hot, bright day. A lamp was lighted in the house, the happy children were chatting together, and supper was waiting. The father and mother lingered for a moment outside and looked down over the shadowy fields; then they went in, without speaking. The great day was over, and they shut the door.

Review Questions
1. Describe Katy and Susan Ellen's personalities. How are they alike? Different?
2. Why did Mr. Hilton want to take the girls into town with him?
3. Why did Mrs. Hilton disapprove?
4. How did Mr. Hilton known Judge Masterson? Did he expect the judge to remember him?
5. What surprise did Mr. Hilton want to bring home for his wife?

Thought Questions
1. What is a "holiday"? How has the definition changed over the years?
2. What do we know about the Hilton's son? Do you think the Hiltons handled their loss well? How did Mr. Hilton show his appreciation for his daughters?
3. Is contentment better than ambition? Is it possible to have both?
4. Do you ever feel like you have to impress people? Is the feeling stronger when you are around friends or strangers? Explain.
5. How would you describe the relationship between the Hilton girls and their parents? Support your argument from the text. What techniques does Jewett use to develop her characters?

"The Schoolboy's Story"
Charles Dickens

Charles Dickens (1812-1870) was a British writer who, besides writing compelling and complex characters, used his writing to address social problems, injustice, and hypocrisy in England. Using his own childhood as a model, Dickens wrote novels about young boys who were struggling to make their way in the world. "The Schoolboy's Story" is similar in plot to Dickens' longer works, including the well-known novels *Oliver Twist* and *David Copperfield*.

Being rather young at present—I am getting on in years, but still I am rather young—I have no particular adventures of my own to fall back upon. It wouldn't much interest anybody here, I suppose, to know what a screw the Reverend is, or what a griffin SHE is, or how they do stick it into parents—particularly hair-cutting, and medical attendance. One of our fellows was charged in his half's account twelve and sixpence for two pills—tolerably profitable at six and threepence a-piece, I should think—and he never took them either, but put them up the sleeve of his jacket.

As to the beef, it's shameful. It's NOT beef. Regular beef isn't veins. You can chew regular beef. Besides which, there's gravy to regular beef, and you never see a drop to ours. Another of our fellows went home ill, and heard the family doctor tell his father that he couldn't account for his complaint unless it was the beer. Of course it was the beer, and well it might be!

However, beef and Old Cheeseman are two different things. So is beer. It was Old Cheeseman I meant to tell about; not the manner in which our fellows get their constitutions destroyed for the sake of profit.

Why, look at the pie-crust alone. There's no flakiness in it. It's solid—like damp lead. Then our fellows get nightmares, and are bolstered for calling out and waking other fellows. Who can wonder!

Old Cheeseman one night walked in his sleep, put his hat on over his night-cap, got hold of a fishing-rod and a cricket-bat, and went down into the parlour, where they naturally thought from his appearance he was a Ghost. Why, he never would have done that if his meals had been wholesome. When we all begin to walk in our sleeps, I suppose they'll be sorry for it.

Old Cheeseman wasn't second Latin Master then; he was a fellow himself. He was first brought there, very small, in a post-chaise, by a woman who was always taking snuff and shaking him—and that was the most he remembered about it. He never went home for the holidays. His accounts (he never learnt any extras) were sent to a Bank, and the Bank paid them; and he had a brown suit twice a-year, and went into boots at twelve. They were always too big for him, too.

In the Midsummer holidays, some of our fellows who lived within walking distance, used to come back and climb the trees outside the playground wall, on purpose to look at Old Cheeseman reading there by himself. He was always as mild as the tea—and THAT'S pretty mild, I should hope!—so when they whistled to him, he looked up and nodded; and when they said, "Halloa, Old Cheeseman, what have you had for dinner?" he said, "Boiled mutton;" and when they said, "Ain't it solitary, Old Cheeseman?" he said, "It is a little dull sometimes," and then they said, "Well good-bye, Old Cheeseman!" and climbed down again. Of course it was imposing on Old Cheeseman to give him nothing but boiled mutton through a whole Vacation, but that was just like the system. When they didn't give him boiled mutton, they gave him rice pudding, pretending it was a treat. And saved the butcher.

So Old Cheeseman went on. The holidays brought him into other trouble besides the loneliness; because when the fellows began to come back, not wanting to, he was always glad to see them; which was aggravating when they were not at all glad to see him, and so he got his head knocked against walls, and that was the way his nose bled. But he was a favourite in general. Once a subscription was raised for him; and, to keep up his spirits, he was presented before the holidays with two white mice, a rabbit, a pigeon, and a beautiful puppy. Old Cheeseman cried about it—especially soon afterwards, when they all ate one another.

Of course Old Cheeseman used to be called by the names of all sorts of cheeses—Double Glo'sterman, Family Cheshireman, Dutchman, North Wiltshireman, and all that. But he never minded it. And I don't mean to say he was old in point of years—because he wasn't—only he was called from the first, Old Cheeseman.

At last, Old Cheeseman was made second Latin Master. He was brought in one morning at the beginning of a new half, and presented to the school in that capacity as "Mr. Cheeseman." Then our fellows all agreed that Old Cheeseman was a spy, and a deserter, who had gone over to the enemy's camp, and sold himself for gold. It was no excuse for him that he had sold himself for very little gold—two pound ten a quarter and his washing, as was reported. It was decided by a Parliament which sat about it, that Old Cheeseman's mercenary motives could alone be taken into account, and that he had "coined our blood for drachmas." The Parliament took the expression out of the quarrel scene between Brutus and Cassius.

When it was settled in this strong way that Old Cheeseman was a tremendous traitor, who had wormed himself into our fellows' secrets on purpose to get himself into favour by giving up everything he knew, all courageous fellows were invited to come forward and enrol themselves in a Society for making a set against him. The President of the Society was First boy, named Bob Tarter. His father was in the West Indies, and he owned, himself, that his father was worth Millions. He had great power among our fellows, and he wrote a parody, beginning – "Who made believe to be so meek/ That we could hardly hear him speak, / Yet turned out an Informing Sneak? / Old Cheeseman."—and on in that way through more than a dozen verses, which he used to go and sing, every morning, close by the new master's desk.

He trained one of the low boys, too, a rosy-cheeked little Brass who didn't care what he did, to go up to him with his Latin Grammar one morning, and say it so: NOMINATIVUS PRONOMINUM—Old Cheeseman, RARO EXPRIMITUR—was never suspected, NISI DISTINCTIONIS—of being an informer, AUT EMPHASIS GRATIA—until he proved one. UT—for instance, VOS DAMNASTIS—when he sold the boys. QUASI—as though, DICAT—he should say, PRETAEREA NEMO—I'm a Judas! All this produced a great effect on Old Cheeseman. He had never had much hair; but what he had, began to get thinner and thinner every day. He grew paler and more worn; and sometimes of an evening he was seen sitting at his desk with a precious long snuff to his candle, and his hands before his face, crying. But no member of the Society could pity him, even if he felt inclined, because the President said it was Old Cheeseman's conscience.

So Old Cheeseman went on, and didn't he lead a miserable life! Of course the Reverend turned up his nose at him, and of course SHE did—because both of them always do that at all the masters—but he suffered from the fellows most, and he suffered from them constantly. He never told about it, that the Society could find out; but he got no credit for that, because the President said it was Old Cheeseman's cowardice.

He had only one friend in the world, and that one was almost as powerless as he was, for it was only Jane. Jane was a sort of wardrobe woman to our fellows, and took care of the boxes. She had come at first, I believe, as a kind of apprentice—some of our fellows say from a Charity, but I don't know—and after her time was out, had stopped at so much a year. So little a year, perhaps I ought to say, for it is far more likely. However, she had put some pounds in the Savings' Bank, and she was a very nice young woman. She was not quite pretty; but she had a very frank, honest, bright face, and all our fellows were fond of her. She was uncommonly neat and cheerful, and uncommonly comfortable and kind. And if anything was the matter with a fellow's mother, he always went and showed the letter to Jane.

Jane was Old Cheeseman's friend. The more the Society went against him, the more Jane stood by him. She used to give him a good-humoured look out of her still-room window, sometimes, that seemed to set him up for the day. She used to pass out of the orchard and the kitchen garden (always kept locked, I believe you!) through the playground, when she might have gone the other way, only to give a turn of her head, as much as to say "Keep up your spirits!" to Old Cheeseman. His slip of a room was so fresh and orderly that it was well known who looked after it while he was at his desk; and when our fellows saw a smoking hot dumpling on his plate at dinner, they knew with indignation who had sent it up.

Under these circumstances, the Society resolved, after a quantity of meeting and debating, that Jane should be requested to cut Old Cheeseman dead; and that if she refused, she must be sent to Coventry herself. So a deputation, headed by the President, was appointed to wait on Jane, and inform her of the vote the Society had been under the painful necessity of passing. She was very much respected for all her good qualities, and there was a story about her having once waylaid the Reverend in his own study, and got a fellow off from severe punishment, of her own kind comfortable heart. So the deputation didn't much like the job. However, they went up, and the President told Jane all about it. Upon which Jane turned very red, burst into tears, informed the President and the deputation, in a way not at all like her usual way, that they were a parcel of malicious young savages, and turned the whole respected body out of the room. Consequently it was entered in the Society's book (kept in astronomical cypher for fear of detection), that all communication with Jane was interdicted: and the President addressed the members on this convincing instance of Old Cheeseman's undermining.

But Jane was as true to Old Cheeseman as Old Cheeseman was false to our fellows—in their opinion, at all events—and steadily continued to be his only friend. It was a great exasperation to the Society, because Jane was as much a loss to them as she was a gain to him; and being more inveterate against him than ever, they treated him worse than ever. At last, one morning, his desk stood empty, his room was peeped into, and found to be vacant, and a whisper went about among the pale faces of our fellows that Old Cheeseman, unable to bear it any longer, had got up early and drowned himself.

The mysterious looks of the other masters after breakfast, and the evident fact that old Cheeseman was not expected, confirmed the Society in this opinion. Some began to discuss whether the President was liable to hanging or only transportation for life, and the President's face showed a great anxiety to know which. However, he said that a jury of his country should find him game; and that in his address he should put it to them to lay their hands upon their hearts and say whether they as Britons approved of informers, and how they thought they would like it themselves. Some of the Society considered that he had better run away until he found a forest where he might change clothes with a wood-cutter, and stain his face with blackberries; but the majority believed that if he stood his ground, his father—belonging as he did to the West Indies, and being worth millions—could buy him off.

All our fellows' hearts beat fast when the Reverend came in, and made a sort of a Roman, or a Field Marshal, of himself with the ruler; as he always did before delivering an address. But their fears were nothing to their astonishment when he came out with the story that Old Cheeseman, "so long our respected friend and fellow-pilgrim in the pleasant plains of knowledge," he called him—O yes! I dare say! Much of that!—was the orphan child of a disinherited young lady who had married against her father's wish, and whose young husband had died, and who had died of sorrow herself, and whose unfortunate baby (Old Cheeseman) had been brought up at the cost of a grandfather who would never consent to see it, baby, boy, or man: which grandfather was now dead, and serve him right—that's my putting in—and which grandfather's large property, there being no will, was now, and all of a sudden and for ever, Old Cheeseman's! Our so long respected friend and fellow-pilgrim in the pleasant plains of knowledge, the Reverend wound up a lot of bothering quotations by saying, would "come among us once more" that day fortnight, when he desired to take leave of us himself, in a more particular manner. With these words, he stared severely round at our fellows, and went solemnly out.

There was precious consternation among the members of the Society, now. Lots of them wanted to resign, and lots more began to try to make out that they had never belonged to it. However, the President stuck up, and said that they must stand or fall together, and that if a breach was made it should be over his body—which was meant to encourage the Society: but it didn't. The President further said, he would consider the position in which they stood, and would give them his best opinion and advice in a few days. This was eagerly looked for, as he knew a good deal of the world on account of his father's being in the West Indies.

After days and days of hard thinking, and drawing armies all over his slate, the President called our fellows together, and made the matter clear. He said it was plain that when Old Cheeseman came on the appointed day, his first revenge would be to impeach the Society, and have it flogged all round. After witnessing with joy the torture of his enemies, and gloating over the cries which agony would extort from them, the probability was that he would invite the Reverend, on pretence of conversation, into a private room—say the parlour into which Parents were shown, where the two great globes were which were never used—and would there reproach him with the various frauds and oppressions he had endured at his hands. At the close of his observations he would make a signal to a Prizefighter concealed in the passage, who would then appear and pitch into the Reverend, till he was left insensible. Old Cheeseman would then make Jane a present of from five to ten pounds, and would leave the establishment in fiendish triumph.

The President explained that against the parlour part, or the Jane part, of these arrangements he had nothing to say; but, on the part of the Society, he counselled deadly resistance. With this view he recommended that all available desks should be filled with stones, and that the first word of the complaint should be the signal to every fellow to let fly at Old Cheeseman. The bold advice put the Society in better spirits, and was unanimously taken. A post about Old Cheeseman's size was put up in the playground, and all our fellows practised at it till it was dinted all over.

When the day came, and Places were called, every fellow sat down in a tremble. There had been much discussing and disputing as to how Old Cheeseman would come; but it was the general opinion that he would appear in a sort of triumphal car drawn by four horses, with two livery servants in front, and the Prizefighter in disguise up behind. So, all our fellows sat listening for the sound of wheels. But no wheels were heard, for Old Cheeseman walked after all, and came into the school without any preparation. Pretty much as he used to be, only dressed in black.

"Gentlemen," said the Reverend, presenting him, "our so long respected friend and fellow-pilgrim in the pleasant plains of knowledge, is desirous to offer a word or two. Attention, gentlemen, one and all!"

Every fellow stole his hand into his desk and looked at the President. The President was all ready, and taking aim at old Cheeseman with his eyes.

What did Old Cheeseman then, but walk up to his old desk, look round him with a queer smile as if there was a tear in his eye, and begin in a quavering, mild voice, "My dear companions and old friends!"

Every fellow's hand came out of his desk, and the President suddenly began to cry.

"My dear companions and old friends," said Old Cheeseman, "you have heard of my good fortune. I have passed so many years under this roof—my entire life so far, I may say—that I hope you have been glad to hear of it for my sake. I could never enjoy it without exchanging congratulations with you. If we have ever misunderstood one another at all, pray, my dear boys, let us forgive and forget. I have a great tenderness for you, and I am sure you return it. I want in the fullness of a grateful heart to shake hands with you every one. I have come back to do it, if you please, my dear boys."

Since the President had begun to cry, several other fellows had broken out here and there: but now, when Old Cheeseman began with him as first boy, laid his left hand affectionately on his shoulder and gave him his right; and when the President said "Indeed, I don't deserve it, sir; upon my honour I don't;" there was sobbing and crying all over the school. Every other fellow said he didn't deserve it, much in the same way; but Old Cheeseman, not minding that a bit, went cheerfully round to every boy, and wound up with every master—finishing off the Reverend last.

Then a snivelling little chap in a corner, who was always under some punishment or other, set up a shrill cry of "Success to Old Cheeseman! Hooray!" The Reverend glared upon him, and said, "MR. Cheeseman, sir." But, Old Cheeseman protesting that he liked his old name a great deal better than his new one, all our fellows took up the cry; and, for I don't know how many minutes, there was such a thundering of feet and hands, and such a roaring of Old Cheeseman, as never was heard.

After that, there was a spread in the dining-room of the most magnificent kind. Fowls, tongues, preserves, fruits, confectionaries, jellies, neguses, barley-sugar temples, trifles, crackers—eat all you can and pocket what you like—all at Old Cheeseman's expense. After that, speeches, whole holiday, double and treble sets of all manners of things for all manners of games, donkeys, pony-chaises and drive yourself, dinner for all the masters at the Seven Bells (twenty pounds a-head our fellows estimated it at), an annual holiday and feast fixed for that day every year, and another on Old Cheeseman's birthday—Reverend bound down before the fellows to allow it, so that he could never back out—all at Old Cheeseman's expense.

And didn't our fellows go down in a body and cheer outside the Seven Bells? O no!

But there's something else besides. Don't look at the next story-teller, for there's more yet. Next day, it was resolved that the Society should make it up with Jane, and then be dissolved. What do you think of Jane being gone, though! "What? Gone for ever?" said our fellows, with long faces.

"Yes, to be sure," was all the answer they could get. None of the people about the house would say anything more. At length, the first boy took upon himself to ask the Reverend whether our old friend Jane was really gone? The Reverend (he has got a daughter at home—turn-up nose, and red) replied severely, "Yes, sir, Miss Pitt is gone." The idea of calling Jane, Miss Pitt! Some said she had been sent away in disgrace for taking money from Old Cheeseman; others said she had gone into Old Cheeseman's service at a rise of ten pounds a year. All that our fellows knew, was, she was gone.

It was two or three months afterwards, when, one afternoon, an open carriage stopped at the cricket field, just outside bounds, with a lady and gentleman in it, who looked at the game a long time and stood up to see it played. Nobody thought much about them, until the same little snivelling chap came in, against all rules, from the post where he was Scout, and said, "It's Jane!" Both Elevens forgot the game directly, and ran crowding round the carriage. It WAS Jane! In such a bonnet! And if you'll believe me, Jane was married to Old Cheeseman.

It soon became quite a regular thing when our fellows were hard at it in the playground, to see a carriage at the low part of the wall where it joins the high part, and a lady and gentleman standing up in it, looking over. The gentleman was always Old Cheeseman, and the lady was always Jane.

The first time I ever saw them, I saw them in that way. There had been a good many changes among our fellows then, and it had turned out that Bob Tarter's father wasn't worth Millions! He wasn't worth anything. Bob had gone for a soldier, and Old Cheeseman had purchased his discharge. But that's not the carriage. The carriage stopped, and all our fellows stopped as soon as it was seen.

"So you have never sent me to Coventry after all!" said the lady, laughing, as our fellows swarmed up the wall to shake hands with her. "Are you never going to do it?"

"Never! never! never!" on all sides.

I didn't understand what she meant then, but of course I do now. I was very much pleased with her face though, and with her good way, and I couldn't help looking at her—and at him too—with all our fellows clustering so joyfully about them.

They soon took notice of me as a new boy, so I thought I might as well swarm up the wall myself, and shake hands with them as the rest did. I was quite as glad to see them as the rest were, and was quite as familiar with them in a moment.

"Only a fortnight now," said Old Cheeseman, "to the holidays. Who stops? Anybody?"

A good many fingers pointed at me, and a good many voices cried "He does!" For it was the year when you were all away; and rather low I was about it, I can tell you.

"Oh!" said Old Cheeseman. "But it's solitary here in the holiday time. He had better come to us."

So I went to their delightful house, and was as happy as I could possibly be. They understand how to conduct themselves toward boys, THEY do. When they take a boy to the play, for instance, they DO take him. They don't go in after it's begun, or come out before it's over. They know how to bring a boy up, too. Look at their own! Though he is very little as yet, what a capital boy he is! Why, my next favourite to Mrs. Cheeseman and Old Cheeseman, is young Cheeseman.

So, now I have told you all I know about Old Cheeseman. And it's not much after all, I am afraid. Is it?

Review Questions
1. Why did Old Cheeseman stay at school over the holidays?
2. What new position did Old Cheeseman take? Why were the boys angry at him?
3. Why did Mr. Cheeseman disappear?
4. What did the boys expect him to do when he came back? What did he do?
5. What was the boys' response to Old Cheeseman's actions?

Thought Questions
1. What would it be like to have to live at school year-round? How does this model of schooling compare to your own?
2. Have you ever been in a group that was being cruel to someone else? What was your response? Is there a correct way to react?
3. Would it be hard to be in Jane's place? Do you think you would have been as loyal? How does Dickens develop Jane's character in this story?
4. How did Old Cheeseman soften the hearts of the Society members? What can you learn from his example?
5. Have you ever said, "I'll never treat my children that way!" when you were angry at your parents? Do you change your behavior based on what you observe in other people?

CHARACTERS

Writing Practice

The best writers are able to inform readers about their characters indirectly. After all, when you interact with people, there is no narrator to tell you "Mark is in a bad mood today." You have to figure it out on your own.

When you are next in a public place (a grocery store, mall, park, etc.), take a minute to observe the people around you. What can you learn about their personalities from the way they talk? Dress? Act? What facial expressions, gestures, and dialogue portray different emotions? How might one characteristic be interpreted differently by two different observers?

Now translate this to short stories. Remember: show, don't tell. Look back through the two stories you have just read. How do Dickens and Jewett develop their characters? What words and actions do they use to show who their characters are?

Using these two stories as a guide, practice showing character traits rather than telling readers about them. Follow the example given and name two things—actions, descriptions, words, or tone—that would portray each of the following emotions:

Example: Anxiousness – wringing hands, pacing the room

- Happiness
- Sadness
- Fear
- Anger
- Excitement

What's Cooking? PLOT

A story without a plot is like a train that is standing still. The plot gives a story excitement and energy. Most plots include an introduction of the characters, some event that sets the stage for the rest of the story, a climax (where the conflicts come to a head), and a conclusion, in which the loose ends are satisfactorily resolved. The plot should also include some form of conflict, either external or internal, as a means of producing growth in the story's characters.

A well-developed plot should follow a logical sequence. It should make sense to the reader. Plots can be organized in many ways. The most common and least confusing type of plot is arranged in chronological (time-based) order. This kind of story follows a sequence of events, such as a day in a character's life, a bus trip across the country, or a student's experiences in college.

In contrast to the example of a story without a plot, it is fitting that you are about to read "The Celestial Railroad," by Nathaniel Hawthorne, a story about a man's travels on a very unique train. Keep the following questions in mind as you read the next two stories:

- How is the story introduced?
- Is there a rising action?
- Is there a climax or turning point?
- Is there a falling action?
- How does the story conclude?
- How is the plot revealed (through action, conversation, or the author's descriptions)?
- Does everything happen in sequence, or are there flashbacks?
- Does the author lay out the plot clearly, or are there events you must guess at?

As a writer, you can choose a plot that is full of action and adventure or one that centers on something as simple as a decision that must be made. Pay attention to the differences in the plots of the two stories you read next, and think about the kind of plot you might like to write.

"The Celestial Railroad"
Nathaniel Hawthorne

Nathaniel Hawthorne (1804-1864), an American writer, was a descendant of Puritans who lived through the Salem witch trials, and some of his writing is critical of self-righteousness in religion. This story takes a more moderate view of religion, instead criticizing the popular distortions of religion in his time. "The Celestial Railroad" is based on John Bunyan's classic novel *The Pilgrim's Progress*. As you read, be on the lookout for issues of religion that still apply today.

    Not a great while ago, passing through the gate of dreams, I visited that region of the earth in which lies the famous City of Destruction. It interested me much to learn that by the public spirit of some of the inhabitants a railroad has recently been established between this populous and flourishing town and the Celestial City. Having a little time upon my hands, I resolved to gratify a liberal curiosity by making a trip thither. Accordingly, one fine morning after paying my bill at the hotel, and directing the porter to stow my luggage behind a coach, I took my seat in the vehicle and set out for the station-house. It was my good fortune to enjoy the company of a gentleman—one Mr. Smooth-it-away—who, though he had never actually visited the Celestial City, yet seemed as well acquainted with its laws, customs, policy, and statistics, as with those of the City of Destruction, of which he was a native townsman. Being, moreover, a director of the railroad corporation and one of its largest stockholders, he had it in his power to give me all desirable information respecting that praiseworthy enterprise.

    Our coach rattled out of the city, and at a short distance from its outskirts passed over a bridge of elegant construction, but somewhat too slight, as I imagined, to sustain any considerable weight. On both sides lay an extensive quagmire, which could not have been more disagreeable either to sight or smell, had all the kennels of the earth emptied their pollution there.

    "This," remarked Mr. Smooth-it-away, "is the famous Slough of Despond—a disgrace to all the neighborhood; and the greater that it might so easily be converted into firm ground."

    "I have understood," said I, "that efforts have been made for that purpose from time immemorial. Bunyan mentions that above twenty thousand cartloads of wholesome instructions had been thrown in here without effect."

"Very probably! And what effect could be anticipated from such unsubstantial stuff?" cried Mr. Smooth-it-away. "You observe this convenient bridge. We obtained a sufficient foundation for it by throwing into the slough some editions of books of morality, volumes of French philosophy and German rationalism; tracts, sermons, and essays of modern clergymen; extracts from Plato, Confucius, and various Hindoo sages together with a few ingenious commentaries upon texts of Scripture,—all of which by some scientific process, have been converted into a mass like granite. The whole bog might be filled up with similar matter."

It really seemed to me, however, that the bridge vibrated and heaved up and down in a very formidable manner; and, in spite of Mr. Smooth-it-away's testimony to the solidity of its foundation, I should be loath to cross it in a crowded omnibus, especially if each passenger were encumbered with as heavy luggage as that gentleman and myself. Nevertheless we got over without accident, and soon found ourselves at the station-house. This very neat and spacious edifice is erected on the site of the little wicket gate, which formerly, as all old pilgrims will recollect, stood directly across the highway, and, by its inconvenient narrowness, was a great obstruction to the traveller of liberal mind and expansive stomach. The reader of John Bunyan will be glad to know that Christian's old friend Evangelist, who was accustomed to supply each pilgrim with a mystic roll, now presides at the ticket office. Some malicious persons it is true deny the identity of this reputable character with the Evangelist of old times, and even pretend to bring competent evidence of an imposture. Without involving myself in a dispute I shall merely observe that, so far as my experience goes, the square pieces of pasteboard now delivered to passengers are much more convenient and useful along the road than the antique roll of parchment. Whether they will be as readily received at the gate of the Celestial City I decline giving an opinion.

A large number of passengers were already at the station-house awaiting the departure of the cars. By the aspect and demeanor of these persons it was easy to judge that the feelings of the community had undergone a very favorable change in reference to the celestial pilgrimage. It would have done Bunyan's heart good to see it. Instead of a lonely and ragged man with a huge burden on his back, plodding along sorrowfully on foot while the whole city hooted after him, here were parties of the first gentry and most respectable people in the neighborhood setting forth toward the Celestial City as cheerfully as if the pilgrimage were merely a summer tour. Among the gentlemen were characters of deserved eminence—magistrates, politicians, and men of wealth, by whose example religion could not but be greatly recommended to their meaner brethren. In the ladies' apartment, too, I rejoiced to distinguish some of those flowers of fashionable society who are so well fitted to adorn the most elevated circles of the Celestial City. There was much pleasant conversation about the news of the day, topics of business and politics, or the lighter matters of amusement; while religion, though indubitably the main thing at heart, was thrown tastefully into the background. Even an infidel would have heard little or nothing to shock his sensibility.

One great convenience of the new method of going on pilgrimage I must not forget to mention. Our enormous burdens, instead of being carried on our shoulders as had been the custom of old, were all snugly deposited in the baggage car, and, as I was assured, would be delivered to their respective owners at the journey's end. Another thing, likewise, the

benevolent reader will be delighted to understand. It may be remembered that there was an ancient feud between Prince Beelzebub and the keeper of the wicket gate, and that the adherents of the former distinguished personage were accustomed to shoot deadly arrows at honest pilgrims while knocking at the door. This dispute, much to the credit as well of the illustrious potentate above mentioned as of the worthy and enlightened directors of the railroad, has been pacifically arranged on the principle of mutual compromise. The prince's subjects are now pretty numerously employed about the station-house, some in taking care of the baggage, others in collecting fuel, feeding the engines, and such congenial occupations; and I can conscientiously affirm that persons more attentive to their business, more willing to accommodate, or more generally agreeable to the passengers, are not to be found on any railroad. Every good heart must surely exult at so satisfactory an arrangement of an immemorial difficulty.

"Where is Mr. Greatheart?" inquired I. "Beyond a doubt the directors have engaged that famous old champion to be chief conductor on the railroad?"

"Why, no," said Mr. Smooth-it-away, with a dry cough. "He was offered the situation of brakeman; but, to tell you the truth, our friend Greatheart has grown preposterously stiff and narrow in his old age. He has so often guided pilgrims over the road on foot that he considers it a sin to travel in any other fashion. Besides, the old fellow had entered so heartily into the ancient feud with Prince Beelzebub that he would have been perpetually at blows or ill language with some of the prince's subjects, and thus have embroiled us anew. So, on the whole, we were not sorry when honest Greatheart went off to the Celestial City in a huff and left us at liberty to choose a more suitable and accommodating man. Yonder comes the engineer of the train. You will probably recognize him at once."

The engine at this moment took its station in advance of the cars, looking, I must confess, much more like a sort of mechanical demon that would hurry us to the infernal regions than a laudable contrivance for smoothing our way to the Celestial City. On its top sat a personage almost enveloped in smoke and flame, which, not to startle the reader, appeared to gush from his own mouth and stomach as well as from the engine's brazen abdomen.

"Do my eyes deceive me?" cried I. "What on earth is this! A living creature? If so, he is own brother to the engine he rides upon!"

"Poh, poh, you are obtuse!" said Mr. Smooth-it-away, with a hearty laugh. "Don't you know Apollyon, Christian's old enemy, with whom he fought so fierce a battle in the Valley of Humiliation? He was the very fellow to manage the engine; and so we have reconciled him to the custom of going on pilgrimage, and engaged him as chief engineer."

"Bravo, bravo!" exclaimed I, with irrepressible enthusiasm; "this shows the liberality of the age; this proves, if anything can, that all musty prejudices are in a fair way to be obliterated. And how will Christian rejoice to hear of this happy transformation of his old antagonist! I promise myself great pleasure in informing him of it when we reach the Celestial City."

The passengers being all comfortably seated, we now rattled away merrily, accomplishing a greater distance in ten minutes than Christian probably trudged over in a day. It was laughable, while we glanced along, as it were, at the tail of a thunderbolt, to observe two dusty foot travellers in the old pilgrim guise, with cockle shell and staff, their mystic rolls of parchment in their hands and their intolerable burdens on their backs. The preposterous obstinacy of these honest people in persisting to groan and stumble along the difficult pathway rather than take advantage of modern improvements, excited great mirth among our wiser brotherhood. We greeted the two pilgrims with many pleasant gibes and a roar of laughter; whereupon they gazed at us with such woeful and absurdly compassionate visages that our merriment grew tenfold more obstreperous. Apollyon also entered heartily into the fun, and contrived to flirt the smoke and flame of the engine, or of his own breath, into their faces, and envelop them in an atmosphere of scalding steam. These little practical jokes amused us mightily, and doubtless afforded the pilgrims the gratification of considering themselves martyrs.

At some distance from the railroad Mr. Smooth-it-away pointed to a large, antique edifice, which, he observed, was a tavern of long standing, and had formerly been a noted stopping-place for pilgrims. In Bunyan's road-book it is mentioned as the Interpreter's House.

"I have long had a curiosity to visit that old mansion," remarked I.

"It is not one of our stations, as you perceive," said my companion. "The keeper was violently opposed to the railroad; and well he might be, as the track left his house of entertainment on one side, and thus was pretty certain to deprive him of all his reputable customers. But the footpath still passes his door, and the old gentleman now and then receives a call from some simple traveller, and entertains him with fare as old-fashioned as himself."

Before our talk on this subject came to a conclusion we were rushing by the place where Christian's burden fell from his shoulders at the sight of the Cross. This served as a theme for Mr. Smooth-it-away, Mr. Live-for-the-world, Mr. Hide-sin-in-the-heart, Mr. Scaly-conscience, and a knot of gentlemen from the town of Shun-repentance, to descant upon the inestimable advantages resulting from the safety of our baggage. Myself, and all the passengers indeed, joined with great unanimity in this view of the matter; for our burdens were rich in many things esteemed precious throughout the world; and, especially, we each of us possessed a great variety of favorite Habits, which we trusted would not be out of fashion even in the polite circles of the Celestial City. It would have been a sad spectacle to see such an assortment of valuable articles tumbling into the sepulchre. Thus pleasantly conversing on the favorable circumstances of our position as compared with those of past pilgrims and of narrow-minded ones at the present day, we soon found ourselves at the foot of the Hill Difficulty. Through the very heart of this rocky mountain a tunnel has been constructed of most admirable architecture, with a lofty arch and a spacious double track; so that, unless the earth and rocks should chance to crumble down, it will remain an eternal monument of the builder's skill and enterprise. It is a great though incidental advantage that the materials from the heart of the Hill Difficulty have been employed in filling up the Valley of Humiliation, thus obviating the necessity of descending into that disagreeable and unwholesome hollow.

"This is a wonderful improvement, indeed," said I. "Yet I should have been glad of an opportunity to visit the Palace Beautiful and be introduced to the charming young ladies—Miss Prudence, Miss Piety, Miss Charity, and the rest—who have the kindness to entertain pilgrims there."

"Young ladies!" cried Mr. Smooth-it-away, as soon as he could speak for laughing. "And charming young ladies! Why, my dear fellow, they are old maids, every soul of them—prim, starched, dry, and angular; and not one of them, I will venture to say, has altered so much as the fashion of her gown since the days of Christian's pilgrimage."

"Ah, well," said I, much comforted, "then I can very readily dispense with their acquaintance."

The respectable Apollyon was now putting on the steam at a prodigious rate, anxious, perhaps, to get rid of the unpleasant reminiscences connected with the spot where he had so disastrously encountered Christian. Consulting Mr. Bunyan's road-book, I perceived that we must now be within a few miles of the Valley of the Shadow of Death, into which doleful region, at our present speed, we should plunge much sooner than seemed at all desirable. In truth, I expected nothing better than to find myself in the ditch on one side or the Quag on the other; but on communicating my apprehensions to Mr. Smooth-it-away, he assured me that the difficulties of this passage, even in its worst condition, had been vastly exaggerated, and that, in its present state of improvement, I might consider myself as safe as on any railroad in Christendom.

Even while we were speaking the train shot into the entrance of this dreaded Valley. Though I plead guilty to some foolish palpitations of the heart during our headlong rush over the causeway here constructed, yet it were unjust to withhold the highest encomiums on the boldness of its original conception and the ingenuity of those who executed it. It was gratifying, likewise, to observe how much care had been taken to dispel the everlasting gloom and supply the defect of cheerful sunshine, not a ray of which has ever penetrated among these awful shadows. For this purpose, the inflammable gas which exudes plentifully from the soil is collected by means of pipes, and thence communicated to a quadruple row of lamps along the whole extent of the passage. Thus a radiance has been created even out of the fiery and sulphurous curse that rests forever upon the valley—a radiance hurtful, however, to the eyes, and somewhat bewildering, as I discovered by the changes which it wrought in the visages of my companions.

In this respect, as compared with natural daylight, there is the same difference as between truth and falsehood, but if the reader have ever travelled through the dark Valley, he will have learned to be thankful for any light that he could get—if not from the sky above, then from the blasted soil beneath. Such was the red brilliancy of these lamps that they appeared to build walls of fire on both sides of the track, between which we held our course at lightning speed, while a reverberating thunder filled the Valley with its echoes. Had the engine run off the track,—a catastrophe, it is whispered, by no means unprecedented,—the bottomless pit, if there be any such place, would undoubtedly have received us. Just as some dismal fooleries of this nature had made my heart quake there came a tremendous shriek, careering along the valley as if a thousand devils had burst their lungs to utter it, but which proved to be merely the whistle of the engine on arriving at a stopping-place.

The spot where we had now paused is the same that our friend Bunyan—a truthful man, but infected with many fantastic notions—has designated, in terms plainer than I like to repeat, as the mouth of the infernal region. This, however, must be a mistake, inasmuch as Mr.

Smooth-it-away, while we remained in the smoky and lurid cavern, took occasion to prove that Tophet has not even a metaphorical existence. The place, he assured us, is no other than the crater of a half-extinct volcano, in which the directors had caused forges to be set up for the manufacture of railroad iron. Hence, also, is obtained a plentiful supply of fuel for the use of the engines. Whoever had gazed into the dismal obscurity of the broad cavern mouth, whence ever and anon darted huge tongues of dusky flame, and had seen the strange, half-shaped monsters, and visions of faces horribly grotesque, into which the smoke seemed to wreathe itself, and had heard the awful murmurs, and shrieks, and deep, shuddering whispers of the blast, sometimes forming themselves into words almost articulate, would have seized upon Mr. Smooth-it-away's comfortable explanation as greedily as we did. The inhabitants of the cavern, moreover, were unlovely personages, dark, smoke-begrimed, generally deformed, with misshapen feet, and a glow of dusky redness in their eyes as if their hearts had caught fire and were blazing out of the upper windows. It struck me as a peculiarity that the laborers at the forge and those who brought fuel to the engine, when they began to draw short breath, positively emitted smoke from their mouth and nostrils.

Among the idlers about the train, most of whom were puffing cigars which they had lighted at the flame of the crater, I was perplexed to notice several who, to my certain knowledge, had heretofore set forth by railroad for the Celestial City. They looked dark, wild, and smoky, with a singular resemblance, indeed, to the native inhabitants, like whom, also, they had a disagreeable propensity to ill-natured gibes and sneers, the habit of which had wrought a settled contortion of their visages. Having been on speaking terms with one of these persons,—an indolent, good-for-nothing fellow, who went by the name of Take-it-easy,—I called him, and inquired what was his business there.

"Did you not start," said I, "for the Celestial City?"

"That's a fact," said Mr. Take-it-easy, carelessly puffing some smoke into my eyes. "But I heard such bad accounts that I never took pains to climb the hill on which the city stands. No business doing, no fun going on, nothing to drink, and no smoking allowed, and a thrumming of church music from morning till night. I would not stay in such a place if they offered me house room and living free."

"But, my good Mr. Take-it-easy," cried I, "why take up your residence here, of all places in the world?"

"Oh," said the loafer, with a grin, "it is very warm hereabouts, and I meet with plenty of old acquaintances, and altogether the place suits me. I hope to see you back again some day soon. A pleasant journey to you."

While he was speaking the bell of the engine rang, and we dashed away after dropping a few passengers, but receiving no new ones. Rattling onward through the Valley, we were dazzled with the fiercely gleaming gas lamps, as before. But sometimes, in the dark of intense brightness, grim faces, that bore the aspect and expression of individual sins, or evil passions, seemed to thrust themselves through the veil of light, glaring upon us, and stretching forth a great, dusky hand, as if to impede our progress. I almost thought that they were my own sins that appalled me there. These were freaks of imagination—nothing more, certainly—mere delusions, which I ought to be heartily ashamed of; but all through the Dark Valley I was tormented, and pestered, and dolefully bewildered with the same kind of waking dreams. The mephitic gases of that region intoxicate the brain. As the light of natural day, however, began to struggle with the glow of the lanterns, these vain imaginations lost their vividness, and finally vanished from the first ray of sunshine that greeted our escape from the Valley of the Shadow of Death. Ere we had gone a mile beyond it I could wellnigh have taken my oath that this whole gloomy passage was a dream.

At the end of the valley, as John Bunyan mentions, is a cavern, where, in his days, dwelt two cruel giants, Pope and Pagan, who had strown the ground about their residence with the bones of slaughtered pilgrims. These vile old troglodytes are no longer there; but into their deserted cave another terrible giant has thrust himself, and makes it his business to seize upon honest travellers and fatten them for his table with plentiful meals of smoke, mist, moonshine, raw potatoes, and sawdust. He is a German by birth, and is called Giant Transcendentalist; but as to his form, his features, his substance, and his nature generally, it is the chief peculiarity of this huge miscreant that neither he for himself, nor anybody for him, has ever been able to describe them. As we rushed by the cavern's mouth we caught a hasty glimpse of him, looking somewhat like an ill-proportioned figure, but considerably more like a heap of fog and duskiness. He shouted after us, but in so strange a phraseology that we knew not what he meant, nor whether to be encouraged or affrighted.

It was late in the day when the train thundered into the ancient city of Vanity, where Vanity Fair is still at the height of prosperity, and exhibits an epitome of whatever is brilliant, gay, and fascinating beneath the sun. As I purposed to make a considerable stay here, it gratified me to learn that there is no longer the want of harmony between the town's-people and pilgrims, which impelled the former to such lamentably mistaken measures as the persecution of Christian and the fiery martyrdom of Faithful. On the contrary, as the new railroad brings with it great trade and a constant influx of strangers, the lord of Vanity Fair is its chief patron, and the capitalists of the city are among the largest stockholders. Many passengers stop to take their pleasure or make their profit in the Fair, instead of going onward to the Celestial City. Indeed, such are the charms of the place that people often affirm it to be the true and only heaven; stoutly contending that there is no other, that those who seek further are mere dreamers, and that, if the fabled brightness of the Celestial City lay but a bare mile beyond the gates of Vanity, they would not be fools enough to go thither. Without subscribing to these perhaps exaggerated encomiums, I can truly say that my abode in the city was mainly agreeable, and my intercourse with the inhabitants productive of much amusement and instruction.

Being naturally of a serious turn, my attention was directed to the solid advantages derivable from a residence here, rather than to the effervescent pleasures which are the grand

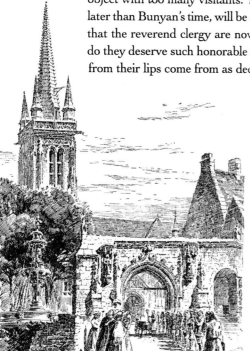

object with too many visitants. The Christian reader, if he have had no accounts of the city later than Bunyan's time, will be surprised to hear that almost every street has its church, and that the reverend clergy are nowhere held in higher respect than at Vanity Fair. And well do they deserve such honorable estimation; for the maxims of wisdom and virtue which fall from their lips come from as deep a spiritual source, and tend to as lofty a religious aim, as those of the sagest philosophers of old. In justification of this high praise I need only mention the names of the Rev. Mr. Shallow-deep, the Rev. Mr. Stumble-at-truth, that fine old clerical character the Rev. Mr. This-to-day, who expects shortly to resign his pulpit to the Rev. Mr. That-to-morrow; together with the Rev. Mr. Bewilderment, the Rev. Mr. Clog-the-spirit, and, last and greatest, the Rev. Dr. Wind-of-doctrine. The labors of these eminent divines are aided by those of innumerable lecturers, who diffuse such a various profundity, in all subjects of human or celestial science, that any man may acquire an omnigenous erudition without the trouble of even learning to read. Thus literature is etherealized by assuming for its medium the human voice; and knowledge, depositing all its heavier particles, except, doubtless, its gold becomes exhaled into a sound, which forthwith steals into the ever-open ear of the community. These ingenious methods constitute a sort of machinery, by which thought and study are done to every person's hand without his putting himself to the slightest inconvenience in the matter. There is another species of machine for the wholesale manufacture of individual morality. This excellent result is affected by societies for all manner of virtuous purposes, with which a man has merely to connect himself, throwing, as it were, his quota of virtue into the common stock, and the president and directors will take care that the aggregate amount be well applied. All these, and other wonderful improvements in ethics, religion, and literature, being made plain to my comprehension by the ingenious Mr. Smooth-it-away, inspired me with a vast admiration of Vanity Fair.

It would fill a volume, in an age of pamphlets, were I to record all my observations in this great capital of human business and pleasure. There was an unlimited range of society—the powerful, the wise, the witty, and the famous in every walk of life; princes, presidents, poets, generals, artists, actors, and philanthropists, —all making their own market at the fair, and deeming no price too exorbitant for such commodities as hit their fancy. It was well worth one's while, even if he had no idea of buying or selling, to loiter through the bazaars and observe the various sorts of traffic that were going forward.

Some of the purchasers, I thought, made very foolish bargains. For instance, a young man having inherited a splendid fortune, laid out a considerable portion of it in the purchase of diseases, and finally spent all the rest for a heavy lot of repentance and a suit of rags. A very pretty girl bartered a heart as clear as crystal, and which seemed her most valuable possession, for another jewel of the same kind, but so worn and defaced as to be utterly worthless. In one shop there were a great many crowns of laurel and myrtle, which soldiers, authors, statesmen, and various other people pressed eagerly to buy; some purchased these paltry wreaths with their lives, others by a toilsome servitude of years, and many sacrificed whatever was most valuable, yet finally slunk away without the crown. There was a sort of stock or scrip, called Conscience, which seemed to be in great demand, and would purchase almost anything. Indeed, few rich commodities were to be obtained without paying a heavy sum in this particular stock, and a man's business was seldom very lucrative unless he knew precisely when and how to throw his hoard of conscience into the market. Yet as this stock was the only thing of permanent value, whoever parted with it was sure to find himself a loser in the long run. Several of the speculations were of a questionable character. Occasionally a member of Congress recruited his pocket by the sale of his constituents; and I was assured that public officers have often sold their country at very moderate prices. Thousands sold their happiness for a whim. Gilded chains were in great demand, and purchased with almost any sacrifice. In truth, those who desired, according to the old adage, to sell anything valuable for a song, might find customers all over the Fair; and there were innumerable messes of pottage, piping hot, for such as chose to buy them with their birthrights. A few articles, however, could not be found genuine at Vanity Fair. If a customer wished to renew his stock of youth the dealers offered him a set of false teeth and an auburn wig; if he demanded peace of mind, they recommended opium or a brandy bottle.

Tracts of land and golden mansions, situate in the Celestial City, were often exchanged, at very disadvantageous rates, for a few years' lease of small, dismal, inconvenient tenements in Vanity Fair. Prince Beelzebub himself took great interest in this sort of traffic, and sometimes condescended to meddle with smaller matters. I once had the pleasure to see him bargaining with a miser for his soul, which, after much ingenious skirmishing on both sides, his highness succeeded in obtaining at about the value of sixpence. The prince remarked with a smile, that he was a loser by the transaction.

Day after day, as I walked the streets of Vanity, my manners and deportment became more and more like those of the inhabitants. The place began to seem like home; the idea of pursuing my travels to the Celestial City was almost obliterated from my mind. I was reminded of it, however, by the sight of the same pair of simple pilgrims at whom we had laughed so heartily when Apollyon puffed smoke and steam into their faces at the commencement of our journey. There they stood amidst the densest bustle of Vanity; the dealers offering them their purple and fine linen and jewels, the men of wit and humor gibing at them, a pair of buxom ladies ogling them askance, while the benevolent Mr. Smooth-it-away whispered some of his wisdom at their elbows, and pointed to a newly-erected temple; but there were these worthy simpletons, making the scene look wild and monstrous, merely by their sturdy repudiation of all part in its business or pleasures.

One of them—his name was Stick-to-the-right—perceived in my face, I suppose, a species of sympathy and almost admiration, which, to my own great surprise, I could not help feeling for this pragmatic couple. It prompted him to address me.

"Sir," inquired he, with a sad, yet mild and kindly voice, "do you call yourself a pilgrim?"

"Yes," I replied, "my right to that appellation is indubitable. I am merely a sojourner here in Vanity Fair, being bound to the Celestial City by the new railroad."

"Alas, friend," rejoined Mr. Stick-to-the-right, "I do assure you, and beseech you to receive the truth of my words, that that whole concern is a bubble. You may travel on it all your lifetime, were you to live thousands of years, and yet never get beyond the limits of Vanity Fair. Yea, though you should deem yourself entering the gates of the blessed city, it will be nothing but a miserable delusion."

"The Lord of the Celestial City," began the other pilgrim, whose name was Mr. Foot-it-to-heaven, "has refused, and will ever refuse, to grant an act of incorporation for this railroad; and unless that be obtained, no passenger can ever hope to enter his dominions. Wherefore every man who buys a ticket must lay his account with losing the purchase money, which is the value of his own soul."

"Poh, nonsense!" said Mr. Smooth-it-away, taking my arm and leading me off, "these fellows ought to be indicted for a libel. If the law stood as it once did in Vanity Fair we should see them grinning through the iron bars of the prison window."

This incident made a considerable impression on my mind, and contributed with other circumstances to indispose me to a permanent residence in the city of Vanity; although, of course, I was not simple enough to give up my original plan of gliding along easily and commodiously by railroad. Still, I grew anxious to be gone. There was one strange thing that troubled me. Amid the occupations or amusements of the Fair, nothing was more common than for a person—whether at feast, theatre, or church, or trafficking for wealth and honors, or whatever he might be doing, to vanish like a soap bubble, and be never more seen of his fellows; and so accustomed were the latter to such little accidents that they went on with their business as quietly as if nothing had happened. But it was otherwise with me.

Finally, after a pretty long residence at the Fair, I resumed my journey toward the Celestial City, still with Mr. Smooth-it-away at my side. At a short distance beyond the suburbs of Vanity we passed the ancient silver mine, of which Demas was the first discoverer, and which is now wrought to great advantage, supplying nearly all the coined currency of the world. A little further onward was the spot where Lot's wife had stood forever under the semblance of a pillar of salt. Curious travellers have long since carried it away piecemeal. Had all regrets been punished as rigorously as this poor dame's were, my yearning for the relinquished delights of Vanity Fair might have produced a similar change in my own corporeal substance, and left me a warning to future pilgrims.

The next remarkable object was a large edifice, constructed of moss-grown stone, but in a modern and airy style of architecture. The engine came to a pause in its vicinity, with the usual tremendous shriek.

"This was formerly the castle of the redoubted giant Despair," observed Mr. Smooth-it-away; "but since his death Mr. Flimsy-faith has repaired it, and keeps an excellent house of entertainment here. It is one of our stopping-places."

"It seems but slightly put together," remarked I, looking at the frail yet ponderous walls. "I do not envy Mr. Flimsy-faith his habitation. Some day it will thunder down upon the heads of the occupants."

"We shall escape at all events," said Mr. Smooth-it-away, "for Apollyon is putting on the steam again."

The road now plunged into a gorge of the Delectable Mountains, and traversed the field

where in former ages the blind men wandered and stumbled among the tombs. One of these ancient tombstones had been thrust across the track by some malicious person, and gave the train of cars a terrible jolt. Far up the rugged side of a mountain I perceived a rusty iron door, half overgrown with bushes and creeping plants, but with smoke issuing from its crevices.

"Is that," inquired I, "the very door in the hillside which the shepherds assured Christian was a by-way to hell?"

"That was a joke on the part of the shepherds," said Mr. Smooth-it-away, with a smile. "It is neither more nor less than the door of a cavern which they use as a smoke-house for the preparation of mutton hams."

My recollections of the journey are now, for a little space, dim and confused, inasmuch as a singular drowsiness here overcame me, owing to the fact that we were passing over the enchanted ground, the air of which encourages a disposition to sleep. I awoke, however, as soon as we crossed the borders of the pleasant land of Beulah. All the passengers were rubbing their eyes, comparing watches, and congratulating one another on the prospect of arriving so seasonably at the journey's end. The sweet breezes of this happy clime came refreshingly to our nostrils; we beheld the glimmering gush of silver fountains, overhung by trees of beautiful foliage and delicious fruit, which were propagated by grafts from the celestial gardens. Once, as we dashed onward like a hurricane, there was a flutter of wings and the bright appearance of an angel in the air, speeding forth on some heavenly mission. The engine now announced the close vicinity of the final station-house by one last and horrible scream, in which there seemed to be distinguishable every kind of wailing and woe, and bitter fierceness of wrath, all mixed up with the wild laughter of a devil or a madman. Throughout our journey, at every stopping-place, Apollyon had exercised his ingenuity in screwing the most abominable sounds out of the whistle of the steam-engine; but in this closing effort he outdid himself and created an infernal uproar, which, besides disturbing the peaceful inhabitants of Beulah, must have sent its discord even through the celestial gates.

While the horrid clamor was still ringing in our ears we heard an exulting strain, as if a thousand instruments of music, with height and depth and sweetness in their tones, at once tender and triumphant, were struck in unison, to greet the approach of some illustrious hero, who had fought the good fight and won a glorious victory, and was come to lay aside his battered arms forever. Looking to ascertain what might be the occasion of this glad harmony, I perceived, on alighting from the cars, that a multitude of shining ones had assembled on the other side of the river, to welcome two poor pilgrims, who were just emerging from its depths. They were the same whom Apollyon and ourselves had persecuted with taunts, and gibes, and scalding steam, at the commencement of our journey—the same whose unworldly aspect and impressive words had stirred my conscience amid the wild revellers of Vanity Fair.

"How amazingly well those men have got on," cried I to Mr. Smooth-it-away. "I wish we were secure of as good a reception."

"Never fear, never fear!" answered my friend. "Come, make haste; the ferry boat will be off directly, and in three minutes you will be on the other side of the river. No doubt you will find coaches to carry you up to the city gates."

A steam ferry boat, the last improvement on this important route, lay at the river side, puffing, snorting, and emitting all those other disagreeable utterances which betoken the departure to be immediate. I hurried on board with the rest of the passengers, most of whom were in great perturbation: some bawling out for their baggage; some tearing their hair and exclaiming that the boat would explode or sink; some already pale with the heaving of the stream; some gazing affrighted at the ugly aspect of the steersman; and some still dizzy with the slumberous influences of the Enchanted Ground. Looking back to the shore, I was amazed to discern Mr. Smooth-it-away waving his hand in token of farewell.

"Don't you go over to the Celestial City?" exclaimed I.

"Oh, no!" answered he with a queer smile, and that same disagreeable contortion of visage which I had remarked in the inhabitants of the Dark Valley. "Oh, no! I have come thus far only for the sake of your pleasant company. Good-by! We shall meet again."

And then did my excellent friend Mr. Smooth-it-away laugh outright, in the midst of which cachinnation a smoke-wreath issued from his mouth and nostrils, while a twinkle of lurid flame darted out of either eye, proving indubitably that his heart was all of a red blaze. The impudent fiend! To deny the existence of Tophet, when he felt its fiery tortures raging within his breast. I rushed to the side of the boat, intending to fling myself on shore; but the wheels, as they began their revolutions, threw a dash of spray over me so cold—so deadly cold, with the chill that will never leave those waters until Death be drowned in his own river—that with a shiver and a heartquake I awoke.

Thank Heaven it was a Dream!

Review Questions
1. What did the narrator say had changed since Pilgrim's Progress was written? How had the City of Destruction changed?
2. Who did the narrator think should be the train conductor? Why wasn't that man chosen?
3. Who did the narrator recognize in the Valley of the Shadow of Death? What did he say?
4. What was the currency in Vanity Fair? What things could you not buy there?
5. Who was Mr. Smooth-it-away? What did he do at the end of the story?

Thought Questions
1. Why do you think Hawthorne wrote this "sequel" to *The Pilgrim's Progress*? This was written in 1843. What would a modern sequel look like? How would it be different?
2. Do you think good and evil have been "watered down" in society since Hawthorne wrote this story? If yes, in what ways?
3. The train-travelers wanted to keep their baggage with them. Do you have any unhealthy habits to which you cling? What does it take to let go of a habit like that?
4. Is it easy to live as a Christian? Should it be, or is hardship a necessary part of faith? Discuss.
5. Do you think the train trip was an effective way to structure the plot of this story? Why or why not?

"The Necklace"
Henri Guy de Maupassant

Henri Guy de Maupassant (1850-1893), was a prolific French short story writer who trained under novelist Gustave Flaubert. Guy de Maupassant's stories include mysteries and commentaries on French social life. He is famous for his attention to realistic detail. Some of his stories have been compared to O. Henry's for their surprise endings, and to Edgar Allan Poe's for their interest in human psychology. "The Necklace" is one of his best-known stories, combining a clever plot with an unexpected ending, while keeping the characters central.

    She was one of those pretty and charming girls born, as though fate had blundered over her, into a family of artisans. She had no marriage portion, no expectations, no means of getting known, understood, loved, and wedded by a man of wealth and distinction; and she let herself be married off to a little clerk in the Ministry of Education. Her tastes were simple because she had never been able to afford any other, but she was as unhappy as though she had married beneath her; for women have no caste or class; their beauty, grace, and charm serving them for birth or family, their natural delicacy, their instinctive elegance, their nimbleness of wit, are their only mark of rank, and put the slum girl on a level with the highest lady in the land.

    She suffered endlessly, feeling herself born for every delicacy and luxury. She suffered from the poorness of her house, from its mean walls, worn chairs, and ugly curtains. All these things, of which other women of her class would not even have been aware, tormented and insulted her. The sight of the little Breton girl who came to do the work in her little house aroused heart-broken regrets and hopeless dreams in her mind. She imagined silent antechambers, heavy with Oriental tapestries, lit by torches in lofty bronze sockets, with two tall footmen in knee-breeches sleeping in large arm-chairs, overcome by the heavy warmth of the stove. She imagined vast saloons hung with antique silks, exquisite pieces of furniture supporting priceless ornaments, and small, charming, perfumed rooms, created just for little parties of intimate friends, men who were famous and sought after, whose homage roused every other woman's envious longings.

    When she sat down for dinner at the round table covered with a three-days-old cloth, opposite her husband, who took the cover off the soup-tureen, exclaiming delightedly:

"Aha! Scotch broth! What could be better?" she imagined delicate meals, gleaming silver, tapestries peopling the walls with folk of a past age and strange birds in faery forests; she imagined delicate food served in marvelous dishes, murmured gallantries, listened to with an inscrutable smile as one trifled with the rosy flesh of trout or wings of asparagus chicken.

She had no clothes, no jewels, nothing. And these were the only things she loved; she felt that she was made for them. She had longed so eagerly to charm, to be desired, to be wildly attractive and sought after.

She had a rich friend, an old school friend whom she refused to visit, because she suffered so keenly when she returned home. She would weep whole days, with grief, regret, despair, and misery.

One evening her husband came home with an exultant air, holding a large envelope in his hand. "Here's something for you," he said.

Swiftly she tore the paper and drew out a printed card on which were these words: "The Minister of Education and Madame Ramponneau request the pleasure of the company of Monsieur and Madame Loisel at the Ministry on the evening of Monday, January the 18th."

Instead of being delighted, as her husband hoped, she flung the invitation petulantly across the table, murmuring: "What do you want me to do with this?"

"Why, darling, I thought you'd be pleased. You never go out, and this is a great occasion. I had tremendous trouble to get it. Every one wants one; it's very select, and very few go to the clerks. You'll see all the really big people there."

She looked at him out of furious eyes, and said impatiently: "And what do you suppose I am to wear at such an affair?"

He had not thought about it; he stammered: "Why, the dress you go to the theatre in. It looks very nice, to me…" He stopped, stupefied and utterly at a loss when he saw that his wife was beginning to cry. Two large tears ran slowly down from the corners of her eyes toward the corners of her mouth.

"What's the matter with you? What's the matter with you?" he faltered.

But with a violent effort she overcame her grief and replied in a calm voice, wiping her wet cheeks: "Nothing. Only I haven't a dress and so I can't go to this party. Give your invitation to some friend of yours whose wife will be turned out better than I shall."

He was heart-broken. "Look here, Mathilde," he persisted. "What would be the cost of a suitable dress, which you could use on other occasions as well, something very simple?

She thought for several seconds, reckoning up prices and also wondering for how large a sum she could ask without bringing upon herself an immediate refusal and an exclamation of horror from the careful-minded clerk. At last she replied with some hesitation: "I don't know exactly, but I think I could do it on four hundred francs."

He grew slightly pale, for this was exactly the amount he had been saving for a gun, intending to get a little shooting next summer on the plain of Nanterre with some friends who went lark-shooting there on Sundays. Nevertheless he said: "Very well. I'll give you four hundred francs. But try and get a really nice dress with the money."

The day of the party drew near, and Madame Loisel seemed sad, uneasy and anxious. Her dress was ready, however. One evening her husband said to her: "What's the matter with you? You've been very odd for the last three days."

"I'm utterly miserable at not having any jewels, not a single stone, to wear," she replied. "I shall look absolutely no one. I would almost rather not go to the party."

"Wear flowers," he said. "They're very smart at this time of the year. For ten francs you could get two or three gorgeous roses."

She was not convinced. "No...there's nothing so humiliating as looking poor in the middle of a lot of rich women."

"How stupid you are!" exclaimed her husband. "Go and see Madame Forestier and ask her to lend you some jewels. You know her quite well enough for that."

She uttered a cry of delight. "That's true. I never thought of it."

Next day she went to see her friend and told her her trouble. Madame Forestier went to her dressing-table, took up a large box, brought it to Madame Loisel, opened it, and said: "Choose, my dear."

First she saw some bracelets, then a pearl necklace, then a Venetian cross in gold and gems, of exquisite workmanship. She tried the effect of the jewels before the mirror, hesitating, unable to make up her mind to leave them, to give them up. She kept on asking: "Haven't you anything else?"

"Yes. Look for yourself. I don't know what you would like best."

Suddenly she discovered, in a black satin case, a superb diamond necklace; her heart began to beat covetously. Her hands trembled as she lifted it. She fastened it round her neck, upon her high dress, and remained in ecstasy at sight of herself. Then, with hesitation, she asked in anguish: "Could you lend me this, just this alone?"

"Yes, of course."

She flung herself on her friend's breast, embraced her frenziedly, and went away with her treasure. The day of the party arrived. Madame Loisel was a success. She was the prettiest woman present, elegant, graceful, smiling, and quite above herself with happiness. All the men stared at her, inquired her name, and asked to be introduced to her. All the Under-Secretaries of State were eager to waltz with her. The Minister noticed her.

She danced madly, ecstatically, drunk with pleasure, with no thought for anything, in the triumph of her beauty, in the pride of her success, in a cloud of happiness made up of this universal homage and admiration, of the desires she had aroused, of the completeness of a victory so dear to her feminine heart.

She left about four o'clock in the morning. Since midnight her husband had been dozing in a deserted little room, in company with three other men whose wives were having a good time. He threw over her shoulders the garments he had brought for them to go home in, modest everyday clothes, whose poverty clashed with the beauty of the ball-dress. She was conscious of this and was anxious to hurry away, so that she should not be noticed by the other women putting on their costly furs.

Loisel restrained her. "Wait a little. You'll catch cold in the open. I'm going to fetch a cab."

But she did not listen to him and rapidly descended the staircase. When they were out in the street they could not find a cab; they began to look for one, shouting at the drivers whom they saw passing in the distance. They walked down toward the Seine, desperate and shivering. At last they found on the quay one of those old night-prowling carriages which are only to be seen in Paris after dark, as though they were ashamed of their shabbiness in the daylight. It brought them to their door in the Rue des Martyrs, and sadly they walked up to their own apartment. It was the end, for her. As for him, he was thinking that he must be at the office at ten.

She took off the garments in which she had wrapped her shoulders, so as to see herself in all her glory before the mirror. But suddenly she uttered a cry. The necklace was no longer round her neck!

"What's the matter with you?" asked her husband, already half undressed.

She turned toward him in the utmost distress. "I...I...I've no longer got Madame Forestier's necklace..."

He started with astonishment. "What! ...Impossible!" They searched in the folds of her dress, in the folds of the coat, in the pockets, everywhere. They could not find it. "Are you sure that you still had it on when you came away from the ball?" he asked.

"Yes, I touched it in the hall at the Ministry."

"But if you had lost it in the street, we should have heard it fall."

"Yes. Probably we should. Did you take the number of the cab?"

"No. You didn't notice it, did you?"

"No."

They stared at one another, dumbfounded. At last Loisel put on his clothes again. "I'll go over all the ground we walked," he said, "and see if I can't find it."

And he went out. She remained in her evening clothes, lacking strength to get into bed, huddled on a chair, without volition or power of thought. Her husband returned about seven. He had found nothing. He went to the police station, to the newspapers, to offer a reward, to the cab companies, everywhere that a ray of hope impelled him. She waited all day long, in the same state of bewilderment at this fearful catastrophe.

Loisel came home at night, his face lined and pale; he had discovered nothing. "You must write to your friend," he said, "and tell her that you've broken the clasp of her necklace and are getting it mended. That will give us time to look about us." She wrote at his dictation.

By the end of a week they had lost all hope. Loisel, who had aged five years, declared: "We must see about replacing the diamonds."

Next day they took the box which had held the necklace and went to the jewelers whose name was inside. He consulted his books. "It was not I who sold this necklace, Madame; I must have merely supplied the clasp."

Then they went from jeweler to jeweler, searching for another necklace like the first, consulting their memories, both ill with remorse and anguish of mind. In a shop at the Palais-Royal they found a string of diamonds which seemed to them exactly like the one they were looking for. It was worth forty thousand francs. They were allowed to have it for thirty-six thousand. They begged the jeweller not to sell it for three days. And they arranged matters on the understanding that it would be taken back for thirty-four thousand francs, if the first one were found before the end of February. Loisel possessed eighteen thousand francs left to him by his father. He intended to borrow the rest.

He did borrow it, getting a thousand from one man, five hundred from another, five louis here, three louis there. He gave notes of hand, entered into ruinous agreements, did business with usurers and the whole tribe of money-lenders. He mortgaged the whole remaining years of his existence, risked his signature without even knowing if he could honor it, and, appalled at the agonizing face of the future, at the black misery about to fall upon him, at the prospect of every possible physical privation and moral torture, he went to get the new necklace and put down upon the jeweler's counter thirty-six thousand francs.

When Madame Loisel took back the necklace to Madame Forestier, the latter said to her in a chilly voice: "You ought to have brought it back sooner; I might have needed it." She did not, as her friend had feared, open the case. If she had noticed the substitution, what would she have thought? What would she have said? Would she not have taken her for a thief?

Madame Loisel came to know the ghastly life of abject poverty. From the very first she played her part heroically. This fearful debt must be paid off. She would pay it. The servant was dismissed. They changed their flat; they took a garret under the roof.

She came to know the heavy work of the house, the hateful duties of the kitchen. She washed the plates, wearing out her pink nails on the coarse pottery and the bottoms of pans. She washed the dirty linen, the shirts and dish-cloths, and hung them out to dry on a string; every morning she took the dustbin down into the street and carried up the water, stopping on each landing to get her breath. And, clad like a poor woman, she went to the fruiterer, to the grocer, to the butcher, a basket on her arm, haggling, insulted, fighting for every wretched halfpenny of her money.

Every month notes had to be paid off, others renewed, time gained.

Her husband worked in the evenings at putting straight a merchant's accounts, and often at night he did copying at twopence-halfpenny a page.

And this life lasted ten years.

At the end of ten years everything was paid off, everything, the usurer's charges and the accumulation of superimposed interest.

Madame Loisel looked old now. She had become like all the other strong, hard, coarse women of poor households. Her hair was badly done, her skirts were awry, her hands were red. She spoke in a shrill voice, and the water slopped all over the floor when she scrubbed it. But sometimes, when her husband was at the office, she sat down by the window and thought of that evening long ago, of the ball at which she had been so beautiful and so much admired. What would have happened if she had never lost those jewels. Who knows? Who knows? How strange life is, how fickle! How little is needed to ruin or to save!

One Sunday, as she had gone for a walk along the Champs-Elysees to freshen herself after the labors of the week, she caught sight suddenly of a woman who was taking a child out for a walk. It was Madame Forestier, still young, still beautiful, still attractive. Madame Loisel was conscious of some emotion. Should she speak to her? Yes, certainly. And now that she had paid, she would tell her all. Why not? She went up to her. "Good morning, Jeanne."

The other did not recognize her, and was surprised at being thus familiarly addressed by a poor woman. "But...Madame..." she stammered. "I don't know...you must be making a mistake."

"No...I am Mathilde Loisel."

Her friend uttered a cry. "Oh! ...my poor Mathilde, how you have changed! ..."

"Yes, I've had some hard times since I saw you last; and many sorrows...and all on your account."

"On my account! ...How was that?"

"You remember the diamond necklace you lent me for the ball at the Ministry?"

"Yes. Well?"

"Well, I lost it."

"How could you? Why, you brought it back."

"I brought you another one just like it. And for the last ten years we have been paying for it. You realize it wasn't easy for us; we had no money...Well, it's paid for at last, and I'm glad indeed."

Madame Forestier had halted. "You say you bought a diamond necklace to replace mine?"

"Yes. You hadn't noticed it? They were very much alike." And she smiled in proud and innocent happiness.

Madame Forestier, deeply moved, took her two hands. "Oh, my poor Mathilde! But mine was imitation. It was worth at the very most five hundred francs!"

Review Questions
1. Why was Madame Loisel unhappy about her husband's surprise?
2. What did her husband give up in order to buy her a new dress?
3. How was Madame Forestier related to Madame Loisel?
4. How much did Madame and Monsieur Loisel pay for the replacement necklace?
5. What did Madame Forestier reveal to Madame Loisel about the necklace that the Loisels had lost and replaced?

Thought Questions
1. Have you ever been discontented? If so, are your reactions generally rational or irrational? If you want something badly and then get it, does that make you content? Why or why not?
2. Have you ever lost or damaged something that was borrowed? What did you do?
3. Would it have been kinder if Madame Forestier had not told Mathilde the truth about the necklace? Is kindness or truth more important in a friendship? Explain your reasoning.
4. Pretend you are going to write an epilogue for the story. What do you think the Loisels would do next? What would you do if you were in their place?
5. What techniques does Guy de Maupassant use to move the plot forward? How does he handle gaps of time in which nothing happens?

PLOT

Writing Practice

Any good plot must be based on conflict. Conflict produces character growth and keeps the action of a story moving. Conflict can be external (when the characters are struggling against someone or something in their environment) or internal (when the characters are struggling with something within themselves).

Now that you have read these two stories with very different plots, think about the causes of conflict in "The Celestial Railroad." Is the main conflict external, internal, or both? What about in "The Necklace"? How is the conflict different in these two stories?

You may have heard of the term, "Murphy's Law." This informal law—most likely named for Air Force engineer Captain Edward A. Murphy, who applied it to his experiments in deceleration in the 1940s—says, "What can go wrong, will go wrong." Although it's not often applied to writing stories, one way to create conflict is to apply Murphy's Law to everyday situations. For example, what could go wrong at a picnic? Think about ants, bad weather, sunburn, poison ivy, etc.

Now it's your turn. List several potential sources of conflict for each of the following events:

- Having a sleepover
- A championship basketball game
- A pie-eating contest
- A horse show
- Moving to a new house

Then take it one step further: how could these dilemmas lead to character development? Remember, even though conflict is necessary for a good plot, even more important is the role of conflict in instigating growth and change.

Do I Sense a Connection? THEME

Reading for enjoyment is one of life's great pleasures. There is nothing better than curling up with a good book on a rainy day and immersing yourself in the story. But reading should not be just a passive activity. The one thing that can make a good book better is when that book makes you think or offers you a deeper message.

If the book had a thousand tiny messages, it could still be interesting, but the individual messages would get so tangled up that each one would have very little impact. For that reason, many writers will tackle a single theme in each book they write. A theme is a general topic that is addressed in various ways throughout the story. Famous themes include love, forgiveness, guilt, and repentance. In longer works, several themes may be present, but short stories—again because of their length—often focus on one main theme.

Each of the following stories has a specific theme. As you read, consider these questions especially:

- What is the theme of the story? Love? Greed? Sacrifice?
- What is the author trying to reveal about human nature?
- What is the worldview of each of the characters?
- What do you think might be the author's worldview? What makes you think so?

Keep in mind that not all themes will be as explicit as the ones in Andersen's and Dostoevsky's stories. Sometimes an unstated theme is more effective because it challenges readers to find the theme on their own. As a writer, think about themes you might want to address, and test out different ways to develop those themes through your plot, characters, and settings.

"God Lives"
Hans Christian Andersen

Hans Christian Andersen (1805-1875) was a Danish writer famous for his children's fairy tales. What endeared Andersen to adults and children alike was that his simple stories carried deeper messages about acceptance, love, and patience. Although most of his stories are considered children's material, they have a lot to say to teens and adults as well. One of Andersen's major themes was the idea that suffering eventually leads to happiness. This can be seen in his famous works "The Little Mermaid" and "The Ugly Duckling." The stories you will read are less familiar. The first is called "God Lives" (sometimes translated "God Can Never Die"). This story is about a simple trick a woman uses to open her husband's eyes to God's love.

It was a Sunday morning. The sun shone brightly and warmly into the room, as the air, mild and refreshing, flowed through the open window. And out under God's blue heaven, where fields and meadows were covered with greens and flowers, all the little birds rejoiced. While joy and contentment were everywhere outside, in the house lived sorrow and misery. Even the wife, who otherwise always was in good spirits, sat that morning at the breakfast table with a downcast expression; finally she arose, without having touched a bite of her food, dried her eyes, and walked toward the door.

It really seemed as if there were a curse hanging over this house. The cost of living was high, the food supply low; taxes had become heavier and heavier; year after year the household belongings had depreciated more and more, and now at last there was nothing to look forward to but poverty and misery. For a long time all this had depressed the husband, who always had been a hard-working and law-abiding citizen; now the thought of the future filled him with despair; yes, many times he even threatened to end his miserable and hopeless existence. Neither the comforting words of his good-humored wife nor the worldly or spiritual counsel of his friends had helped him; these had only made him more silent and sorrowful. It is easy to understand that his poor wife finally should lose her courage, too. However, there was quite another reason for her sadness, which we soon shall hear.

When the husband saw that his wife also grieved and wanted to leave the room, he stopped her and said, "I won't let you go until you have told me what is wrong with you!"

After a moment of silence, she sighed and said, "Oh, my dear husband, I dreamed last night that God was dead, and that all the angels followed Him to His grave!"

"How can you believe or think such foolish stuff!" answered the husband. "You know, of course, that God can never die!"

The good wife's face sparkled with happiness, and as she affectionately squeezed both her husband's hands, she exclaimed, "Then our dear God is still alive!"

"Why, of course," said the husband. "How could you ever doubt it!"

Then she embraced him, and looked at him with loving eyes, expressing confidence, peace, and happiness, as she said, "But, my dear husband, if God is still alive, why do we not believe and trust in Him! He has counted every hair on our heads; not a single one is lost without His knowledge. He clothes the lilies in the field; He feeds the sparrows and the ravens."

It was as if a veil lifted from his eyes and as if a heavy load fell from his heart when she spoke these words. He smiled for the first time in a long while, and thanked his dear, pious wife for the trick she had played on him, through which she had revived his belief in God and restored his trust. And in the room the sun shone even more friendly on the happy people's faces; a gentle breeze caressed their smiling cheeks, and the birds sang even louder their heartfelt thanks to God.

Review Questions
1. What issues were the husband and wife facing?
2. Why was the woman upset on this particular day?
3. Describe the woman's dream.
4. What was her husband's response to the dream?
5. What trick did the woman play on her husband? What was she trying to accomplish?

Thought Questions
1. Have you ever felt as if God were dead? When? What would the world be like if God was dead or did not exist?
2. Is it harder to believe God is in control when things do not go the way you want? Is it easier to believe in God when life is going well?
3. The verses in Matthew about the sparrows and the lilies are very well known. Have you ever watched the sparrows outside looking for food? Do you think about God providing for their needs? Why or why not?
4. What do you think of the wife's method of restoring her husband's faith?
5. Does Andersen state the theme of this story? If so, how? If not, how does he reveal it?

"The Teapot"
Hans Christian Andersen

The second story you will read by Andersen is called "The Teapot." Like many of Andersen's stories, it applies feelings and thoughts to a common household object. You may notice that this particular teapot suffers from a vice as often found in humans as in teapots.

There was a proud Teapot, proud of being made of porcelain, proud of its long spout and its broad handle. It had something in front of it and behind it; the spout was in front, and the handle behind, and that was what it talked about. But it didn't mention its lid, for it was cracked and it was riveted and full of defects, and we don't talk about our defects—other people do that. The cups, the cream pitcher, the sugar bowl—in fact, the whole tea service—thought much more about the defects in the lid and talked more about it than about the sound handle and the distinguished spout. The Teapot knew this.

"I know them," it told itself. "And I also know my imperfections, and I realize that in that very knowledge is my humility and my modesty. We all have many defects, but then we also have virtues. The cups have a handle, the sugar bowl has a lid, but of course I have both, and one thing more, one thing they can never have; I have a spout, and that makes me the queen of the tea table. The sugar bowl and the cream pitcher are permitted to be serving maids of delicacies, but I am the one who gives forth, the adviser. I spread blessings abroad among thirsty mankind. Inside of me the Chinese leaves give flavor to boiling, tasteless water."

This was the way the Teapot talked in its fresh young life. It stood on the table that was prepared for tea and it was lifted up by the most delicate hand. But that most delicate hand was very awkward. The Teapot was dropped; the spout broke off, and the handle broke off; the lid is not worth talking about; enough has been said about that. The Teapot lay in a faint on the floor, while the boiling water ran out of it. It was a great shock it got, but the worst thing of all was that the others laughed at it—and not at the awkward hand.

"I'll never be able to forget that!" said the Teapot, when later on it talked to itself about its past life. "They called me an invalid, and stood me in a corner, and the next day gave me to a woman who was begging for food. I fell into poverty, and was speechless both outside and inside, but as I stood there my better life began. One is one thing and then becomes quite another. They put earth in me, and for a Teapot that's the same as being buried, but in that earth they planted a flower bulb. Who put it there and gave it to me, I don't know; but it was planted there, a substitution for the Chinese leaves and the boiling water, the broken handle and spout. And the bulb lay in the earth, inside of me, and it became my heart, my living heart, a thing I never had before. There was life in me; there were power and might; my pulse beat. The bulb put out sprouts; thoughts and feeling sprang up and burst forth into flower. I saw it, I bore it, and I forgot myself in its beauty. It is a blessing to forget oneself in others!

"It didn't thank me, it didn't even think of me—everybody admired it and praised it. It made me very happy; how much more happy it must have made it!

"One day I heard them say it deserved a better pot. They broke me in two—that really hurt—and the flower was put into a better pot; then they threw me out into the yard, where I lie as an old potsherd. But I have my memory; that I can never lose!"

Review Questions
1. Of what was the Teapot proud? Of what was it ashamed?
2. Why did the Teapot feel like it was the queen of the tea table?
3. How was the Teapot broken?
4. What new pride did the Teapot discover as a flower pot?
5. What did the Teapot hold onto when its situation in life became worse?

Thought Questions
1. Why do people like to talk about the imperfections of others? Does it really make you feel better about yourself in the long run?
2. What is wrong with being proud of your physical characteristics? Would it be good if you always criticized your looks? How could that become a form of pride?
3. The Teapot said, "It is a blessing to forget oneself in others!" Explain this statement. Have you seen this in your own life? How?
4. Why are memories important?
5. What is the theme of this story? How do you know?

"Father Zossima's Brother"

Fyodor Dostoevsky

Fyodor Dostoevsky (1821-1881) was a Russian novelist, journalist, and short story writer. He had a talent for understanding the minds of his characters. He combined this talent with a focus on man's relationship with God and other moral and philosophical questions. "Father Zossima's Brother," the first selection, is an excerpt from the novel *The Brothers Karamazov*, book six, chapter two. This selection deals with God's power to change people.

Beloved fathers and teachers, I was born in a distant province in the north, in the town of V. My father was a gentleman by birth, but of no great consequence or position. He died when I was only two years old, and I don't remember him at all. He left my mother a small house built of wood, and a fortune, not large, but sufficient to keep her and her children in comfort. There were two of us, my elder brother Markel and I. He was eight years older than I was, of hasty, irritable temperament, but kind-hearted and never ironical. He was remarkably silent, especially at home with me, his mother, and the servants. He did well at school, but did not get on with his school-fellows, though he never quarreled, at least so my mother has told me. Six months before his death, when he was seventeen, he made friends with a political exile who had been banished from Moscow to our town for freethinking, and led a solitary existence there. He was a good scholar who had gained distinction in philosophy in the university. Something made him take a fancy to Markel, and he used to ask him to see him. The young man would spend whole evenings with him during that winter, till the exile was summoned to Petersburg to take up his post again at his own request, as he had powerful friends.

It was the beginning of Lent, and Markel would not fast, he was rude and laughed at it. "That's all silly twaddle, and there is no God," he said, horrifying my mother, the servants, and me too. For though I was only nine, I too was aghast at hearing such words. We had four servants, all serfs. I remember my mother selling one of the four, the cook Afimya, who was lame and elderly, for sixty paper roubles, and hiring a free servant to take her place.

In the sixth week in Lent, my brother, who was never strong and had a tendency to consumption, was taken ill. He was tall but thin and delicate-looking, and of very pleasing countenance. I suppose he caught cold, anyway the doctor, who came, soon whispered to my mother that it was galloping consumption, that he would not live through the spring. My mother began weeping, and, careful not to alarm my brother, she entreated him to go to church, to confess and take the sacrament, as he was still able to move about. This made him angry, and he said something profane about the church. He grew thoughtful, however; he guessed at once that he was seriously ill, and that that was why his mother was begging him to confess and take the sacrament. He had been aware, indeed, for a long time past, that he was far from well, and had a year before coolly observed at dinner to your mother and me, "My life won't be long among you, I may not live another year," which seemed now like a prophecy.

Three days passed and Holy Week had come. And on Tuesday morning my brother began going to church. "I am doing this simply for your sake, mother, to please and comfort you," he said. My mother wept with joy and grief. "His end must be near," she thought, "if there's such a change in him." But he was not able to go to church long, he took to his bed, so he had to confess and take the sacrament at home.

It was a late Easter, and the days were bright, fine, and full of fragrance. I remember he used to cough all night and sleep badly, but in the morning he dressed and tried to sit up in an arm-chair. That's how I remember him sitting, sweet and gentle, smiling, his face bright and joyous, in spite of his illness. A marvelous change passed over him, his spirit seemed transformed. The old nurse would come in and say, "Let me light the lamp before the holy image, my dear." And once he would not have allowed it and would have blown it out.

"Light it, light it, dear, I was a wretch to have prevented you doing it. You are praying when you light the lamp, and I am praying when I rejoice seeing you. So we are praying to the same God."

Those words seemed strange to us, and mother would go to her room and weep, but when she went in to him she wiped her eyes and looked cheerful. "Mother, don't weep, darling," he would say, "I've long to live yet, long to rejoice with you, and life is glad and joyful."

"Ah, dear boy, how can you talk of joy when you lie feverish at night, coughing as though you would tear yourself to pieces?"

"Don't cry, mother," he would answer, "life is paradise, and we are all in paradise, but we won't see it; if we would, we should have heaven on earth the next day."

Everyone wondered at his words, he spoke so strangely and positively; we were all touched and wept. Friends came to see us. "Dear ones," he would say to them, "what have I done that you should love me so, how can you love anyone like me, and how was it I did not know, I did not appreciate it before?"

When the servants came in to him he would say continually, "Dear, kind people, why are you doing so much for me, do I deserve to be waited on? If it were God's will for me to live, I would wait on you, for all men should wait on one another."

Mother shook her head as she listened. "My darling, it's your illness makes you talk like that."

"Mother darling," he would say, "there must be servants and masters, but if so I will be the servant of my servants, the same as they are to me. And another thing, mother, every one of us has sinned against all men, and I more than any."

Mother positively smiled at that, smiled through her tears. "Why, how could you have sinned against all men, more than all? Robbers and murderers have done that, but what sin have you committed yet, that you hold yourself more guilty than all?"

"Mother, little heart of mine," he said (he had begun using such strange caressing words at that time), "little heart of mine, my joy, believe me, everyone is really responsible to all men for all men and for everything. I don't know how to explain it to you, but I feel it is so, painfully even. And how is it we went on then living, getting angry and not knowing?"

So he would get up every day, more and more sweet and joyous and full of love. When the doctor, an old German called Eisenschmidt, came:

"Well, doctor, have I another day in this world?" he would ask, joking.

"You'll live many days yet," the doctor would answer, "and months and years too."

"Months and years!" he would exclaim. "Why reckon the days? One day is enough for a man to know all happiness. My dear ones, why do we quarrel, try to outshine each other and keep grudges against each other? Let's go straight into the garden, walk and play there, love, appreciate, and kiss each other, and glorify life."

"Your son cannot last long," the doctor told my mother, as she accompanied him the door. "The disease is affecting his brain."

The windows of his room looked out into the garden, and our garden was a shady one, with old trees in it which were coming into bud. The first birds of spring were flitting in the branches, chirruping and singing at the windows. And looking at them and admiring them, he began suddenly begging their forgiveness too: "Birds of heaven, happy birds, forgive me, for I have sinned against you too." None of us could understand that at the time, but he shed tears of joy. "Yes," he said, "there was such a glory of God all about me: birds, trees, meadows, sky; only I lived in shame and dishonored it all and did not notice the beauty and glory."

"You take too many sins on yourself," mother used to say, weeping.

"Mother, darling, it's for joy, not for grief I am crying. Though I can't explain it to you, I like to humble myself before them, for I don't know how to love them enough. If I have sinned against everyone, yet all forgive me, too, and that's heaven. Am I not in heaven now?"

And there was a great deal more I don't remember. I remember I went once into his room when there was no one else there. It was a bright evening, the sun was setting, and the whole room was lighted up. He beckoned me, and I went up to him. He put his hands on my shoulders and looked into my face tenderly, lovingly; he said nothing for a minute, only looked at me like that.

"Well," he said, "run and play now, enjoy life for me too."

I went out then and ran to play. And many times in my life afterwards I remembered even with tears how he told me to enjoy life for him too. There were many other marvelous and beautiful sayings of his, though we did not understand them at the time. He died the third week after Easter. He was fully conscious though he could not talk; up to his last hour he did not change. He looked happy, his eyes beamed and sought us, he smiled at us, beckoned us. There was a great deal of talk even in the town about his death. I was impressed by all this at the time, but not too much so, though I cried a good deal at his funeral. I was young then, a child, but a lasting impression, a hidden feeling of it all, remained in my heart, ready to rise up and respond when the time came. So indeed it happened.

Review Questions
1. Why did the mother want her son to go to church?
2. What eventually convinced him to go?
3. How did Markel change after he returned to the church?
4. What was Father Zossima's reaction to his brother's change of heart?
5. What did Father Zossima mean at the end of the story when he said, "A lasting impression, a hidden feeling of it all, remained in my heart, ready to rise up and respond when the time came"? Is this kind of memory different than the one at the end of "The Teapot"?

Thought Questions
1. If you knew that you were going to die next week, how would you spend your last few days? How would you treat the people around you? What causes you to take things around you for granted? Is it a reversible process?
2. Is joy the same thing as happiness? Can you have one without the other?
3. How do your sins affect the world around you? What is your responsibility in relation to the creation?
4. Do you enjoy life? What does that mean? What does it look like?
5. What is the theme of this story? Does Father Zossima state it explicitly?

"The Startling Painting"
Fyodor Dostoevsky

"The Startling Painting," also by Dostoevsky, deals with images of Christ's death. This selection is an excerpt from part three, chapter six of Dostoevsky's novel *The Idiot*.

    The picture represented Christ who has only just been taken from the cross. I believe artists usually paint Christ, both on the cross and after He has been taken from the cross, still with extraordinary beauty of face. They strive to preserve that beauty even in His most terrible agonies. In Rogozhin's picture there's no trace of beauty. It is in every detail the corpse of a man who has endured infinite agony before the crucifixion; who has been wounded, tortured, beaten by the guards and the people when He carried the cross on His back and fell beneath its weight, and after that has undergone the agony of crucifixion, lasting for six hours at least (according to my reckoning).

    It's true it's the face of a man only just taken from the cross—that is to say, still bearing traces of warmth and life. Nothing is rigid in it yet, so that there's still a look of suffering in the face of the dead man, as though he were still feeling it (that has been very well caught by the artist). Yet the face has not been spared in the least. It is simple nature, and the corpse of a man, whoever he might be, must really look like that after such suffering. I know that the Christian Church laid it down, even in the early ages, that Christ's suffering was not symbolical but actual, and that His body was therefore fully and completely subject to the laws of nature on the cross. In the picture the face is fearfully crushed by blows, swollen, covered with fearful, swollen and blood-stained bruises, the eyes are open and squinting: the great wide-open whites of the eyes glitter with a sort of deathly, glassy light.

    But, strange to say, as one looks at this corpse of a tortured man, a peculiar and curious questions arises; if just such a corpse (and it must have been just like that) was seen by all His disciples, by those who were to become His chief apostles, by the women that followed Him and stood by the cross, by all who believed in Him and worshiped Him, how could they believe that that martyr would rise again? The question instinctively arises: if death is so awful and the laws of nature so mighty, how can they be overcome? How can they be overcome when even He did not conquer them, He who vanquished nature in His lifetime, who exclaimed, "Maiden, arise!" and the maiden arose—"Lazarus, come forth!" and the dead man came forth?

Looking at such a picture, one conceives of nature in the shape of an immense, merciless, dumb beast, or more correctly, much more correctly, speaking, though it sounds strange, in the form of a huge machine of the most modern construction which, dull and insensible, has aimlessly clutched, crushed and swallowed up a great priceless Being, a Being worth all nature and its laws, worth the whole earth, which was created perhaps solely for the sake of the advent of that Being.

Review Questions
1. Who was the artist of the painting the narrator was studying?
2. What was unique about this particular painting?
3. How did the narrator respond to the painting?
4. What question did the painting raise in the narrator's mind?
5. How did the narrator conceive of nature after observing the painting?

Thought Questions
1. How do you picture Jesus at his birth? His death? Has your view been influenced by art or movies? How does your view of Jesus' death influence what you believe about his message?
2. Was Jesus conquered by nature? Why or why not? How do you think Dostoevsky might respond, based on this story?
3. Even though Jesus died a horrible death, his apostles still continued to proclaim his message. What does this tell you about their faith? Would this make sense if Jesus had not risen?
4. Josh McDowell's book, *More Than a Carpenter* asks, "What good is a dead Messiah?"[2] What do you think? If Jesus' story had ended with the cross, would Christianity exist today? Would it be worth believing?
5. What is the theme of this story? Do Dostoevsky and Andersen present their themes in different ways? If so, how? Which author's method do you prefer, and why?

---

[2]McDowell, Josh. *More Than a Carpenter.* Wheaton: Tyndale, 1977. This phrase is the title of chapter six.

THEME

Writing Practice

Consider each of the following themes. Think about what kind of story might be suitable to each theme. Write down at least one idea.

Example: Sin — a child stealing cookies from the cookie jar

- Pride
- Guilt
- Love
- Anger
- Forgiveness

(Hint: stories about most themes relating to human nature can be found somewhere in the Bible). Think about how you would reveal your theme to readers without sacrificing your characters' individuality and making them too stereotypical.

Was it a Dark and Stormy Night?
MOOD

There is a vast difference between the mood and tone of familiar fairy tales, such as those written by Andersen, and the murder thrillers of Edgar Allan Poe. The latter are often described as "dark," even if they do not take place at night. The difference is in the mood or tone of the story.

Setting can play a role in creating mood, as can the time of day, but word choice is very important. The form of a story can also establish its mood. Poetry is a good example. When spoken aloud, the rhythm of poetry can give emphasis to a military story by setting a marching pace, or it can set a peaceful tone by flowing smoothly and gently.

As you read the following stories in poetic form, think about what mood is created. Is it peaceful? Angry? Frightening? Compare the moods of each of these five pieces. (Read at least part of each piece aloud if possible.)

Several of these selections were written in older forms of English, which can be challenging to read. Don't feel that you must read very quickly to make it through the entire selection of these longer pieces; instead, try to read at a pace that allows you to get a good feel for the rhythm and mood of the poem. Read them aloud at least once, imagining that you are telling the story to someone else, and try to read with expression.

"The Casket Scenes"
William Shakespeare

William Shakespeare (circa 1564-1616) was an English playwright and poet often regarded as one of the greatest English writers. Shakespeare's plays and sonnets range in genre from history to tragedy and comedy, and in theme from revenge and war to love and marriage. Although his language can be challenging to understand, once you make sense of it, it is full of subtle humor and wit. The first selection, "The Casket Scenes," is an excerpt from the play *The Merchant of Venice* (Act 2 Scenes 7 and 9, and Act 3 Scene 2). The heroine, Portia, is a wealthy heiress, but suitors wishing to marry her must first complete a task her father designed to test their character. These scenes describe the test and three suitors' fates.

Belmont. A room in PORTIA'S house.
Flourish of cornets. Enter PORTIA, with the PRINCE OF MOROCCO, and their trains.

PORTIA
Go draw aside the curtains and discover
The several caskets to this noble prince.
Now make your choice.

MOROCCO
The first, of gold, which this inscription bears,
'Who chooseth me shall gain what many men desire;'
The second, silver, which this promise carries,
'Who chooseth me shall get as much as he deserves;'
This third, dull lead, with warning all as blunt,
'Who chooseth me must give and hazard all he hath.'
How shall I know if I do choose the right?

PORTIA
The one of them contains my picture, prince:
If you choose that, then I am yours withal.

MOROCCO
Some god direct my judgment! Let me see;
I will survey the inscriptions back again.
What says this leaden casket?
'Who chooseth me must give and hazard all he hath.'
Must give: for what? for lead? hazard for lead?
This casket threatens. Men that hazard all
Do it in hope of fair advantages:
A golden mind stoops not to shows of dross;
I'll then nor give nor hazard aught for lead.
What says the silver with her virgin hue?
'Who chooseth me shall get as much as he deserves.'
As much as he deserves! Pause there, Morocco,
And weigh thy value with an even hand:
If thou be'st rated by thy estimation,
Thou dost deserve enough; and yet enough
May not extend so far as to the lady:
And yet to be afeard of my deserving
Were but a weak disabling of myself.
As much as I deserve! Why, that's the lady:
I do in birth deserve her, and in fortunes,
In graces and in qualities of breeding;
But more than these, in love I do deserve.
What if I stray'd no further, but chose here?
Let's see once more this saying graved in gold
'Who chooseth me shall gain what many men desire.'
Why, that's the lady; all the world desires her;
From the four corners of the earth they come,
To kiss this shrine, this mortal-breathing saint:
The Hyrcanian deserts and the vasty wilds
Of wide Arabia are as thoroughfares now
For princes to come view fair Portia:
The watery kingdom, whose ambitious head
Spits in the face of heaven, is no bar
To stop the foreign spirits, but they come,
As o'er a brook, to see fair Portia.
One of these three contains her heavenly picture.
Is't like that lead contains her? 'Twere damnation
To think so base a thought: it were too gross
To rib her cerecloth in the obscure grave.
Or shall I think in silver she's immured,
Being ten times undervalued to tried gold?
O sinful thought! Never so rich a gem
Was set in worse than gold. They have in England
A coin that bears the figure of an angel
Stamped in gold, but that's insculp'd upon;

But here an angel in a golden bed
Lies all within. Deliver me the key:
Here do I choose, and thrive I as I may!

PORTIA
There, take it, prince; and if my form lie there,
Then I am yours.

He unlocks the golden casket

MOROCCO
O h —! what have we here?
A carrion Death, within whose empty eye
There is a written scroll! I'll read the writing. [Reads]
"All that glitters is not gold;
Often have you heard that told:
Many a man his life hath sold
But my outside to behold:
Gilded tombs do worms enfold.
Had you been as wise as bold,
Young in limbs, in judgment old,
Your answer had not been inscroll'd:
Fare you well; your suit is cold."
Cold, indeed; and labour lost:
Then, farewell, heat, and welcome, frost!
Portia, adieu. I have too grieved a heart
To take a tedious leave: thus losers part.

Exit with his train. Flourish of cornets.

PORTIA
A gentle riddance. Draw the curtains, go.
Let all of his complexion choose me so.

Exeunt

Belmont. A room in PORTIA'S house.
Enter NERISSA with a Servitor.

NERISSA
Quick, quick, I pray thee; draw the curtain straight:
The Prince of Arragon hath ta'en his oath,
And comes to his election presently.

Flourish of cornets. Enter the PRINCE OF ARRAGON, PORTIA, and their trains.

PORTIA
Behold, there stand the caskets, noble prince:
If you choose that wherein I am contain'd,
Straight shall our nuptial rites be solemnized:
But if you fail, without more speech, my lord,
You must be gone from hence immediately.

ARRAGON
I am enjoin'd by oath to observe three things:
First, never to unfold to any one
Which casket 'twas I chose; next, if I fail
Of the right casket, never in my life
To woo a maid in way of marriage: Lastly,
If I do fail in fortune of my choice,
Immediately to leave you and be gone.

PORTIA
To these injunctions every one doth swear
That comes to hazard for my worthless self.

ARRAGON
And so have I address'd me. Fortune now
To my heart's hope! Gold; silver; and base lead.
'Who chooseth me must give and hazard all he hath.'
You shall look fairer, ere I give or hazard.
What says the golden chest? ha! let me see:
'Who chooseth me shall gain what many men desire.'
What many men desire! that 'many' may be meant
By the fool multitude, that choose by show,
Not learning more than the fond eye doth teach;
Which pries not to the interior, but, like the martlet,
Builds in the weather on the outward wall,
Even in the force and road of casualty.
I will not choose what many men desire,
Because I will not jump with common spirits
And rank me with the barbarous multitudes.
Why, then to thee, thou silver treasure-house;
Tell me once more what title thou dost bear:
'Who chooseth me shall get as much as he deserves:'
And well said too; for who shall go about
To cozen fortune and be honourable
Without the stamp of merit? Let none presume
To wear an undeserved dignity.
O, that estates, degrees and offices
Were not derived corruptly, and that clear honour
Were purchased by the merit of the wearer!

How many then should cover that stand bare!
How many be commanded that command!
How much low peasantry would then be glean'd
From the true seed of honour! and how much honour
Pick'd from the chaff and ruin of the times
To be new-varnish'd! Well, but to my choice:
'Who chooseth me shall get as much as he deserves.'
I will assume desert. Give me a key for this,
And instantly unlock my fortunes here.

He opens the silver casket.

PORTIA
Too long a pause for that which you find there.

ARRAGON
What's here? the portrait of a blinking idiot,
Presenting me a schedule! I will read it.
How much unlike art thou to Portia!
How much unlike my hopes and my deservings!
'Who chooseth me shall have as much as he deserves.'
Did I deserve no more than a fool's head?
Is that my prize? are my deserts no better?

PORTIA
To offend, and judge, are distinct offices
And of opposed natures.

ARRAGON
What is here? [Reads]
"The fire seven times tried this:
Seven times tried that judgment is,
That did never choose amiss.
Some there be that shadows kiss;
Such have but a shadow's bliss:
There be fools alive, I wis,
Silver'd o'er; and so was this.
Take what wife you will to bed,
I will ever be your head:
So be gone: you are sped."
Still more fool I shall appear
By the time I linger here
With one fool's head I came to woo,
But I go away with two.
Sweet, adieu. I'll keep my oath,
Patiently to bear my wroth.

Exeunt Arragon and train.

PORTIA
Thus hath the candle singed the moth.
O, these deliberate fools! when they do choose,
They have the wisdom by their wit to lose.

NERISSA
The ancient saying is no heresy,
Hanging and wiving goes by destiny.

PORTIA
Come, draw the curtain, Nerissa.

Enter a Servant

Servant
Where is my lady?

PORTIA
Here: what would my lord?

Servant
Madam, there is alighted at your gate
A young Venetian, one that comes before
To signify the approaching of his lord;
From whom he bringeth sensible regrets,
To wit, besides commends and courteous breath,
Gifts of rich value. Yet I have not seen
So likely an ambassador of love:
A day in April never came so sweet,
To show how costly summer was at hand,
As this fore-spurrer comes before his lord.

PORTIA
No more, I pray thee: I am half afeard
Thou wilt say anon he is some kin to thee,
Thou spend'st such high-day wit in praising him.
Come, come, Nerissa; for I long to see
Quick Cupid's post that comes so mannerly.

NERISSA
Bassanio, lord Love, if thy will it be!

Exeunt

Belmont. A room in PORTIA'S house.
Enter BASSANIO, PORTIA, GRATIANO, NERISSA, and Attendants.

PORTIA
I pray you, tarry: pause a day or two
Before you hazard; for, in choosing wrong,
I lose your company: therefore forbear awhile.
There's something tells me, but it is not love,
I would not lose you; and you know yourself,
Hate counsels not in such a quality.
But lest you should not understand me well,—
And yet a maiden hath no tongue but thought,—
I would detain you here some month or two
Before you venture for me. I could teach you
How to choose right, but I am then forsworn;
So will I never be: so may you miss me;
But if you do, you'll make me wish a sin,
That I had been forsworn. Beshrew your eyes,
They have o'erlook'd me and divided me;
One half of me is yours, the other half yours,
Mine own, I would say; but if mine, then yours,
And so all yours. O, these naughty times
Put bars between the owners and their rights!
And so, though yours, not yours. Prove it so,
Let fortune go to h— for it, not I.
I speak too long; but 'tis to 'peize the time,
To eke it and to draw it out in length,
To stay you from election.

BASSANIO
Let me choose
For as I am, I live upon the rack.

PORTIA
Upon the rack, Bassanio! then confess
What treason there is mingled with your love.

BASSANIO
None but that ugly treason of mistrust,
Which makes me fear the enjoying of my love:
There may as well be amity and life
'Tween snow and fire, as treason and my love.

PORTIA
Ay, but I fear you speak upon the rack,
Where men enforced do speak anything.

BASSANIO
Promise me life, and I'll confess the truth.

PORTIA
Well then, confess and live.

BASSANIO
'Confess' and 'love'
Had been the very sum of my confession:
O happy torment, when my torturer
Doth teach me answers for deliverance!
But let me to my fortune and the caskets.

PORTIA
Away, then! I am lock'd in one of them:
If you do love me, you will find me out.
Nerissa and the rest, stand all aloof.
Let music sound while he doth make his choice;
Then, if he lose, he makes a swan-like end,
Fading in music: that the comparison
May stand more proper, my eye shall be the stream
And watery death-bed for him. He may win;
And what is music then? Then music is
Even as the flourish when true subjects bow
To a new-crowned monarch: such it is
As are those dulcet sounds in break of day
That creep into the dreaming bridegroom's ear,
And summon him to marriage. Now he goes,
With no less presence, but with much more love,
Than young Alcides, when he did redeem
The virgin tribute paid by howling Troy
To the sea-monster: I stand for sacrifice
The rest aloof are the Dardanian wives,
With bleared visages, come forth to view
The issue of the exploit. Go, Hercules!
Live thou, I live: with much, much more dismay
I view the fight than thou that makest the fray.

Music, whilst BASSANIO comments on the caskets to himself.

SONG
Tell me where is fancy bred,
Or in the heart, or in the head?
How begot, how nourished?
Reply, reply.
It is engender'd in the eyes,

With gazing fed; and fancy dies
In the cradle where it lies.
Let us all ring fancy's knell
I'll begin it,—Ding, dong, bell.

ALL
Ding, dong, bell.

BASSANIO
So may the outward shows be least themselves:
The world is still deceived with ornament.
In law, what plea so tainted and corrupt,
But, being seasoned with a gracious voice,
Obscures the show of evil? In religion,
What d— error, but some sober brow
Will bless it and approve it with a text,
Hiding the grossness with fair ornament?
There is no vice so simple but assumes
Some mark of virtue on his outward parts:
How many cowards, whose hearts are all as false
As stairs of sand, wear yet upon their chins
The beards of Hercules and frowning Mars;
Who, inward search'd, have livers white as milk;
And these assume but valour's excrement
To render them redoubted! Look on beauty,
And you shall see 'tis purchased by the weight;
Which therein works a miracle in nature,
Making them lightest that wear most of it:
So are those crisped snaky golden locks
Which make such wanton gambols with the wind,
Upon supposed fairness, often known
To be the dowry of a second head,
The skull that bred them in the sepulchre.
Thus ornament is but the guiled shore
To a most dangerous sea; the beauteous scarf
Veiling an Indian beauty; in a word,
The seeming truth which cunning times put on
To entrap the wisest. Therefore, thou gaudy gold,
Hard food for Midas, I will none of thee;
Nor none of thee, thou pale and common drudge
'Tween man and man: but thou, thou meagre lead,
Which rather threatenest than dost promise aught,
Thy paleness moves me more than eloquence;
And here choose I; joy be the consequence!

PORTIA
[Aside] How all the other passions fleet to air,
As doubtful thoughts, and rash-embraced despair,
And shuddering fear, and green-eyed jealousy! O love,
Be moderate; allay thy ecstasy,
In measure rein thy joy; scant this excess.
I feel too much thy blessing: make it less,
For fear I surfeit.

BASSANIO
What find I here? [Opening the leaden casket]
Fair Portia's counterfeit! What demi-god
Hath come so near creation? Move these eyes?
Or whether, riding on the balls of mine,
Seem they in motion? Here are sever'd lips,
Parted with sugar breath: so sweet a bar
Should sunder such sweet friends. Here in her hairs
The painter plays the spider and hath woven
A golden mesh to entrap the hearts of men,
Faster than gnats in cobwebs; but her eyes,—
How could he see to do them? having made one,
Methinks it should have power to steal both his
And leave itself unfurnish'd. Yet look, how far
The substance of my praise doth wrong this shadow
In underprizing it, so far this shadow
Doth limp behind the substance. Here's the scroll,
The continent and summary of my fortune. [Reads]
"You that choose not by the view,
Chance as fair and choose as true!
Since this fortune falls to you,
Be content and seek no new,
If you be well pleased with this
And hold your fortune for your bliss,
Turn you where your lady is
And claim her with a loving kiss."
A gentle scroll. Fair lady, by your leave;
I come by note, to give and to receive.
Like one of two contending in a prize,
That thinks he hath done well in people's eyes,
Hearing applause and universal shout,
Giddy in spirit, still gazing in a doubt
Whether these pearls of praise be his or no;
So, thrice fair lady, stand I, even so;
As doubtful whether what I see be true,
Until confirm'd, sign'd, ratified by you.

"The Casket Scenes"

PORTIA
You see me, Lord Bassanio, where I stand,
Such as I am: though for myself alone
I would not be ambitious in my wish,
To wish myself much better; yet, for you
I would be trebled twenty times myself;
A thousand times more fair, ten thousand times more rich;
That only to stand high in your account,
I might in virtue, beauties, livings, friends,
Exceed account; but the full sum of me
Is sum of something, which, to term in gross,
Is an unlesson'd girl, unschool'd, unpractised;
Happy in this, she is not yet so old
But she may learn; happier than this,
She is not bred so dull but she can learn;
Happiest of all is that her gentle spirit
Commits itself to yours to be directed,
As from her lord, her governor, her king.
Myself and what is mine to you and yours
Is now converted: but now I was the lord
Of this fair mansion, master of my servants,
Queen o'er myself: and even now, but now,
This house, these servants and this same myself
Are yours, my lord: I give them with this ring;
Which when you part from, lose, or give away,
Let it presage the ruin of your love
And be my vantage to exclaim on you.

BASSANIO
Madam, you have bereft me of all words,
Only my blood speaks to you in my veins;
And there is such confusion in my powers,
As after some oration fairly spoke
By a beloved prince, there doth appear
Among the buzzing pleased multitude;
Where every something, being blent together,
Turns to a wild of nothing, save of joy,
Express'd and not express'd. But when this ring
Parts from this finger, then parts life from hence:
O, then be bold to say Bassanio's dead!

NERISSA
My lord and lady, it is now our time,
That have stood by and seen our wishes prosper,
To cry, good joy: good joy, my lord and lady.

Review Questions
1. What task had Portia's father created for her suitors?
2. Who was the first suitor? Which casket did he choose? Why?
3. Who was the second suitor? Which casket did he choose? Why?
4. Who was the final suitor? Which casket did he choose? Why?
5. Which casket held Portia's picture?

Thought Questions
1. If you had been the first suitor, which casket would you have chosen? Why? When did you figure out which casket held Portia's picture?
2. What did the words on the lead casket, "Who chooseth me must give and hazard all he hath" mean? How could these words be compared to wedding vows, in which the bride and groom promise to love and care for each other unconditionally?
3. When you look at people, do you tend to look first at outward appearances? Can that ever be a good thing?
4. What do you think of the casket test? Was it a good way for Portia's father to evaluate her suitors in his absence? Why or why not?
5. What is the mood of this piece? Does it shift from the first scene to the last? If so, can you pick out specific words or phrases that create a change of mood?

"Iago's Intentions"
William Shakespeare

The next selection, also by Shakespeare, is an excerpt from Act 1 Scene 1 of the tragedy *Othello, the Moor of Venice*. In this scene, Iago tells his friend Roderigo that another soldier has received the position that he, Iago, thinks he deserved. With Roderigo's help, Iago plots revenge on both his commander and the rival who was promoted in his place.

Venice. A street.
Enter RODERIGO and IAGO

RODERIGO
Tush! never tell me; I take it much unkindly
That thou, Iago, who hast had my purse
As if the strings were thine, shouldst know of this.

IAGO
'Sblood, but you will not hear me:
If ever I did dream of such a matter, Abhor me.

RODERIGO
Thou told'st me thou didst hold him in thy hate.

IAGO
Despise me, if I do not. Three great ones of the city,
In personal suit to make me his lieutenant,
Off-capp'd to him: and, by the faith of man,
I know my price, I am worth no worse a place:
But he; as loving his own pride and purposes,
Evades them, with a bombast circumstance
Horribly stuff'd with epithets of war;
And, in conclusion,
Nonsuits my mediators; for, 'Certes,' says he,
'I have already chose my officer.'
And what was he?
Forsooth, a great arithmetician,

One Michael Cassio, a Florentine,
A fellow almost d— in a fair wife;
That never set a squadron in the field,
Nor the division of a battle knows
More than a spinster; unless the bookish theoric,
Wherein the toged consuls can propose
As masterly as he: mere prattle, without practise,
Is all his soldiership. But he, sir, had the election:
And I, of whom his eyes had seen the proof
At Rhodes, at Cyprus and on other grounds
Christian and heathen, must be be-lee'd and calm'd
By debitor and creditor: this counter-caster,
He, in good time, must his lieutenant be,
And I—God bless the mark!—his Moorship's ancient.

RODERIGO
By heaven, I rather would have been his hangman.

IAGO
Why, there's no remedy; 'tis the curse of service,
Preferment goes by letter and affection,
And not by old gradation, where each second
Stood heir to the first. Now, sir, be judge yourself,
Whether I in any just term am affined
To love the Moor.

RODERIGO
I would not follow him then.

IAGO
O, sir, content you;
I follow him to serve my turn upon him:
We cannot all be masters, nor all masters
Cannot be truly follow'd. You shall mark
Many a duteous and knee-crooking knave,
That, doting on his own obsequious bondage,
Wears out his time, much like his master's ass,
For nought but provender, and when he's old, cashier'd:
Whip me such honest knaves. Others there are
Who, trimm'd in forms and visages of duty,
Keep yet their hearts attending on themselves,
And, throwing but shows of service on their lords,
Do well thrive by them and when they have lined their coats
Do themselves homage: these fellows have some soul;
And such a one do I profess myself. For, sir,
It is as sure as you are Roderigo,

"Iago's Intentions"

Were I the Moor, I would not be Iago:
In following him, I follow but myself;
Heaven is my judge, not I for love and duty,
But seeming so, for my peculiar end:
For when my outward action doth demonstrate
The native act and figure of my heart
In compliment extern, 'tis not long after
But I will wear my heart upon my sleeve
For daws to peck at: I am not what I am.

RODERIGO
What a full fortune does the thicklips owe
If he can carry't thus!

IAGO
Call up her father,
Rouse him: make after him, poison his delight,
Proclaim him in the streets; incense her kinsmen,
And, though he in a fertile climate dwell,
Plague him with flies: though that his joy be joy,
Yet throw such changes of vexation on't,
As it may lose some colour.

RODERIGO
Here is her father's house; I'll call aloud.

IAGO
Do, with like timorous accent and dire yell
As when, by night and negligence, the fire
Is spied in populous cities.

RODERIGO
What, ho, Brabantio! Signior Brabantio, ho!

IAGO
Awake! what, ho, Brabantio! thieves! thieves! thieves!
Look to your house, your daughter and your bags!
Thieves! thieves!

BRABANTIO appears above, at a window

BRABANTIO
What is the reason of this terrible summons?
What is the matter there?

RODERIGO
Signior, is all your family within?

IAGO
Are your doors lock'd?

BRABANTIO
Why, wherefore ask you this?

IAGO
'Zounds, sir, you're robb'd; for shame, put on your gown;
Your heart is burst, you have lost half your soul;
Even now, now, very now, an old black ram
Is topping your white ewe. Arise, arise;
Awake the snorting citizens with the bell,
Or else the devil will make a grandsire of you:
Arise, I say.

BRABANTIO
What, have you lost your wits?

RODERIGO
Most reverend signior, do you know my voice?

BRABANTIO
Not I what are you?

RODERIGO
My name is Roderigo.

BRABANTIO
The worser welcome:
I have charged thee not to haunt about my doors:
In honest plainness thou hast heard me say
My daughter is not for thee; and now, in madness,
Being full of supper and distempering draughts,
Upon malicious bravery, dost thou come
To start my quiet.

RODERIGO
Sir, sir, sir,—

BRABANTIO
But thou must needs be sure
My spirit and my place have in them power
To make this bitter to thee.

RODERIGO
Patience, good sir.

BRABANTIO
What tell'st thou me of robbing? this is Venice;
My house is not a grange.

RODERIGO
Most grave Brabantio,
In simple and pure soul I come to you.

IAGO
'Zounds, sir, you are one of those that will not
serve God, if the devil bid you. Because we come to
do you service and you think we are ruffians, you'll
have your daughter covered with a Barbary horse;
you'll have your nephews neigh to you; you'll have
coursers for cousins and gennets for germans.

BRABANTIO
What profane wretch art thou?

IAGO
I am one, sir, that comes to tell you your daughter
and the Moor are now making the beast with two backs.

BRABANTIO
Thou art a villain.

IAGO
You are—a senator.

BRABANTIO
This thou shalt answer; I know thee, Roderigo.

RODERIGO
Sir, I will answer any thing. But, I beseech you,
If't be your pleasure and most wise consent,
As partly I find it is, that your fair daughter,
At this odd-even and dull watch o' the night,
Transported, with no worse nor better guard
But with a knave of common hire, a gondolier,
To the gross clasps of a lascivious Moor—
If this be known to you and your allowance,
We then have done you bold and saucy wrongs;

But if you know not this, my manners tell me
We have your wrong rebuke. Do not believe
That, from the sense of all civility,
I thus would play and trifle with your reverence:
Your daughter, if you have not given her leave,
I say again, hath made a gross revolt;
Tying her duty, beauty, wit and fortunes
In an extravagant and wheeling stranger
Of here and every where. Straight satisfy yourself:
If she be in her chamber or your house,
Let loose on me the justice of the state
For thus deluding you.

BRABANTIO
Strike on the tinder, ho!
Give me a taper! call up all my people!
This accident is not unlike my dream:
Belief of it oppresses me already.
Light, I say! light!

Exit above

IAGO
Farewell; for I must leave you:
It seems not meet, nor wholesome to my place,
To be produced—as, if I stay, I shall—
Against the Moor: for, I do know, the state,
However this may gall him with some cheque,
Cannot with safety cast him, for he's embark'd
With such loud reason to the Cyprus wars,
Which even now stand in act, that, for their souls,
Another of his fathom they have none,
To lead their business: in which regard,
Though I do hate him as I do hell-pains.
Yet, for necessity of present life,
I must show out a flag and sign of love,
Which is indeed but sign. That you shall surely find him,
Lead to the Sagittary the raised search;
And there will I be with him. So, farewell.

Exit
Enter, below, BRABANTIO, and Servants with torches

BRABANTIO
It is too true an evil: gone she is;
And what's to come of my despised time

Is nought but bitterness. Now, Roderigo,
Where didst thou see her? O unhappy girl!
With the Moor, say'st thou? Who would be a father!
How didst thou know 'twas she? O she deceives me
Past thought! What said she to you? Get more tapers:
Raise all my kindred. Are they married, think you?

RODERIGO
Truly, I think they are.

BRABANTIO
O heaven! How got she out? O treason of the blood!
Fathers, from hence trust not your daughters' minds
By what you see them act. Is there not charms
By which the property of youth and maidhood
May be abused? Have you not read, Roderigo,
Of some such thing?

RODERIGO
Yes, sir, I have indeed.

BRABANTIO
Call up my brother. O, would you had had her!
Some one way, some another. Do you know
Where we may apprehend her and the Moor?

RODERIGO
I think I can discover him, if you please,
To get good guard and go along with me.

BRABANTIO
Pray you, lead on. At every house I'll call;
I may command at most. Get weapons, ho!
And raise some special officers of night.
On, good Roderigo: I'll deserve your pains.

Exeunt

Review Questions
1. Who was Iago? What was his relationship to the Moor?
2. Who was Brabantio? What was his relationship to the situation?
3. Was Iago on good terms with the Moor (Othello)? Why or why not?
4. Why did he feel that he deserved the position of lieutenant more than Michael Cassio did?
5. Why was Iago planning to stay in the service of Othello? What was his ulterior motive?

Thought Questions
1. Have you ever been passed over for a privilege that you deserved? Does Iago's response seem reasonable? Explain.
2. In *Julius Caesar*, another play by Shakespeare, Cassius says to Brutus, "Upon what meat does this our Caesar feed / that he is grown so great? / Age, thou art shamed / Rome, thou have lost the breed of noble bloods."[3] What do these lines mean? How do they relate to Iago's complaints?
3. Do you think Iago gained anything by blackening Othello's name? If not, why did he do it? Have you ever done something out of pure spite? How did it make you feel?
4. How would you feel if someone you thought was your friend betrayed your trust? Why are friends able to harm you more than enemies can?
5. Compare the mood in this piece with the excerpts from *The Merchant of Venice*. What are some major differences? How does Shakespeare produce those differences?

---

[3] Shakespeare, Julius Caesar. Act 1, Scene 2.

"The Pardoner's Tale"
Geoffrey Chaucer

Geoffrey Chaucer (circa 1343-1400) was an English poet, one of the first who chose to write in English rather than Latin or Greek. Chaucer was also involved in politics, and he maintained a place near the center of power in England almost his entire life. His most famous work was *The Canterbury Tales*, a collection of stories told as if by a group of travelers exchanging stories to pass the time. "The Pardoner's Tale" is a part of that collection. A pardoner was a man of the church who sold pardons (forgiveness) for sins.

In Flanders, once, there was a company
Of young companions given to folly,
Riot and gambling, brothels and taverns;
And, to the music of harps, lutes, gitterns,
They danced and played at dice both day and night.
And ate also and drank beyond their might,
Whereby they made the devil's sacrifice
Within that devil's temple, wicked wise,
By superfluity both vile and vain.
So d— their oaths and so profane
That it was terrible to hear them swear;
Our Blessed Saviour's Body did they tear;
They thought the Jews had rent Him not enough;
And each of them at others' sins would laugh.
Then entered dancing-girls of ill repute,
Graceful and slim, and girls who peddled fruit,
Harpers and bawds and women selling cake,
Who do their office for the Devil's sake,
To kindle and blow the fire of lechery,
Which is so closely joined with gluttony;
I call on holy writ, now, to witness

That lust is in all wine and drunkenness.
Lo, how the drunken Lot unnaturally
Lay with his daughters two, unwittingly;
So drunk he was he knew not what he wrought.
Herod, as in his story's clearly taught,
When full of wine and merry at a feast,
Sitting at table idly gave behest
To slay John Baptist, who was all guiltless.
Seneca says a good word too, doubtless;
He says there is no difference he can find
Between a man that's quite out of his mind
And one that's drunken, save perhaps in this
That when a wretch in madness fallen is,
The state lasts longer than does drunkenness.
O gluttony; full of all wickedness,
O first cause of confusion to us all,
Beginning of damnation and our fall,
Till Christ redeemed us with His blood again!
Behold how dearly, to be brief and plain,
Was purchased this accursed villainy;
Corrupt was all this world with gluttony!
Adam our father, and his wife also,
From Paradise to labour and to woe
Were driven for that vice, no doubt; indeed
The while that Adam fasted, as I read,
He was in Paradise; but then when he
Ate of the fruit forbidden of the tree,
Anon he was cast out to woe and pain.
O gluttony, of you we may complain!
Oh, knew a man how many maladies

Follow on excess and on gluttonies,
Surely he would be then more moderate
In diet, and at table more sedate.
Alas! The throat so short, the tender mouth,
Causing that east and west and north and south,
In earth, in air, in water men shall swink
To get a glutton dainty meat and drink!
Of this same matter Paul does wisely treat:
"Meat for the belly and belly for the meat:
And both shall God destroy," as Paul does say.
Alas! A foul thing is it, by my fay,
To speak this word, and fouler is the deed,
When man so guzzles of the white and red
That of his own throat makes he his privy,
Because of this cursed superfluity.
The apostle, weeping, says most piteously:
"For many walk, of whom I've told you, aye,
Weeping I tell you once again they're dross,
For they are foes of Christ and of the Cross,
Whose end is death, whose belly is their god."
O gut! O belly! O you stinking cod,
Filled full of dung, with all corruption found!
At either end of you foul is the sound.
With how great cost and labour do they find
Your food! These cooks, they pound and strain and grind;
Substance to accident they turn with fire,
All to fulfill your gluttonous desire!
Out of the hard and riven bones knock they
The marrow, for they throw nothing away
That may go through the gullet soft and sweet;

With spicery, with leaf, bark, root, replete
Shall be the sauces made for your delight,
To furnish you a sharper appetite.
But truly, he that such delights entice
Is dead while yet he wallows in this vice.
A lecherous thing is wine, and drunkenness
Is full of striving and of wretchedness.
O drunken man, disfigured is your face,
Sour is your breath, foul are you to embrace,
And through your drunken nose there comes a sound
As if you snored out "Samson, Samson" round;
And yet God knows that Samson drank no wine.
You fall down just as if you were stuck swine;
Your tongue is loose, your honest care obscure;
For drunkenness is very sepulture
Of any mind a man may chance to own.
In whom strong drink has domination shown
He can no counsel keep for any dread.
Now keep you from the white and from the red,
And specially from the white wine grown at Lepe
That is for sale in Fish Street or in Cheap.
This wine of Spain, it mixes craftily
With other wines that chance to be near by,
From which there rise such fumes, as well may be,
That when a man has drunk two draughts, or three,
And thinks himself to be at home in Cheap,
He finds that he's in Spain, and right at Lepe,
Not at Rochelle nor yet at Bordeaux town,
And then will he snore out "Samson, Samson."
But hearken, masters, one word more I pray:

The greatest deeds of all, I'm bold to say,
Of victories in the Old Testament,
Through the True God, Who is omnipotent,
Were gained by abstinence and after prayer:
Look in the Bible, you may learn this there.
Lo, Attila, the mighty conqueror,
Died in his sleep, in shame and dishonour,
And bleeding at the nose for drunkenness;
A great captain should live in soberness.
Above all this, advise yourself right well
What was commanded unto Lemuel
Not Samuel, but Lemuel, say I
The Bible's words you cannot well deny:
Drinking by magistrates is called a vice.
No more of this, for it may well suffice.
And now that I have told of gluttony,
I'll take up gambling, showing you thereby
The curse of chance, and all its evils treat;
From it proceeds false swearing and deceit,
Blaspheming, murder, and—what's more—the waste
Of time and money; add to which, debased
And shamed and lost to honour quite is he,
Who once a common gambler's known to be.
And ever the higher one is of estate,
The more he's held disgraced and desolate.
And if a prince plays similar hazardry
In all his government and policy,
He loses in the estimate of men
His good repute, and finds it not again.
Chilon, who was a wise ambassador,
Was sent to Corinth, all in great honour,
From Lacedaemon, to make alliance.
And when he came, he noticed there, by chance,
All of the greatest people of the land
Playing at hazard there on every hand.
Wherefore, and all as soon as it might be,
He stole off home again to his country,
And said: "I will not thus debase my name;
Nor will I take upon me so great shame
You to ally with common hazarders.
Send, if you will, other ambassadors;
For, my truth, I say I'd rather die
Than you with gamblers like to them ally.
For you that are so glorious in honours
Shall never ally yourselves with hazarders
By my consent, or treaty I have made."

This wise philosopher, 'twas thus he said.
Let us look, then, at King Demetrius.
The king of Parthia, as the book tells us,
Sent him a pair of golden dice, in scorn,
Because the name of gambler he had borne;
Wherefore he marked his reputation down
As valueless despite his wide renown.
Great lords may find sufficient other play
Seemly enough to while the time away.
Now will I speak of oaths both false and great
A word or two, whereof the old books treat.
Great swearing is a thing abominable,
And vain oaths yet more reprehensible.
The High God did forbid swearing at all,
As witness Matthew; but in especial
Of swearing says the holy Jeremiah,
"Thou shalt not swear in vain, to be a liar,
But swear in judgment and in righteousness";
But idle swearing is a wickedness.
Behold, in the first table of the Law,
That should be honoured as High God's, sans flaw,
This second one of His commandments plain:
"Thou shalt not take the Lord God's name in vain."
Nay, sooner He forbids us such swearing
Than homicide or many a wicked thing;
I say that, as to order, thus it stands;
'Tis known by him who His will understands
That the great second law of God is that.
Moreover, I will tell you full and flat,
That retribution will not quit his house
Who in his swearing is too outrageous.
"By God's own precious heart, and by His nails,
And by the blood of Christ that's now at Hales,
Seven is my chance, and yours is five and trey!"
"By God's good arms, if you do falsely play,
This dagger through your heart I'll stick for you!"
Such is the whelping of the bitched bones two:
Perjury, anger, cheating, homicide.
Now for the love of Christ, Who for us died,
Forgo this swearing oaths, both great and small;
But, sirs, now will I tell to you my tale.
Now these three roisterers, whereof I tell,
Long before prime was rung by any bell,
Were sitting in a tavern for to drink;
And as they sat they heard a small bell clink
Before a corpse being carried to his grave;

Whereat one of them called unto his knave:
"Go run," said he, "and ask them civilly
What corpse it is that's just now passing by,
And see that you report the man's name well."
"Sir," said the boy, "it needs not that they tell.
I learned it, ere you came here, full two hours;
He was, by gad, an old comrade of yours;
And he was slain, all suddenly, last night,
When drunk, as he sat on his bench upright;
An unseen thief, called Death, came stalking by,
Who hereabouts makes all the people die,
And with his spear he clove his heart in two
And went his way and made no more ado.
He's slain a thousand with this pestilence;
And, master, ere you come in his presence,
It seems to me to be right necessary
To be forewarned of such an adversary:
Be ready to meet him for evermore.
My mother taught me this, I say no more."
"By holy Mary," said the innkeeper,
"The boy speaks truth, for Death has slain, this year,
A mile or more hence, in a large village,
Both man and woman, child and hind and page.
I think his habitation must be there;
To be advised of him great wisdom 'twere,
Before he did a man some dishonour."
"Yea, by God's arms!" exclaimed this roisterer,
"Is it such peril, then, this Death to meet?
I'll seek him in the road and in the street,
As I now vow to God's own noble bones!
Hear, comrades, we're of one mind, as each owns;
Let each of us hold up his hand to other
And each of us become the other's brother,
And we three will go slay this traitor Death;
He shall be slain who's stopped so many a breath,
By God's great dignity, ere it be night."
Together did these three their pledges plight
To live and die, each of them for the other,
As if he were his very own blood brother.
And up they started, drunken, in this rage,
And forth they went, and toward that village
Whereof the innkeeper had told before.
And so, with many a grisly oath, they swore
And Jesus' blessed body once more rent
"Death shall be dead if we find where he went."
When they had gone not fully half a mile,

Just as they would have trodden over a stile,
An old man, and a poor, with them did meet.
This ancient man full meekly them did greet,
And said thus: "Now, lords, God keep you and see!"
The one that was most insolent of these three
Replied to him: "What? Churl of evil grace,
Why are you all wrapped up, except your face?
Why do you live so long in so great age?"
This ancient man looked upon his visage
And thus replied: "Because I cannot find
A man, nay, though I walked from here to Ind,
Either in town or country who'll engage
To give his youth in barter for my age;
And therefore must I keep my old age still,
As long a time as it shall be God's will.
Not even Death, alas! my life will take;
Thus restless I my wretched way must make,
And on the ground, which is my mother's gate,
I knock with my staff early, aye, and late,
And cry: 'O my dear mother, let me in!
Lo, how I'm wasted, flesh and blood and skin!
Alas! When shall my bones come to their rest?
Mother, with you fain would I change my chest,
That in my chamber so long time has been,
Aye! For a haircloth rag to wrap me in!'
But yet to me she will not show that grace,
And thus all pale and withered is my face.
"But, sirs, in you it is no courtesy
To speak to an old man despitefully,
Unless in word he trespass or in deed.
In holy writ you may, yourselves, well read
'Before an old man, hoar upon the head,
You should arise.' Which I advise you read,
Nor to an old man any injury do
More than you would that men should do to you
In age, if you so long time shall abide;
And God be with you, whether you walk or ride.
I must pass on now where I have to go."
"Nay, ancient churl, by God it sha'n't be so,"
Cried out this other hazarder, anon;
"You sha'n't depart so easily, by Saint John!
You spoke just now of that same traitor Death,
Who in this country stops our good friends' breath.
Hear my true word, since you are his own spy,
Tell where he is or you shall rue it, aye
By God and by the holy Sacrament!

Indeed you must be, with this Death, intent
To slay all us young people, you false thief."
"Now, sirs," said he, "if you're so keen, in brief,
To find out Death, turn up this crooked way,
For in that grove I left him, by my fay,
Under a tree, and there he will abide;
Nor for your boasts will he a moment hide.
See you that oak? Right there you shall him find.
God save you, Who redeemed all humankind,
And mend your ways!"— thus said this ancient man.
And every one of these three roisterers ran
Till he came to that tree; and there they found,
Of florins of fine gold, new-minted, round,
Well-nigh eight bushels full, or so they thought.
No longer, then, after this Death they sought,
But each of them so glad was of that sight,
Because the florins were so fair and bright,
That down they all sat by this precious hoard.
The worst of them was first to speak a word.
"Brothers," said he, "take heed to what I say;
My wits are keen, although I mock and play.
This treasure here Fortune to us has given
That mirth and jollity our lives may liven,
And easily as it's come, so will we spend.
Eh! By God's precious dignity! Who'd pretend,
Today, that we should have so fair a grace?
But might this gold be carried from this place
Home to my house, or if you will, to yours
For well we know that all this gold is ours
Then were we all in high felicity.
But certainly by day this may not be;
For men would say that we were robbers strong,
And we'd, for our own treasure, hang ere long.
This treasure must be carried home by night
All prudently and slyly, out of sight.
So I propose that cuts among us all
Be drawn, and let's see where the cut will fall;
And he that gets the short cut, blithe of heart
Shall run to town at once, and to the mart,
And fetch us bread and wine here, privately.
And two of us shall guard, right cunningly,
This treasure well; and if he does not tarry,
When it is night we'll all the treasure carry
Where, by agreement, we may think it best."
That one of them the cuts brought in his fist
And bade them draw to see where it might fall;

And it fell on the youngest of them all;
And so, forth toward the town he went anon.
And just as soon as he had turned and gone,
That one of them spoke thus unto the other:
"You know well that you are my own sworn brother,
So to your profit I will speak anon.
You know well how our comrade is just gone;
And here is gold, and that in great plenty,
That's to be parted here among us three.
Nevertheless, if I can shape it so
That it be parted only by us two,
Shall I not do a turn that is friendly?"
The other said: "Well, now, how can that be?
He knows well that the gold is with us two.
What shall we say to him? What shall we do?"
"Shall it be secret?" asked the first rogue, then,
"And I will tell you in eight words, or ten,
What we must do, and how bring it about."
"Agreed," replied the other, "Never doubt,
That, on my word, I nothing will betray."
"Now," said the first, "we're two, and I dare say
The two of us are stronger than is one.
Watch when he sits, and soon as that is done
Arise and make as if with him to play;
And I will thrust him through the two sides, yea,
The while you romp with him as in a game,
And with your dagger see you do the same;
And then shall all this gold divided be,
My right dear friend, just between you and me;
Then may we both our every wish fulfill
And play at dice all at our own sweet will."
And thus agreed were these two rogues, that day,
To slay the third, as you have heard me say.
This youngest rogue who'd gone into the town,
Often in fancy rolled he up and down
The beauty of those florins new and bright.
"O Lord," thought he, "if so be that I might
Have all this treasure to myself alone,
There is no man who lives beneath the throne
Of God that should be then so merry as I."
And at the last the Fiend, our enemy,
Put in his thought that he should poison buy
With which he might kill both his fellows; aye,
The Devil found him in such wicked state,
He had full leave his grief to consummate;
For it was utterly the man's intent

To kill them both and never to repent.
And on he strode, no longer would he tarry,
Into the town, to an apothecary,
And prayed of him that he'd prepare and sell
Some poison for his rats, and some as well
For a polecat that in his yard had lain,
The which, he said, his capons there had slain,
And fain he was to rid him, if he might,
Of vermin that thus damaged him by night.
The apothecary said: "And you shall have
A thing of which, so God my spirit save,
In all this world there is no live creature
That's eaten or has drunk of this mixture
As much as equals but a grain of wheat,
That shall not sudden death thereafter meet;
Yea, die he shall, and in a shorter while
Than you require to walk but one short mile;
This poison is so violent and strong."
This wicked man the poison took along
With him boxed up, and then he straightway ran
Into the street adjoining, to a man,
And of him borrowed generous bottles three;
And into two his poison then poured he;
The third one he kept clean for his own drink.
For all that night he was resolved to swink
In carrying the florins from that place.
And when this roisterer, with evil grace,
Had filled with wine his mighty bottles three,
Then to his comrades forth again went he.
What is the need to tell about it more?
For just as they had planned his death before,
Just so they murdered him, and that anon.
And when the thing was done, then spoke the one:
"Now let us sit and drink and so be merry,
And afterward we will his body bury."
And as he spoke, one bottle of the three
He took wherein the poison chanced to be
And drank and gave his comrade drink also,
For which, and that anon, lay dead these two.
I feel quite sure that Doctor Avicena
Within the sections of his Canon never
Set down more certain signs of poisoning
Than showed these wretches two at their ending.
Thus ended these two homicides in woe;
Died thus the treacherous poisoner also.
O cursed sin, full of abominableness!

O treacherous homicide! O wickedness!
O gluttony, lechery, and hazardry!
O blasphemer of Christ with villainy,
And with great oaths, habitual for pride!
Alas! Mankind, how may this thing betide
That to thy dear Creator, Who thee wrought,
And with His precious blood salvation bought,
Thou art so false and so unkind, alas!
Now, good men, God forgive you each trespass,
And keep you from the sin of avarice.
My holy pardon cures and will suffice,
So that it brings me gold, or silver brings,
Or else, I care not – brooches, spoons or rings.
Bow down your heads before this holy bull!
Come up, you wives, and offer of your wool!
Your names I'll enter on my roll, anon,
And into Heaven's bliss you'll go, each one.
For I'll absolve you, by my special power,
You that make offering, as clean this hour
As you were born. And lo, sirs, thus I preach.
And Jesus Christ, who is our souls' great leech,
So grant you each his pardon to receive;
For that is best; I will not you deceive.
But, sirs, one word forgot I in my tale;
I've relics in my pouch that cannot fail,
As good as England ever saw, I hope,
The which I got by kindness of the pope.
If gifts your change of heart and mind reveal,
You'll get my absolution while you kneel.
Come forth, and kneel down here before, anon,
And humbly you'll receive my full pardon;
Or else receive a pardon as you wend,
All new and fresh as every mile shall end,
So that you offer me each time, anew,
More gold and silver, all good coins and true.
It is an honour to each one that's here
That you may have a competent pardoner
To give you absolution as you ride,
For all adventures that may still betide.
Perchance from horse may fall down one or two,
Breaking his neck, and it might well be you.
See what insurance, then, it is for all
That I within your fellowship did fall,
Who may absolve you, both the great and less,
When soul from body passes, as I guess.
I think our host might just as well begin,

For he is most-enveloped in all sin.
Come forth, sir host, and offer first anon,
And you shall kiss the relics, every one,
Aye, for a groat! Unbuckle now your purse."
"Nay, nay," said he, "then may I have Christ's curse!
It sha'n't be," said he, "as I've hope for riches,
Why, you would have me kissing your old breeches,
And swear they were the relics of a saint,
Though with your excrement 'twere dabbed like paint.
By cross Saint Helen found in Holy Land,
I would I had your ballocks in my hand
Instead of relics in a reliquary;
Let's cut them off, and them I'll help you carry;
They shall be shrined within a hog's fat turd."
This pardoner, he answered not a word;
So wrathy was he no word would he say.
"Now," said our host, "I will no longer play
With you, nor any other angry man."
But at this point the worthy knight began,
When that he saw how all the folk did laugh:
"No more of this, for it's gone far enough;
Sir pardoner, be glad and merry here;
And you, sir host, who are to me so dear,
I pray you that you kiss the pardoner.
And, pardoner, I pray you to draw near,
And as we did before, let's laugh and play."
And then they kissed and rode forth on their way.

Review Questions
1. What was the great sin against which the pardoner was preaching?
2. Why did the young men want to find Death?
3. What actually killed the friend of the three young men?
4. How did the old man prevent the ruffians from killing him?
5. What did the young men find under the tree?

Thought Questions
1. How would you describe the pardoner? Do you think he is supposed to be a likeable character? Why or why not?
2. What is gluttony? Does it always have to relate to food or drink? How is this sin different today than it was during Chaucer's time? How is it the same? In what areas of your life do you struggle with gluttony?
3. When the old man directed the three rogues to "Death," they found gold. Why is this symbolic? Do riches always lead to death?
4. What is a pardoner? Can humans buy forgiveness? Explain. Is the idea of a pardoner consistent with the Bible?
5. Even though this is a story about death, is the mood of the story grim or humorous? How does Chaucer achieve that effect?

Paradise Lost, Book 1
John Milton

John Milton (1608-1674) was an English poet who was interested not only in writing but also in political, civil, and religious rights. Milton's greatest work was *Paradise Lost*, a twelve-book epic poem first published in 1667. *Paradise Lost* deals with the events of man's fall and exile from Eden. This selection is the first book of the poem. Milton's language may be offsetting at first, so take time to read slowly, and be sure that you understand what is going on. Reading aloud may help, because much of Milton's older English is phonetic (spelled the way it is pronounced). Remember that in reading poetry, the punctuation (not the line breaks) tells you where to pause.

THE ARGUMENT

This first Book proposes first in brief the whole Subject, Man's disobedience, and the loss thereupon of Paradise wherein he was plac't: Then touches the prime cause of his fall, the Serpent, or rather Satan in the Serpent; who revolting from God, and drawing to his side many Legions of Angels, was by the command of God driven out of Heaven with all his Crew into the great Deep.

Which action past over, the Poem hasts into the midst of things, presenting Satan with his Angels now fallen into Hell, describ'd here, not in the Center (for Heaven and Earth may be suppos'd as yet not made, certainly not yet accurst) but in a place of utter darknesse, fitliest call'd Chaos: Here Satan with his Angels lying on the burning Lake, thunder-struck and, astonish't, after a certain space recovers, as from confusion, calls up him who next in Order and Dignity lay by him; they confer of thir miserable fall. Satan awakens all his Legions, who lay till then in the same manner confounded; They rise, thir Numbers, array of Battel, thir chief Leaders nam'd, according to the Idols known afterwards in Canaan and the Countries adjoyning. To these Satan directs his Speech, comforts them with hope yet of regaining Heaven, but tells them lastly of a new World and new kind of Creature to be created, according to an ancient Prophesie or report in Heaven; for that Angels were long before this visible Creation, was the opinion of many ancient Fathers.

To find out the truth of this Prophesie, and what to determin thereon he refers to a full Councell. What his Associates thence attempt. Pandemonium the Palace of Satan rises, suddenly built out of the Deep: The infernal Peers there sit in Counsel.

BOOK 1
Of Man's First Disobedience, and the Fruit
Of that Forbidden Tree, whose mortal tast
Brought Death into the World, and all our woe,
With loss of Eden, till one greater Man
Restore us, and regain the blissful Seat,
Sing Heav'nly Muse, that on the secret top
Of Oreb, or of Sinai, didst inspire
That Shepherd, who first taught the chosen Seed,
In the Beginning how the Heav'ns and Earth
Rose out of Chaos: or if Sion Hill
Delight thee more, and Siloa's Brook that flow'd
Fast by the Oracle of God; I thence
Invoke thy aid to my adventrous Song,
That with no middle flight intends to soar
Above th' Aonian Mount, while it pursues
Things unattempted yet in Prose or Rhime.
And chiefly Thou O Spirit, that dost prefer
Before all Temples th' upright heart and pure,
Instruct me, for Thou know'st; Thou from the first
Wast present, and with mighty wings outspread
Dove-like satst brooding on the vast Abyss
And mad'st it pregnant: What in me is dark
Illumin, what is low raise and support;
That to the highth of this great
Argument I may assert Eternal Providence,
And justifie the wayes of God to men.

Say first, for Heav'n hides nothing from thy view
Nor the deep Tract of Hell, say first what cause
Mov'd our Grand Parents in that happy State,
Favour'd of Heav'n so highly, to fall off
From thir Creator, and transgress his Will
For one restraint, Lords of the World besides?
Who first seduc'd them to that foul revolt?
Th' infernal Serpent; he it was, whose guile
Stird up with Envy and Revenge, deceiv'd
The Mother of Mankind, what time his Pride
Had cast him out from Heav'n, with all his Host
Of Rebel Angels, by whose aid aspiring
To set himself in Glory above his Peers,
He trusted to have equal'd the most High,
If he oppos'd; and with ambitious aim
Against the Throne and Monarchy of God
Rais'd impious War in Heav'n and Battel proud

With vain attempt. Him the Almighty Power
Hurl'd headlong flaming from th' Ethereal Skie
With hideous ruine and combustion down
To bottomless perdition, there to dwell
In Adamantine Chains and penal Fire,
Who durst defie th' Omnipotent to Arms.
Nine times the Space that measures Day and Night
To mortal men, he with his horrid crew
Lay vanquisht, rowling in the fiery Gulfe
Confounded though immortal: But his doom
Reserv'd him to more wrath; for now the thought
Both of lost happiness and lasting pain
Torments him; round he throws his baleful eyes
That witness'd huge affliction and dismay
Mixt with obdurate pride and stedfast hate:
At once as far as Angels kenn he views
The dismal Situation waste and wilde,
A Dungeon horrible, on all sides round
As one great Furnace flam'd, yet from those flames
No light, but rather darkness visible
Serv'd onely to discover sights of woe,
Regions of sorrow, doleful shades, where peace
And rest can never dwell, hope never comes
That comes to all; but torture without end
Still urges, and a fiery Deluge, fed
With ever-burning Sulphur unconsum'd:
Such place Eternal Justice had prepar'd
For those rebellious, here thir Prison ordain'd
In utter darkness, and thir portion set
As far remov'd from God and light of Heav'n
As from the Center thrice to th' utmost Pole.
O how unlike the place from whence they fell!
There the companions of his fall, o'rewhelm'd
With Floods and Whirlwinds of tempestuous fire,
He soon discerns, and weltring by his side
One next himself in power, and next in crime,
Long after known in Palestine, and nam'd Beelzebub. To whom th' Arch-Enemy,
And thence in Heav'n call'd Satan, with bold words
Breaking the horrid silence thus began.

If thou beest he; But O how fall'n! how chang'd
From him, who in the happy Realms of Light
Cloth'd with transcendent brightness didst outshine
Myriads though bright: If he Whom mutual league,
United thoughts and counsels, equal hope,

And hazard in the Glorious Enterprize,
Joynd with me once, now misery hath joynd
In equal ruin: into what Pit thou seest
From what highth fall'n, so much the stronger prov'd
He with his Thunder: and till then who knew
The force of those dire Arms? yet not for those
Nor what the Potent Victor in his rage
Can else inflict, do I repent or change,
Though chang'd in outward lustre; that fixt mind
And high disdain, from sence of injur'd merit,
That with the mightiest rais'd me to contend,
And to the fierce contention brought along
Innumerable force of Spirits arm'd
That durst dislike his reign, and me preferring,
His utmost power with adverse power oppos'd
In dubious Battel on the Plains of Heav'n,
And shook his throne. What though the field be lost?
All is not lost; the unconquerable Will,
And study of revenge, immortal hate,
And courage never to submit or yield:
And what is else not to be overcome?
That Glory never shall his wrath or might
Extort from me. To bow and sue for grace
With suppliant knee, and deifie his power,
Who from the terrour of this Arm so late
Doubted his Empire, that were low indeed,
That were an ignominy and shame beneath
This downfall; since by Fate the strength of Gods
And this Empyreal substance cannot fail,
Since through experience of this great event
In Arms not worse, in foresight much advanc't,
We may with more successful hope resolve
To wage by force or guile eternal Warr
 Irreconcileable, to our grand Foe,
Who now triumphs, and in th' excess of joy
Sole reigning holds the Tyranny of Heav'n.

So spake th' Apostate Angel, though in pain,
Vaunting aloud, but rackt with deep despare:
And him thus answer'd soon his bold Compeer.

O Prince, O Chief of many Throned Powers,
That led th' imbattelld Seraphim to Warr
Under thy conduct, and in dreadful deeds
Fearless, endanger'd Heav'ns perpetual King;
And put to proof his high Supremacy,

Whether upheld by strength, or Chance, or Fate,
Too well I see and rue the dire event,
That with sad overthrow and foul defeat
Hath lost us Heav'n, and all this mighty Host
In horrible destruction laid thus low,
As far as Gods and Heav'nly Essences
Can perish: for the mind and spirit remains
Invincible, and vigour soon returns,
Though all our Glory extinct, and happy state
Here swallow'd up in endless misery.
But what if he our Conquerour, (whom I now
Of force believe Almighty, since no less
Then such could hav orepow'rd such force as ours)
Have left us this our spirit and strength intire
Strongly to suffer and support our pains,
That we may so suffice his vengeful ire,
Or do him mightier service as his thralls
By right of Warr, what e're his business be
Here in the heart of Hell to work in Fire,
Or do his Errands in the gloomy Deep;
What can it then avail though yet we feel
Strength undiminisht, or eternal being
To undergo eternal punishment?
Whereto with speedy words th' Arch-fiend reply'd.

Fall'n Cherube, to be weak is miserable
Doing or Suffering: but of this be sure,
To do ought good never will be our task,
But ever to do ill our sole delight,
As being the contrary to his high will
Whom we resist. If then his Providence
Out of our evil seek to bring forth good,
Our labour must be to pervert that end,
And out of good still to find means of evil;
Which oft times may succeed, so as perhaps
Shall grieve him, if I fail not, and disturb
His inmost counsels from their destind aim.
But see the angry Victor hath recall'd
His Ministers of vengeance and pursuit
Back to the Gates of Heav'n: The Sulphurous Hail
Shot after us in storm, oreblown hath laid
The fiery Surge, that from the Precipice
Of Heav'n receiv'd us falling, and the Thunder,
Wing'd with red Lightning and impetuous rage,
Perhaps hath spent his shafts, and ceases now
To bellow through the vast and boundless Deep.

Let us not slip th' occasion, whether scorn,
Or satiate fury yield it from our Foe.
Seest thou yon dreary Plain, forlorn and wilde,
The seat of desolation, voyd of light,
Save what the glimmering of these livid flames
Casts pale and dreadful? Thither let us tend
From off the tossing of these fiery waves,
There rest, if any rest can harbour there,
And reassembling our afflicted Powers,
Consult how we may henceforth most offend
Our Enemy, our own loss how repair,
How overcome this dire Calamity,
What reinforcement we may gain from Hope,
If not what resolution from despare.

Thus Satan talking to his neerest Mate
With Head up-lift above the wave, and Eyes
That sparkling blaz'd, his other Parts besides
Prone on the Flood, extended long and large
Lay floating many a rood, in bulk as huge
As whom the Fables name of monstrous size,
Titanian, or Earth-born, that warr'd on Jove,
Briarios or Typhon, whom the Den
By ancient Tarsus held, or that Sea-beast
Leviathan, which God of all his works
Created hugest that swim th' Ocean stream:
Him haply slumbring on the Norway foam
The Pilot of some small night-founder'd Skiff,
Deeming some Island, oft, as Sea-men tell,
With fixed Anchor in his skaly rind
Moors by his side under the Lee, while Night
Invests the Sea, and wished Morn delayes:
So stretcht out huge in length the Arch-fiend lay
Chain'd on the burning Lake, nor ever thence
Had ris'n or heav'd his head, but that the will
And high permission of all-ruling Heaven
Left him at large to his own dark designs,
That with reiterated crimes he might
Heap on himself damnation, while he sought
Evil to others, and enrag'd might see
How all his malice serv'd but to bring forth
Infinite goodness, grace and mercy shewn
On Man by him seduc't, but on himself
Treble confusion, wrath and vengeance pour'd.
Forthwith upright he rears from off the Pool
His mighty Stature; on each hand the flames

Drivn backward slope thir pointing spires, and rowld
In billows, leave i'th' midst a horrid Vale.
Then with expanded wings he stears his flight
Aloft, incumbent on the dusky Air
That felt unusual weight, till on dry Land
He lights, if it were Land that ever burn'd
With solid, as the Lake with liquid fire;
And such appear'd in hue, as when the force
Of subterranean wind transports a Hill
Torn from Pelorus, or the shatter'd side
Of thundring Ætna, whose combustible
And fewel'd entrals thence conceiving Fire,
Sublim'd with Mineral fury, aid the Winds,
And leave a singed bottom all involv'd
With stench and smoak: Such resting found the sole
Of unblest feet. Him followed his next Mate,
Both glorying to have scap't the Stygian flood
As Gods, and by their own recover'd strength,
Not by the sufferance of supernal Power.

Is this the Region, this the Soil, the Clime,
Said then the lost Arch-Angel, this the seat
That we must change for Heav'n, this mournful gloom
For that celestial light? Be it so, since he
Who now is Sovran can dispose and bid
What shall be right: fardest from him is best
Whom reason hath equald, force hath made supream
Above his equals. Farewel happy Fields
Where Joy for ever dwells: Hail horrours, hail
Infernal world, and thou profoundest Hell
Receive thy new Possessor: One who brings
A mind not to be chang'd by Place or Time.
The mind is its own place, and in it self
Can make a Heav'n of Hell, a Hell of Heav'n.
What matter where, if I be still the same,
And what I should be, all but less than he
Whom Thunder hath made greater? Here at least
We shall be free; th' Almighty hath not built
Here for his envy, will not drive us hence:
Here we may reign secure, and in my choyce
To reign is worth ambition though in Hell:
Better to reign in Hell, then serve in Heav'n.
But wherefore let we then our faithful friends,
Th' associates and copartners of our loss
Lye thus astonisht on th' oblivious Pool,
And call them not to share with us thir part

In this unhappy Mansion, or once more
With rallied Arms to try what may be yet
Regained in Heav'n, or what more lost in Hell?

So Satan spake, and him Beelzebub
Thus answer'd. Leader of those Armies bright,
Which but th' Onmipotent none could have foyld,
If once they hear that voyce, thir liveliest pledge
Of hope in fears and dangers, heard so oft
In worst extreams, and on the perilous edge
Of battel when it rag'd, in all assaults
Thir surest signal, they will soon resume
New courage and revive, though now they lye
Groveling and prostrate on yon Lake of fire,
As we erewhile, astounded and amaz'd,
No wonder, fall'n such a pernicious highth.

He scarce had ceas't when the superior Fiend
Was moving toward the shore; his ponderous shield
Ethereal temper, massy, large and round,
Behind him cast; the broad circumference
Hung on his shoulders like the Moon, whose Orb
Through Optic Glass the Tuscan Artist views
At Ev'ning from the top of Fesole,
Or in Valdarno, to descry new Lands,
Rivers or Mountains in her spotty Globe.
His Spear, to equal which the tallest Pine
Hewn on Norwegian hills, to be the Mast
Of some great Ammirall, were but a wand,
He walk't with to support uneasie steps
Over the burning Marle, not like those steps
On Heavens Azure, and the torrid Clime
Smote on him sore besides, vaulted with Fire;
Nathless he so endur'd, till on the Beach
Of that inflamed Sea, he stood and call'd
His Legions, Angel Forms, who lay intrans't
Thick as Autumnal Leaves that strow the Brooks
In Vallombrosa, where th' Etrurian shades
High overarch't imbowr; or scatterd sedge
Afloat, when with fierce Winds Orion arm'd
Hath vext the Red-Sea Coast, whose waves orethrew
Busiris and his Memphian Chivalry,
While with perfidious hatred they pursu'd
The Sojourners of Goshen, who beheld
From the safe shore their floating Carkases
And broken Chariot Wheels, so thick bestrown

Abject and lost lay these, covering the Flood,
Under amazement of thir hideous change.
He call'd so loud, that all the hollow Deep
Of Hell resounded. Princes, Potentates,
Warriers, the Flowr of Heav'n, once yours, now lost,
If such astonishment as this can sieze
Eternal spirits; or have ye chos'n this place
After the toyl of Battel to repose
Your wearied vertue, for the ease you find
To slumber here, as in the Vales of Heav'n?
Or in this abject posture have ye sworn
To adore the Conquerour? who now beholds
Cherube and Seraph rowling in the Flood
With scatter'd Arms and Ensigns, till anon
His swift pursuers from Heav'n Gates discern
Th' advantage, and descending tread us down
Thus drooping, or with linked Thunderbolts
Transfix us to the bottom of this Gulfe.
Awake, arise, or be for ever fall'n.

They heard, and were abasht, and up they sprung
Upon the wing, as when men wont to watch
On duty, sleeping found by whom they dread,
Rouse and bestir themselves ere well awake.
Nor did they not perceave the evil plight
In which they were, or the fierce pains not feel;
Yet to thir Generals Voyce they soon obeyd
Innumerable. As when the potent Rod
Of Amrams Son in Egipt's evill day
Wav'd round the Coast, up call'd a pitchy cloud
Of Locusts, warping on the Eastern Wind,
That ore the Realm of impious Pharaoh hung
Like Night, and darken'd all the Land of Nile:
So numberless were those bad Angels seen
Hovering on wing under the Cope of Hell
'Twixt upper, nether, and surrounding Fires;
Till, as a signal giv'n, th' uplifted Spear
Of thir great Sultan waving to direct
Thir course, in even ballance down they light
On the firm brimstone, and fill all the Plain;
A multitude, like which the populous North
Pour'd never from her frozen loyns, to pass
Rhene or the Danaw, when her barbarous Sons
Came like a Deluge on the South, and spread
Beneath Gibraltar to the Lybian sands.
Forthwith from every Squadron and each Band

The Heads and Leaders thither hast where stood
Thir great Commander; Godlike shapes and forms
Excelling human, Princely Dignities,
And Powers that earst in Heaven sat on Thrones;
Though of their Names in heav'nly Records now
Be no memorial, blotted out and ras'd
By thir Rebellion, from the Books of Life.
Nor had they yet among the Sons of Eve
Got them new Names, till wandring ore the Earth,
Through Gods high sufferance for the tryal of man,
By falsities and lyes the greatest part
Of Mankind they corrupted to forsake
God thir Creator, and th' invisible
Glory of him that made them, to transform
Oft to the Image of a Brute, adorn'd
With gay Religions full of Pomp and Gold,
And Devils to adore for Deities:
Then were they known to men by various Names,
And various Idols through the Heathen World.
Say, Muse, thir Names then known, who first, who last,
Rous'd from the slumber, on that fiery Couch,
At thir great Emperors call, as next in worth
Came singly where he stood on the bare strand,
While the promiscuous croud stood yet aloof?
The chief were those who from the Pit of Hell
Roaming to seek thir prey on earth, durst fix
Thir Seats long after next the Seat of God,
Thir Altars by his Altar, gods ador'd
Among the Nations round, and durst abide
Jehovah thundring out of Sion, thron'd
Between the Cherubim; yea, often plac'd
Within his Sanctuary it selfe thir Shrines,
Abominations; and with cursed things
His holy Rites, and solemn Feasts profan'd,
And with thir darkness durst affront his light.
First Moloch, horrid King besmear'd with blood
Of human sacrifice, and parents tears,
Though for the noyse of Drums and Timbrels loud
Thir childrens cries unheard, that past through fire
To his grim Idol. Him the Ammonite
Worshipt in Rabba and her watry Plain,
In Argob and in Basan, to the stream
Of utmost Arnon. Nor content with such
Audacious neighbourhood, the wisest heart
Of Solomon he led by fraud to build
His Temple right against the Temple of God

On that opprobrious Hill, and made his Grove
The pleasant Vally of Hinnom, Tophet thence
And black Gehenna call'd, the Type of Hell.
Next Chemos, th' obscene dread of Moabs Sons,
From Aroer to Nebo, and the wild
Of Southmost Abarim; in Hesebon
And Horonaim, Seons Realm, beyond
The flowry Dale of Sibma clad with Vines,
And Eleale to th' Asphaltick Pool.
Peor his other Name, when he entic'd
Israel in Sittim on thir march from Nile
To do him wanton rites, which cost them woe.
Yet thence his lustful Orgies he enlarg'd
Even to that Hill of scandal, by the Grove
Of Moloch homicide, lust hard by hate;
Till good Josiah drove them thence to Hell.
With these came they, who from the bordring flood
Of old Euphrates to the Brook that parts
Egipt from Syrian ground, had general Names
Of Baalim and Ashtaroth, those male,
These feminine. For Spirits when they please
Can either Sex assume, or both; so soft
And uncompounded is thir Essence pure,
Not ti'd or manacl'd with joynt or limb,
Nor founded on the brittle strength of bones,
Like cumbrous flesh; but in what shape they choose
Dilated or condens't, bright or obscure,
Can execute thir aerie purposes,
And works of love or enmity fulfill.
For those the Race of Israel oft forsook
Thir living strength, and unfrequented left
His righteous Altar, bowing lowly down
To bestial gods; for which thir heads as low
Bow'd down in Battel, sunk before the Spear
Of despicable foes. With these in troop
Came Astoreth, whom the Phoenicians call'd Astarte, Queen of Heav'n,
with crescent Horns;
To whose bright Image nightly by the Moon
Sidonian Virgins paid thir Vows and Songs,
In Sion also not unsung, where stood
Her Temple on th' offensive Mountain, built
By that uxorious King, whose heart though large,
Beguil'd by fair Idolatresses, fell
To Idols foul. Thammuz came next behind,
Whose annual wound in Lebanon allur'd
The Syrian Damsels to lament his fate

In amorous dittyes all a Summers day,
While smooth Adonis from his native Rock
Ran purple to the Sea, suppos'd with blood
Of Thammuz yearly wounded: the Love-tale
Infected Sions daughters with like heat,
Whose wanton passions in the sacred Porch Ezekiel saw, when by the
Vision led
His eye survay'd the dark Idolatries
Of alienated Judah. Next came one
Who mourn'd in earnest, when the Captive Ark
Maim'd his brute Image, head and hands lopt of
In his own Temple, on the grunsel edge,
Where he fell flat, and sham'd his Worshipers:
Dagon his Name, Sea Monster, upward Man
And downward Fish: yet had his Temple high
Rear'd in Azotus, dreaded through the Coast
Of Palestine, in Gath and Ascalon,
And Accaron and Gaza's frontier bounds.
Him follow'd Rimmon, whose delightful Seat
Was fair Damascus, on the fertil Banks
Of Abbana and Pharphar, lucid streams.
He also against the house of God was bold:
A Leper once he lost and gain'd a King,
Ahaz his sottish Conquerour, whom he drew
Gods Altar to disparage and displace
For one of Syrian mode, whereon to burn
His odious offrings, and adore the Gods
Whom he had vanquisht. After these appear'd
A crew who under Names of old renown,
Osiris, Isis, Orus and their Train
With monstrous shapes and sorceries abus'd
Fanatic Egipt and her Priests, to seek
Thir wandring Gods disguis'd in brutish forms
Rather then human. Nor did Israel scape
Th' infection when thir borrow'd Gold compos'd
The Calf in Oreb: and the Rebel King
Doubl'd that sin in Bethel and in Dan,
Lik'ning his Maker to the Grazed Ox,
Jehovah, who in one Night when he pass'd
From Egipt marching, equal'd with one stroke
Both her first born and all her bleating Gods.
Belial came last, then whom a Spirit more lewd
Fell not from Heaven, or more gross to love
Vice for it selfe: To him no Temple stood
Or Altar smoak'd; yet who more oft then hee
In Temples and at Altars, when the Priest

Turns Atheist, as did Ely's Sons, who fill'd
With lust and violence the house of God.
In Courts and Palaces he also Reigns
And in luxurious Cities, where the noyse
Of riot ascends above thir loftiest Towrs,
And injury and outrage: And when Night
Darkens the Streets, then wander forth the Sons
Of Belial, flown with insolence and wine.
Witness the Streets of Sodom, and that night
In Gibeah, when hospitable Doors
Yielded thir Matrons to avoide worse rape.
These were the prime in order and in might;
The rest were long to tell, though far renown'd,
Th' Ionian Gods, of Javans Issue held
Gods, yet confest later then Heav'n and Earth
Thir boasted Parents; Titan Heav'ns first born
With his enormous brood, and birthright seis'd
By younger Saturn, hee from mightier Jove
His own and Rhea's Son like measure found;
So Jove usurping reign'd: these first in Creet
And Ida known, thence on the Snowy top
Of cold Olympus rul'd the middle Air
Thir highest Heav'n; or on the Delphian Cliff,
Or in Dodona, and through all the bounds
Of Doric Land; or who with Saturn old
Fled over Adria to th' Hesperian Fields,
And ore the Celtic roam'd the utmost Isles.
All these and more came flocking; but with looks
Down cast and damp, yet such wherein appear'd
Obscure some glimpse of joy, to have found thir chief
Not in despair, to have found themselves not lost
In loss it selfe; which on his count'nance cast
Like doubtfull hew: but he his wonted pride
Soon recollecting, with high words, that bore
Semblance of worth not substance, gently rais'd
Thir fainted courage, and dispel'd thir fears.
Then strait commands that at the warlike sound
Of Trumpets loud and Clarions be upreard
His mighty Standard; that proud honour claim'd
Azazel as his right, a Cherube tall:
Who forthwith from the glittering Staff unfurld
Th' Imperial Ensign, which full high advanc't
Shon like a Meteor streaming to the Wind
With Gemms and Golden lustre rich imblaz'd,
Seraphic arms and Trophies: all the while
Sonorous mettal blowing Martial sounds:

At which the universal Host upsent
A shout that tore Hells Concave, and beyond
Frighted the Reign of Chaos and old Night.
All in a moment through the gloom were seen
Ten thousand Banners rise into the Air
With orient colours waving: with them rose
A forrest huge of spears: and thronging helms
Appear'd, and serried shields in thick array
Of depth immeasurable: Anon they move
In perfect Phalanx to the Dorian mood
Of flutes and soft Recorders; such as rais'd
To highth of noblest temper Hero's old
Arming to Battel, and in stead of rage
Deliberate valour breath'd, firm and unmov'd
With dread of death to flight or foul retreat,
Nor wanting power to mitigate and swage
With solemn touches, troubl'd thoughts, and chase
Anguish and doubt and fear and sorrow and pain
From mortal or immortal minds. Thus they
Breathing united force with fixed thought
Mov'd on in silence to soft Pipes that charm'd
Thir painful steps o're the burnt soyle; and now
Advanc't in view they stand, a horrid Front
Of dreadful length and dazling Arms, in guise
Of Warriers old with order'd Spear and Shield,
Awaiting what command thir mighty Chief
Had to impose: He through the armed Files
Darts his experience't eye, and soon traverse
The whole Battalion views, thir order due,
Thir visages and stature as of Gods,
Thir number last he summs. And now his heart
Distends with pride, and hardning in his strength
Glories: For never since created man,
Met such imbodied force, as nam'd with these
Could merit more then that small infantry
Warr'd on by Cranes: though all the Giant brood
Of Phlegra with th' Heroic Race were joyn'd
That fought at Theb's and Ilium, on each side
Mixt with auxiliar Gods; and what resounds
In Fable or Romance of Uthers Son
Begirt with British and Armoric Knights;
And all who since, Baptiz'd or Infidel
Jousted in Aspramont or Montalban,
Damasco, or Marocco, or Trebisond,
Or whom Biserta sent from Afric shore
When Charlemain with all his Peerage fell

By Fontarabbia. Thus far these beyond
Compare of mortal prowess, yet observ'd
Thir dread Commander: he above the rest
In shape and gesture proudly eminent
Stood like a Tow'r; his form had yet not lost
All her Original brightness, nor appear'd
Less then Archangel ruin'd, and th' excess
Of Glory obscur'd: As when the Sun new ris'n
Looks through the Horizontal misty Air
Shorn of his Beams, or from behind the Moon
In dim Eclips disastrous twilight sheds
On half the Nations, and with fear of change
Perplexes Monarchs. Dark'n'd so, yet shon
Above them all th' Archangel: but his face
Deep scars of Thunder had intrench't, and care
Sat on his faded cheek, but under browes
Of dauntless courage, and considerate Pride
Waiting revenge: cruel his eye, but cast
Signs of remorse and passion to behold
The fellows of his crime, the followers rather
(Farr other once beheld in bliss) condemn'd
For ever now to have thir lot in pain,
Millions of Spirits for his fault amerc't
Of Heav'n, and from Eternal Splendors flung
For his revolt, yet faithfull how they stood,
Thir Glory witherd. As when Heaven's Fire
Hath scath'd the forrest oakes, or mountain pines,
With singed top thir stately growth though bare
Stands on the blasted Heath. He now prepar'd
To speak; where-at thir doubl'd Ranks they bend
From wing to wing, and half enclose him round
With all his peeres: attention held them mute.
Thrice he assay'd, and thrice in spight of scorn,
Tears such as Angels weep, burst forth: at last
Words interwove with sighs found out thir way.

O Myriads of immortal Spirits, O powers
Matchless, but with th' Almighty, and that strife
Was not inglorious, though th' event was dire,
As this place testifies, and this dire change
Hateful to utter: but what powre of mind
Foreseeing or presaging, from the Depth
Of knowledge past or present, could have fear'd,
How such united force of Gods, how such
As stood like these, could ever know repulse?
For who can yet beleeve, though after loss,

That all these puissant legions, whose exile
Hath emptied heav'n, shall faile to re-ascend
Selfe-rais'd, and repossess thir native seat?
For me, be witness all the host of heav'n,
If counsells different, or danger shunn'd
By me, have lost our hopes. But he who reigns
Monarch in heav'n, till then as one secure
Sat on his throne, upheld by old repute,
Consent or custome, and his regal state
Put forth at full, but still his strength conceal'd,
Which tempted our attempt, and wrought our fall.
Henceforth his might we know, and know our own
So as not either to provoke, or dread
New warr, provok't; our better part remains
To worke in close designe, by fraud or guile
What force effected not: that he no less
At length from us may find, who overcomes
By force, hath overcome but half his foe.
Space may produce new Worlds; whereof so rife
There went a fame in Heav'n that he ere long
Intended to create, and therein plant
A generation, whom his choice regard
Should favour equal to the sonns of Heaven:
Thither, if but to prie, shall be perhaps
Our first eruption, thither or elsewhere:
For this infernal pit shall never hold
Celestial Spirits in bondage, nor th' Abysse
Long under darkness cover. But these thoughts
Full counsell must mature: Peace is despaird,
For who can think Submission? warr then, warr
Open or understood must be resolv'd.

He spake: and to confirm his words, out-flew
Millions of flaming swords, drawn from the thighs
Of mighty Cherubim; the sudden blaze
Far round illumin'd hell: highly they rag'd
Against the Highest, and fierce with grasped arms
Clash'd on their sounding shields the din of warr,
Hurling defiance toward the vault of heav'n.

There stood a hill not farr whose griesly top
Belch'd fire and rowling smoak; the rest entire
Shon with a glossie scurf, undoubted signe
That in his womb was hid metallic Ore,
The work of Sulphur. Thither wing'd with speed
A numerous brigad hasten'd. As when bands

Of pioners with spade and pickaxe arm'd
Forerun the Royal Camp, to trench a Field,
Or cast a Rampart. Mammon led them on,
Mammon, the least erected Spirit that fell
From heav'n, for ev'n in heav'n his looks and thoughts
Were always downward bent, admiring more
The riches of Heav'ns pavement, trod'n Gold,
Then aught divine or holy else enjoy'd
In vision beatific: by him first
Men also, and by his suggestion taught,
Ransack'd the Center, and with impious hands
Rifl'd the bowels of thir mother Earth
For Treasures better hid. Soon had his crew
Op'nd into the Hill a spacious wound
And dig'd out ribs of Gold. Let none admire
That riches grow in Hell; that soyle may best
Deserve the precious bane. And here let those
Who boast in mortall things, and wondring tell
Of Babel, and the works Memphian Kings,
Learn how thir greatest Monuments of Fame,
And Strength and Art are easily outdone
By Spirits reprobate, and in an hour
What in an age they with incessant toyle
And hands innumerable scarce perform.
Nigh on the Plain in many cells prepar'd,
That underneath had veins of liquid fire
Sluc'd from the Lake, a second multitude
With wondrous Art founded the massie Ore,
Severing each kinde, and scum'd the Bullion dross:
A third as soon had form'd within the ground
A various mould, and from the boyling cells
By strange conveyance fill'd each hollow nook,
As in an Organ from one blast of wind
To many a row of pipes the sound-bord breaths.
Anon out of the earth a fabric huge
Rose like an exhalation, with the sound
Of Dulcet Symphonies and voices sweet,
Built like a Temple, where pilasters round
Were set, and Doric pillars overlaid
With golden Architrave; nor did there want
Cornice or freeze, with bossy Sculptures grav'n,
The roof was fretted Gold. Not Babilon,
Nor great Alcairo such magnificence
Equal'd in all thir glories, to inshrine
Belus or Serapis thir Gods, or seat
Thir Kings, when Egipt with Assyria strove

In wealth and luxurie. Th' ascending pile
Stood fixt her stately highth, and strait the dores
Op'ning thir brazen foulds discover wide
Within, her ample spaces, o're the smooth
And level pavement: from the arched roof
Pendant by suttle Magic many a row
Of Starry Lamps and blazing Cressets fed
With Naphtha and Asphaltus yielded light
As from a sky. The hasty multitude
Admiring enter'd and the work some praise
And some the Architect: his hand was known
In Heav'n by many a Towred structure high,
Where Scepter'd Angels held thir residence,
And sat as Princes, whom the supreme King
Exalted to such power, and gave to rule,
Each in his hierarchie, the orders bright.
Nor was his name unheard or unador'd
In ancient Greece; and in Ausonian land
Men call'd him Mulciber; and how he fell
From Heav'n, they fabl'd, thrown by angry Jove
Sheer o're the chrystall battlements: from Morn
To Noon he fell, from Noon to dewy eeve,
A Summers day; and with the setting sun
Dropt from the zenith like a falling starr,
On Lemnos th' Ægean Ile: thus they relate,
Erring; for he with this rebellious rout
Fell long before; nor aught avail'd him now
To have built in heav'n high Towers; nor did he scape
By all his engins, but was headlong sent
With his industrious crew to build in hell.
Mean while the winged Haralds by command
Of sovran power, with awfull ceremony
And trumpets sound throughout the host proclaime
A solemn councell forthwith to be held
At Pandæmonium, the high Capitall
Of Satan and his peers: thir summons call'd
From every band and squared regiment
By place or choice the worthiest; they anon
With hunderds and with thousands trooping came
Attended: all accesse was throng'd, the gates
And porches wide, but chief the spacious hall
(Though like a cover'd field, where champions bold
Wont ride in arm'd, and at the Soldans chair
Defy'd the best of Paynim chivalry
To mortall combat or carreer with lance)
Thick swarm'd, both on the ground and in the air,

Brusht with the hisse of russling wings. As bees
In spring time, when the Sun with Taurus rides,
Poure forth thir populous youth about the hive
In clusters; they among fresh dews and flowers
Flie to and fro, or on the smoothed plank,
The suburb of thir straw built cittadell,
New rub'd with baume, expatiate and confer
Thir state affairs. So thick the aerie crowd
Swarm'd and were straitn'd; till the signal giv'n,
Behold a wonder! they but now who seemd
In bigness to surpass earths giant sons
Now lesse then smallest dwarfs, in narrow room
Throng numberless, like that pigmean race
Beyond the Indian Mount, or Faerie Elves,
Whose midnight revells, by a forrest side
Or fountain some belated peasant sees,
Or dreams hee sees, while over head the Moon
Sits arbitress, and neerer to the earth
Wheels her pale course, they on thir mirth and dance
Intent, with jocond music charme his eare;
At once with joy and fear his heart rebounds.
Thus incorporeal spirits to smallest forms
Reduc'd thir shapes immense, and were at large,
Though without number still amidst the hall
Of that infernall Court. But far within
And in thir own dimensions like themselves
The great Seraphic Lords and Cherubim
In close recesse and secret conclave sat
A thousand Demy-gods on golden seats,
Frequent and full. After short silence then
And summons read, the great consult began.

Review Questions
1. What is the subject of Book 1, according to the argument?
2. Who are the main characters in Book 1?
3. Describe the setting of Hell.
4. What caused Satan's fall from Heaven? What were his plans for revenge? According to Milton, did Satan acknowledge the supremacy of God?
5. What did Satan hope to accomplish by attacking man?

Thought Questions
1. Is Milton's account consistent with the Bible?
2. What does Book 1 tell you about Satan's feelings toward man?
3. What is meant by the phrase, "The mind is its own place, and by it selfe can make a Heav'n of Hell, a Hell of Heav'n"? Do you agree? Is this the same thing as Satan's statement, "Better to reign in Hell, then serve in Heav'n"? Discuss.
4. Milton's poem pictures Satan weeping briefly over having led the other fallen angels to exile from Heaven. Do you think that leaders should be judged more harshly because they are capable of leading others astray?
5. Some readers have said that Satan is actually the hero of Milton's epic. Does this selection have a heroic feel? Why or why not? What is the mood of this section of the poem?

"Christmas Bells"
Henry W. Longfellow

Henry Wadsworth Longfellow (1807-1882) was an American poet whose works became popular song lyrics because of their easy rhymes and simple rhythms. Longfellow was very interested in myth and legend, but he also wrote about more common themes such as joy and loss. Longfellow wrote "Christmas Bells" during the American Civil War. It became popular as a Christmas carol, called "I Heard the Bells on Christmas Day," after it was set to music. Today, the most recognized version is the one composed by American Johnny Marks in the 1950s.

I heard the bells on Christmas Day
Their old, familiar carols play,
    And wild and sweet
    The words repeat
Of peace on earth, good-will to men!

And thought how, as the day had come,
The belfries of all Christendom
    Had rolled along
    The unbroken song
Of peace on earth, good-will to men!

Till, ringing, singing on its way,
The world revolved from night to day,
    A voice, a chime,
    A chant sublime
Of peace on earth, good-will to men!

Then from each black, accursed mouth
The cannon thundered in the South,
   And with the sound
   The carols drowned
Of peace on earth, good-will to men!

It was as if an earthquake rent
The hearth-stones of a continent,
   And made forlorn
   The households born
Of peace on earth, good-will to men!

And in despair I bowed my head;
"There is no peace on earth," I said:
   "For hate is strong,
   And mocks the song
Of peace on earth, good-will to men!"

Then pealed the bells more loud and deep:
"God is not dead; nor doth He sleep!
   The Wrong shall fail,
   The Right prevail,
With peace on earth, good-will to men!"

Review Questions
1. About what subject do the bells ring, according to Longfellow?
2. How does the narrator describe Christmas carols?
3. How is the American Civil War referenced in the middle stanzas?
4. What produces the author's despair in the sixth stanza?
5. What is the bells' answer?

Thought Questions
1. What does "Peace on Earth" mean to you? Military peace? Internal peace?
2. Is it easier to imagine peace on earth at Christmastime? Why? Why can't you carry that feeling throughout the year? Would it be as precious if you could?
3. Can there ever truly be peace on earth? If yes, when and how? Should peace be our ultimate goal for the world? Explain. Is peace ever a bad thing?
4. The Christmas carol based on this poem usually leaves out the fourth and fifth stanzas (about the war). How does the mood of the poem change when they are included?
5. Does the poem have a different mood when you read it without the music? Why?

MOOD

Writing Practice

Compare the moods of the poems that you have read—Paradise Lost, The Canterbury Tales, The Merchant of Venice, Othello, and "Christmas Bells." Look closely at the words in the poems. How do the authors convey mood? What adjectives do they use? What verbs? Read a section of each one aloud. Does the rhythm of the lines affect the mood?

Look at the following neutral scene. Then compare it to the second scene. What is the mood of the second scene? Notice what words have been changed and what has been added from the original scene.

In the living room, a woman sits in front of the television. Her fingers weave the strips of paper automatically. She is making a Moravian star. She pauses to glance down at her work, and she runs one hand through her hair.

> In the living room, the lights are dim. A woman sits stiffly in front of the television. Her gnarled fingers weave the strips of paper automatically. She is making another Moravian star. A pile of stars already litters the carpet. She pauses to glance down at her work, and she runs a shaky hand through her gray-streaked hair.

Now rewrite this scene to reflect a different mood (happiness, fright, sadness, excitement). Try to choose words and details that reflect this mood. If you're feeling brave, try turning the scene into poetry. Experiment with rhyme and rhythm to see how each one affects the mood.

May I Ask Who is Speaking? POINT OF VIEW

Imagine someone is telling you a story. You are not convinced by what they are saying, so you ask who told them the story. Why? Because you realize that the point of view of the source factors into how the story is told. In the writing world, point of view is important for the same reason. The narrator plays an important role in what is included, what is left out, and how the story is presented.

There are several important elements in point of view. The first is "person." A first-person story uses the words I, me, and my. Reading a first-person story is like having a personal conversation or reading a diary because the narrator is a character in the story. First person allows you to see only what the character sees and experience events only from his or her perspective. Third person[4], on the other hand, uses the words he, she, and it to tell the story. In this form, the narrator is watching the events of the story from the outside. Third person can either focus on one character or jump from person to person to follow the action.

"Perspective" is the second aspect of point of view. Limited perspective stays within the viewpoint of one character at a time. The reader "sees" through the eyes of that character, and thus sees nothing that the character cannot see. In contrast, the omniscient (all-knowing) perspective can "see" events that happen outside the character's range of vision. In other words, if someone is sneaking up behind Richard, a story with omniscient viewpoint can give the reader this information.

Finally, whereas some narration is objective and must rely on characters' words and actions instead of their thoughts and feelings, narration that is subjective may include this information.

As you read the next two stories, pay attention to the author's treatment of point of view. Because short stories are limited by length, many short story writers stay within the point of view of one character. This technique allows the reader to focus his or her attention on that main character and preserves the focus of the story. However, single viewpoint is not the only point of view acceptable for short stories. Many older classic short stories, for example, address more than one point of view.

When you write, while you should keep your reader's needs in mind, you should also think about the best way to tell your particular story.

---

[4]Second-person ("you") narration is extremely rare. The series *Choose Your Own Adventure* is one example.

"The Hammer of God"
G. K. Chesterton

Gilbert Keith Chesterton (1874-1936) was an English writer who wrote theological and political works as well as fiction. Although his nonfiction writings were more controversial, he is widely known for his fiction, including a collection of detective stories about a small priest named Father Brown. "The Hammer of God" is one of the many Father Brown stories Chesterton composed. This particular story deals with the difference between God's justice and the justice of man.

The little village of Bohun Beacon was perched on a hill so steep that the tall spire of its church seemed only like the peak of a small mountain. At the foot of the church stood a smithy, generally red with fires and always littered with hammers and scraps of iron; opposite to this, over a rude cross of cobbled paths, was "The Blue Boar," the only inn of the place. It was upon this crossway, in the lifting of a leaden and silver daybreak, that two brothers met in the street and spoke; though one was beginning the day and the other finishing it. The Rev. and Hon. Wilfred Bohun was very devout, and was making his way to some austere exercises of prayer or contemplation at dawn. Colonel the Hon. Norman Bohun, his elder brother, was by no means devout, and was sitting in evening dress on the bench outside "The Blue Boar," drinking what the philosophic observer was free to regard either as his last glass on Tuesday or his first on Wednesday. The colonel was not particular.

The Bohuns were one of the very few aristocratic families really dating from the Middle Ages, and their pennon had actually seen Palestine. But it is a great mistake to suppose that such houses stand high in chivalric tradition. Few except the poor preserve traditions. Aristocrats live not in traditions but in fashions. The Bohuns had been Mohocks under Queen Anne and Mashers under Queen Victoria. But like more than one of the really ancient houses, they had rotted in the last two centuries into mere drunkards and dandy degenerates, till there had even come a whisper of insanity.

Certainly there was something hardly human about the colonel's wolfish pursuit of pleasure, and his chronic resolution not to go home till morning had a touch of the hideous clarity of insomnia. He was a tall, fine animal, elderly, but with hair still startlingly yellow. He would have looked merely blonde and leonine, but his blue eyes were sunk so deep in his face that they looked black. They were a little too close together. He had very long yellow moustaches; on each side of them a fold or furrow from nostril to jaw, so that a sneer seemed cut into his face. Over his evening clothes he wore a curious pale yellow coat that looked more like a very light dressing gown than an overcoat, and on the back of his head was stuck an extraordinary broad-brimmed hat of a bright green colour, evidently some oriental curiosity caught up at random. He was proud of appearing in such incongruous attires — proud of the fact that he always made them look congruous.

His brother the curate had also the yellow hair and the elegance, but he was buttoned up to the chin in black, and his face was clean-shaven, cultivated, and a little nervous. He seemed to live for nothing but his religion; but there were some who said (notably the blacksmith, who was a Presbyterian) that it was a love of Gothic architecture rather than of God, and that his haunting of the church like a ghost was only another and purer turn of the almost morbid thirst for beauty which sent his brother raging after women and wine. This charge was doubtful, while the man's practical piety was indubitable. Indeed, the charge was mostly an ignorant misunderstanding of the love of solitude and secret prayer, and was founded on his being often found kneeling, not before the altar, but in peculiar places, in the crypts or gallery, or even in the belfry.

He was at the moment about to enter the church through the yard of the smithy, but stopped and frowned a little as he saw his brother's cavernous eyes staring in the same direction. On the hypothesis that the colonel was interested in the church he did not waste any speculations. There only remained the blacksmith's shop, and though the blacksmith was a Puritan and none of his people, Wilfred Bohun had heard some scandals about a beautiful and rather celebrated wife. He flung a suspicious look across the shed, and the colonel stood up laughing to speak to him.

"Good morning, Wilfred," he said. "Like a good landlord I am watching sleeplessly over my people. I am going to call on the blacksmith."

Wilfred looked at the ground, and said: "The blacksmith is out. He is over at Greenford."

"I know," answered the other with silent laughter; "that is why I am calling on him."

"Norman," said the cleric, with his eye on a pebble in the road, "are you ever afraid of thunderbolts?"

"What do you mean?" asked the colonel. "Is your hobby meteorology?"

"I mean," said Wilfred, without looking up, "do you ever think that God might strike you in the street?"

"I beg your pardon," said the colonel; "I see your hobby is folk-lore."

"I know your hobby is blasphemy," retorted the religious man, stung in the one live place of his nature. "But if you do not fear God, you have good reason to fear man."

The elder raised his eyebrows politely. "Fear man?" he said.

"Barnes the blacksmith is the biggest and strongest man for forty miles round," said the clergyman sternly. "I know you are no coward or weakling, but he could throw you over the wall."

This struck home, being true, and the lowering line by mouth and nostril darkened and deepened. For a moment he stood with the heavy sneer on his face. But in an instant Colonel Bohun had recovered his own cruel good humour and laughed, showing two dog-like front teeth under his yellow moustache. "In that case, my dear Wilfred," he said quite carelessly, "it was wise for the last of the Bohuns to come out partially in armour."

And he took off the queer round hat covered with green, showing that it was lined within with steel. Wilfred recognised it indeed as a light Japanese or Chinese helmet torn down from a trophy that hung in the old family hall.

"It was the first hat to hand," explained his brother airily; "always the nearest hat—and the nearest woman."

"The blacksmith is away at Greenford," said Wilfred quietly; "the time of his return is unsettled."

And with that he turned and went into the church with bowed head, crossing himself like one who wishes to be quit of an unclean spirit. He was anxious to forget such grossness in the cool twilight of his tall Gothic cloisters; but on that morning it was fated that his still round of religious exercises should be everywhere arrested by small shocks. As he entered the church, hitherto always empty at that hour, a kneeling figure rose hastily to its feet and came toward the full daylight of the doorway. When the curate saw it he stood still with surprise. For the early worshipper was none other than the village idiot, a nephew of the blacksmith, one who neither would nor could care for the church or for anything else.

He was always called "Mad Joe," and seemed to have no other name; he was a dark, strong, slouching lad, with a heavy white face, dark straight hair, and a mouth always open. As he passed the priest, his moon-calf countenance gave no hint of what he had been doing or thinking of. He had never been known to pray before. What sort of prayers was he saying now? Extraordinary prayers surely.

Wilfred Bohun stood rooted to the spot long enough to see the idiot go out into the sunshine, and even to see his dissolute brother hail him with a sort of avuncular jocularity. The last thing he saw was the colonel throwing pennies at the open mouth of Joe, with the serious appearance of trying to hit it.

This ugly sunlit picture of the stupidity and cruelty of the earth sent the ascetic finally to his prayers for purification and new thoughts. He went up to a pew in the gallery, which brought him under a coloured window which he loved and always quieted his spirit; a blue window with an angel carrying lilies. There he began to think less about the half-wit, with his livid face and mouth like a fish. He began to think less of his evil brother, pacing like a lean lion in his horrible hunger. He sank deeper and deeper into those cold and sweet colours of silver blossoms and sapphire sky.

In this place half an hour afterwards he was found by Gibbs, the village cobbler, who had been sent for him in some haste. He got to his feet with promptitude, for he knew that no small matter would have brought Gibbs into such a place at all. The cobbler was, as in many villages, an atheist, and his appearance in church was a shade more extraordinary than Mad Joe's. It was a morning of theological enigmas.

"What is it?" asked Wilfred Bohun rather stiffly, but putting out a trembling hand for his hat.

The atheist spoke in a tone that, coming from him, was quite startlingly respectful, and even, as it were, huskily sympathetic.

"You must excuse me, sir," he said in a hoarse whisper, "but we didn't think it right not to let you know at once. I'm afraid a rather dreadful thing has happened, sir. I'm afraid your brother—"

Wilfred clenched his frail hands. "What devilry has he done now?" he cried in voluntary passion.

"Why, sir," said the cobbler, coughing, "I'm afraid he's done nothing, and won't do anything. I'm afraid he's done for. You had really better come down, sir."

The curate followed the cobbler down a short winding stair which brought them out at an entrance rather higher than the street. Bohun saw the tragedy in one glance, flat underneath him like a plan. In the yard of the smithy were standing five or six men mostly in black, one in an inspector's uniform. They included the doctor, the Presbyterian minister, and the priest from the Roman Catholic chapel, to which the blacksmith's wife belonged. The latter was speaking to her, indeed, very rapidly, in an undertone, as she, a magnificent woman with red-gold hair, was sobbing blindly on a bench. Between these two groups, and just clear of the main heap of hammers, lay a man in evening dress, spread-eagled and flat on his face. From the height above Wilfred could have sworn to every item of his costume and appearance, down to the Bohun rings upon his fingers; but the skull was only a hideous splash, like a star of blackness and blood.

Wilfred Bohun gave but one glance, and ran down the steps into the yard. The doctor, who was the family physician, saluted him, but he scarcely took any notice. He could only stammer out: "My brother is dead. What does it mean? What is this horrible mystery?"

There was an unhappy silence; and then the cobbler, the most outspoken man present, answered: "Plenty of horror, sir," he said; "but not much mystery."

"What do you mean?" asked Wilfred, with a white face.

"It's plain enough," answered Gibbs. "There is only one man for forty miles round that could have struck such a blow as that, and he's the man that had most reason to."

"We must not prejudge anything," put in the doctor, a tall, black-bearded man, rather nervously; "but it is competent for me to corroborate what Mr. Gibbs says about the nature of the blow, sir; it is an incredible blow. Mr. Gibbs says that only one man in this district could have done it. I should have said myself that nobody could have done it."

A shudder of superstition went through the slight figure of the curate. "I can hardly understand," he said.

"Mr. Bohun," said the doctor in a low voice, "metaphors literally fail me. It is inadequate to say that the skull was smashed to bits like an eggshell. Fragments of bone were driven into the body and the ground like bullets into a mud wall. It was the hand of a giant."

He was silent a moment, looking grimly through his glasses; then he added: "The thing has one advantage—that it clears most people of suspicion at one stroke. If you or I or any normally made man in the country were accused of this crime, we should be acquitted as an infant would be acquitted of stealing the Nelson column."

"That's what I say," repeated the cobbler obstinately; "there's only one man that could have done it, and he's the man that would have done it. Where's Simeon Barnes, the blacksmith?"

"He's over at Greenford," faltered the curate.

"More likely over in France," muttered the cobbler.

"No; he is in neither of those places," said a small and colourless voice, which came from the little Roman priest who had joined the group. "As a matter of fact, he is coming up the road at this moment."

The little priest was not an interesting man to look at, having stubbly brown hair and a round and stolid face. But if he had been as splendid as Apollo no one would have looked at him at that moment. Everyone turned round and peered at the pathway which wound across the plain below, along which was indeed walking, at his own huge stride and with a hammer on his shoulder, Simeon the smith. He was a bony and gigantic man, with deep, dark, sinister eyes and a dark chin beard. He was walking and talking quietly with two other men; and though he was never specially cheerful, he seemed quite at his ease.

"My God!" cried the atheistic cobbler, "and there's the hammer he did it with."

"No," said the inspector, a sensible-looking man with a sandy moustache, speaking for the first time. "There's the hammer he did it with over there by the church wall. We have left it and the body exactly as they are."

All glanced round and the short priest went across and looked down in silence at the tool where it lay. It was one of the smallest and the lightest of the hammers, and would not have caught the eye among the rest; but on the iron edge of it were blood and yellow hair.

After a silence the short priest spoke without looking up, and there was a new note in his dull voice. "Mr. Gibbs was hardly right," he said, "in saying that there is no mystery. There is at least the mystery of why so big a man should attempt so big a blow with so little a hammer."

"Oh, never mind that," cried Gibbs, in a fever. "What are we to do with Simeon Barnes?"

"Leave him alone," said the priest quietly. "He is coming here of himself. I know those two men with him. They are very good fellows from Greenford, and they have come over about the Presbyterian chapel."

Even as he spoke the tall smith swung round the corner of the church, and strode into his own yard. Then he stood there quite still, and the hammer fell from his hand. The inspector, who had preserved impenetrable propriety, immediately went up to him.

"I won't ask you, Mr. Barnes," he said, "whether you know anything about what has happened here. You are not bound to say. I hope you don't know, and that you will be able to prove it. But I must go through the form of arresting you in the King's name for the murder of Colonel Norman Bohun."

"You are not bound to say anything," said the cobbler in officious excitement. "They've got to prove everything. They haven't proved yet that it is Colonel Bohun, with the head all smashed up like that."

"That won't wash," said the doctor aside to the priest. "That's out of the detective stories. I was the colonel's medical man, and I knew his body better than he did. He had very fine hands, but quite peculiar ones. The second and third fingers were the same length. Oh, that's the colonel right enough."

As he glanced at the brained corpse upon the ground the iron eyes of the motionless blacksmith followed them and rested there also.

"Is Colonel Bohun dead?" said the smith quite calmly. "Then he's damned."

"Don't say anything! Oh, don't say anything," cried the atheist cobbler, dancing about in an ecstasy of admiration of the English legal system. For no man is such a legalist as the good Secularist.

The blacksmith turned on him over his shoulder the august face of a fanatic.

"It's well for you infidels to dodge like foxes because the world's law favours you," he said; "but God guards His own in His pocket, as you shall see this day."

Then he pointed to the colonel and said: "When did this dog die in his sins?"

"Moderate your language," said the doctor.

"Moderate the Bible's language, and I'll moderate mine. When did he die?"

"I saw him alive at six o'clock this morning," stammered Wilfred Bohun.

"God is good," said the smith. "Mr. Inspector, I have not the slightest objection to being arrested. It is you who may object to arresting me. I don't mind leaving the court without a stain on my character. You do mind perhaps leaving the court with a bad set-back in your career."

The solid inspector for the first time looked at the blacksmith with a lively eye; as did everybody else, except the short, strange priest, who was still looking down at the little hammer that had dealt the dreadful blow.

"There are two men standing outside this shop," went on the blacksmith with ponderous lucidity, "good tradesmen in Greenford whom you all know, who will swear that they saw me from before midnight till daybreak and long after in the committee room of our Revival Mission, which sits all night, we save souls so fast. In Greenford itself twenty people could swear to me for all that time. If I were a heathen, Mr. Inspector, I would let you walk on to your downfall. But as a Christian man I feel bound to give you your chance, and ask you whether you will hear my alibi now or in court."

The inspector seemed for the first time disturbed, and said, "Of course I should be glad to clear you altogether now."

The smith walked out of his yard with the same long and easy stride, and returned to his two friends from Greenford, who were indeed friends of nearly everyone present. Each of them said a few words which no one ever thought of disbelieving. When they had spoken, the innocence of Simeon stood up as solid as the great church above them.

One of those silences struck the group which are more strange and insufferable than any speech. Madly, in order to make conversation, the curate said to the Catholic priest: "You seem very much interested in that hammer, Father Brown."

"Yes, I am," said Father Brown; "why is it such a small hammer?"

The doctor swung round on him. "By George, that's true," he cried; "who would use a little hammer with ten larger hammers lying about?"

Then he lowered his voice in the curate's ear and said: "Only the kind of person that can't lift a large hammer. It is not a question of force or courage between the sexes. It's a question of lifting power in the shoulders. A bold woman could commit ten murders with a light hammer and never turn a hair. She could not kill a beetle with a heavy one."

Wilfred Bohun was staring at him with a sort of hypnotised horror, while Father Brown listened with his head a little on one side, really interested and attentive. The doctor went on with more hissing emphasis: "Why do these idiots always assume that the only person who hates the wife's lover is the wife's husband? Nine times out of ten the person who most hates the wife's lover is the wife. Who knows what insolence or treachery he had shown her—look there!" He made a momentary gesture toward the red-haired woman on the bench. She had lifted her head at last and the tears were drying on her splendid face. But the eyes were fixed on the corpse with an electric glare that had in it something of idiocy.

The Rev. Wilfred Bohun made a limp gesture as if waving away all desire to know; but Father Brown, dusting off his sleeve some ashes blown from the furnace, spoke in his indifferent way. "You are like so many doctors," he said; "your mental science is really suggestive. It is your physical science that is utterly impossible. I agree that the woman wants to kill the co-respondent much more than the petitioner does. And I agree that a woman will always pick up a small hammer instead of a big one. But the difficulty is one of physical impossibility. No woman ever born could have smashed a man's skull out flat like that." Then he added reflectively, after a pause: "These people haven't grasped the whole of it. The man was actually wearing an iron helmet, and the blow scattered it like broken glass. Look at that woman. Look at her arms."

Silence held them all up again, and then the doctor said rather sulkily: "Well, I may be wrong; there are objections to everything. But I stick to the main point. No man but an idiot would pick up that little hammer if he could use a big hammer."

With that the lean and quivering hands of Wilfred Bohun went up to his head and seemed to clutch his scanty yellow hair. After an instant they dropped, and he cried: "That was the word I wanted; you have said the word."

Then he continued, mastering his discomposure: "The words you said were, 'No man but an idiot would pick up the small hammer.'"

"Yes," said the doctor. "Well?"

"Well," said the curate, "no man but an idiot did." The rest stared at him with eyes arrested and riveted, and he went on in a febrile and feminine agitation.

"I am a priest," he cried unsteadily, "and a priest should be no shedder of blood. I—I mean that he should bring no one to the gallows. And I thank God that I see the criminal clearly now—because he is a criminal who cannot be brought to the gallows."

"You will not denounce him?" inquired the doctor.

"He would not be hanged if I did denounce him," answered Wilfred with a wild but curiously happy smile. "When I went into the church this morning I found a madman praying there—that poor Joe, who has been wrong all his life. God knows what he prayed; but with such strange folk it is not incredible to suppose that their prayers are all upside down. Very likely a lunatic would pray before killing a man. When I last saw poor Joe he was with my brother. My brother was mocking him."

"By Jove!" cried the doctor, "this is talking at last. But how do you explain—"

The Rev. Wilfred was almost trembling with the excitement of his own glimpse of the truth. "Don't you see; don't you see," he cried feverishly; "that is the only theory that covers both the queer things, that answers both the riddles. The two riddles are the little hammer and the big blow. The smith might have struck the big blow, but would not have chosen the little hammer. His wife would have chosen the little hammer, but she could not have struck the big blow. But the madman might have done both. As for the little hammer—why, he was mad and might have picked up anything. And for the big blow, have you never heard, doctor, that a maniac in his paroxysm may have the strength of ten men?"

The doctor drew a deep breath and then said, "By golly, I believe you've got it."

Father Brown had fixed his eyes on the speaker so long and steadily as to prove that his large grey, ox-like eyes were not quite so insignificant as the rest of his face. When silence had fallen he said with marked respect: "Mr. Bohun, yours is the only theory yet propounded which holds water every way and is essentially unassailable. I think, therefore, that you deserve to be told, on my positive knowledge, that it is not the true one." And with that the old little man walked away and stared again at the hammer.

"That fellow seems to know more than he ought to," whispered the doctor peevishly to Wilfred. "Those popish priests are deucedly sly."

"No, no," said Bohun, with a sort of wild fatigue. "It was the lunatic. It was the lunatic."

The group of the two clerics and the doctor had fallen away from the more official group containing the inspector and the man he had arrested. Now, however, that their own party had broken up, they heard voices from the others. The priest looked up quietly and then looked down again as he heard the blacksmith say in a loud voice:

"I hope I've convinced you, Mr. Inspector. I'm a strong man, as you say, but I couldn't have flung my hammer bang here from Greenford. My hammer hasn't got wings that it should come flying half a mile over hedges and fields."

The inspector laughed amicably and said: "No, I think you can be considered out of it, though it's one of the rummiest coincidences I ever saw. I can only ask you to give us all the assistance you can in finding a man as big and strong as yourself. By George! you might be useful, if only to hold him! I suppose you yourself have no guess at the man?"

"I may have a guess," said the pale smith, "but it is not at a man." Then, seeing the scared eyes turn toward his wife on the bench, he put his huge hand on her shoulder and said: "Nor a woman either."

"What do you mean?" asked the inspector jocularly. "You don't think cows use hammers, do you?"

"I think no thing of flesh held that hammer," said the blacksmith in a stifled voice; "mortally speaking, I think the man died alone."

Wilfred made a sudden forward movement and peered at him with burning eyes.

"Do you mean to say, Barnes," came the sharp voice of the cobbler, "that the hammer jumped up of itself and knocked the man down?"

"Oh, you gentlemen may stare and snigger," cried Simeon; "you clergymen who tell us on Sunday in what a stillness the Lord smote Sennacherib. I believe that One who walks invisible in every house defended the honour of mine, and laid the defiler dead before the door of it. I believe the force in that blow was just the force there is in earthquakes, and no force less."

Wilfred said, with a voice utterly undescribable: "I told Norman myself to beware of the thunderbolt."

"That agent is outside my jurisdiction," said the inspector with a slight smile.

"You are not outside His," answered the smith; "see you to it," and, turning his broad back, he went into the house.

The shaken Wilfred was led away by Father Brown, who had an easy and friendly way with him. "Let us get out of this horrid place, Mr. Bohun," he said. "May I look inside your church? I hear it's one of the oldest in England. We take some interest, you know," he added with a comical grimace, "in old English churches."

Wilfred Bohun did not smile, for humour was never his strong point. But he nodded rather eagerly, being only too ready to explain the Gothic splendours to someone more likely to be sympathetic than the Presbyterian blacksmith or the atheist cobbler.

"By all means," he said; "let us go in at this side." And he led the way into the high side entrance at the top of the flight of steps. Father Brown was mounting the first step to follow him when he felt a hand on his shoulder, and turned to behold the dark, thin figure of the doctor, his face darker yet with suspicion.

"Sir," said the physician harshly, "you appear to know some secrets in this black business. May I ask if you are going to keep them to yourself?"

"Why, doctor," answered the priest, smiling quite pleasantly, "there is one very good reason why a man of my trade should keep things to himself when he is not sure of them, and that is that it is so constantly his duty to keep them to himself when he is sure of them. But if you think I have been discourteously reticent with you or anyone, I will go to the extreme limit of my custom. I will give you two very large hints."

"Well, sir?" said the doctor gloomily.

"First," said Father Brown quietly, "the thing is quite in your own province. It is a matter of physical science. The blacksmith is mistaken, not perhaps in saying that the blow was divine, but certainly in saying that it came by a miracle. It was no miracle, doctor, except in so far as man is himself a miracle, with his strange and wicked and yet half-heroic heart. The force that smashed that skull was a force well known to scientists—one of the most frequently debated of the laws of nature."

The doctor, who was looking at him with frowning intentness, only said: "And the other hint?"

"The other hint is this," said the priest. "Do you remember the blacksmith, though he believes in miracles, talking scornfully of the impossible fairy tale that his hammer had wings and flew half a mile across country?"

"Yes," said the doctor, "I remember that."

"Well," added Father Brown, with a broad smile, "that fairy tale was the nearest thing to the real truth that has been said today." And with that he turned his back and stumped up the steps after the curate.

The Reverend Wilfred, who had been waiting for him, pale and impatient, as if this little delay were the last straw for his nerves, led him immediately to his favourite corner of the church, that part of the gallery closest to the carved roof and lit by the wonderful window with the angel. The little Latin priest explored and admired everything exhaustively, talking cheerfully but in a low voice all the time. When in the course of his investigation he found the side exit and the winding stair down which Wilfred had rushed to find his brother dead, Father Brown ran not down but up, with the agility of a monkey, and his clear voice came from an outer platform above.

"Come up here, Mr. Bohun," he called. "The air will do you good."

Bohun followed him, and came out on a kind of stone gallery or balcony outside the building, from which one could see the illimitable plain in which their small hill stood, wooded away to the purple horizon and dotted with villages and farms. Clear and square, but quite small beneath them, was the blacksmith's yard, where the inspector still stood taking notes and the corpse still lay like a smashed fly.

"Might be the map of the world, mightn't it?" said Father Brown.

"Yes," said Bohun very gravely, and nodded his head.

Immediately beneath and about them the lines of the Gothic building plunged outwards into the void with a sickening swiftness akin to suicide. There is that element of Titan energy in the architecture of the Middle Ages that, from whatever aspect it be seen, it always seems to be rushing away, like the strong back of some maddened horse. This church was hewn out of ancient and silent stone, bearded with old fungoids and stained with the nests of birds. And yet, when they saw it from below, it sprang like a fountain at the stars; and when they saw it, as now, from above, it poured like a cataract into a voiceless pit. For these two men on the tower were left alone with the most terrible aspect of Gothic; the monstrous foreshortening and disproportion, the dizzy perspectives, the glimpses of great things small and small things great; a topsy-turvydom of stone in the mid-air. Details of stone, enormous by their proximity, were relieved against a pattern of fields and farms, pygmy in their distance. A carved bird or beast at a corner seemed like some vast walking or flying dragon wasting the pastures and villages below. The whole atmosphere was dizzy and dangerous, as if men were upheld in air amid the gyrating wings of colossal genii; and the whole of that old church, as tall and rich as a cathedral, seemed to sit upon the sunlit country like a cloudburst.

"I think there is something rather dangerous about standing on these high places even to pray," said Father Brown. "Heights were made to be looked at, not to be looked from."

"Do you mean that one may fall over," asked Wilfred.

"I mean that one's soul may fall if one's body doesn't," said the other priest.

"I scarcely understand you," remarked Bohun indistinctly.

"Look at that blacksmith, for instance," went on Father Brown calmly; "a good man, but not a Christian—hard, imperious, unforgiving. Well, his Scotch religion was made up by men who prayed on hills and high crags, and learnt to look down on the world more than to look up at heaven. Humility is the mother of giants. One sees great things from the valley; only small things from the peak."

"But he—he didn't do it," said Bohun tremulously.

"No," said the other in an odd voice; "we know he didn't do it."

After a moment he resumed, looking tranquilly out over the plain with his pale grey eyes. "I knew a man," he said, "who began by worshipping with others before the altar, but who grew fond of high and lonely places to pray from, corners or niches in the belfry or the spire. And once in one of those dizzy places, where the whole world seemed to turn under him like a wheel, his brain turned also, and he fancied he was God. So that, though he was a good man, he committed a great crime."

Wilfred's face was turned away, but his bony hands turned blue and white as they tightened on the parapet of stone.

"He thought it was given to him to judge the world and strike down the sinner. He would never have had such a thought if he had been kneeling with other men upon a floor. But he saw all men walking about like insects. He saw one especially strutting just below him, insolent and evident by a bright green hat — a poisonous insect."

Rooks cawed round the corners of the belfry; but there was no other sound till Father Brown went on.

"This also tempted him, that he had in his hand one of the most awful engines of nature; I mean gravitation, that mad and quickening rush by which all earth's creatures fly back to her heart when released. See, the inspector is strutting just below us in the smithy. If I were to toss a pebble over this parapet it would be something like a bullet by the time it struck him. If I were to drop a hammer — even a small hammer—"

Wilfred Bohun threw one leg over the parapet, and Father Brown had him in a minute by the collar.

"Not by that door," he said quite gently; "that door leads to hell."

Bohun staggered back against the wall, and stared at him with frightful eyes. "How do you know all this?" he cried. "Are you a devil?"

"I am a man," answered Father Brown gravely; "and therefore have all devils in my heart. Listen to me," he said after a short pause. "I know what you did — at least, I can guess the great part of it. When you left your brother you were racked with no unrighteous rage, to the extent even that you snatched up a small hammer, half inclined to kill him with his foulness on his mouth. Recoiling, you thrust it under your buttoned coat instead, and rushed into the church. You pray wildly in many places, under the angel window, upon the platform above, and a higher platform still, from which you could see the colonel's Eastern hat like the back of a green beetle crawling about. Then something snapped in your soul, and you let God's thunderbolt fall."

Wilfred put a weak hand to his head, and asked in a low voice: "How did you know that his hat looked like a green beetle?"

"Oh, that," said the other with the shadow of a smile, "that was common sense. But hear me further. I say I know all this; but no one else shall know it. The next step is for you; I shall take no more steps; I will seal this with the seal of confession. If you ask me why, there are many reasons, and only one that concerns you. I leave things to you because you have not yet gone very far wrong, as assassins go. You did not help to fix the crime on the smith when it was easy; or on his wife, when that was easy. You tried to fix it on the imbecile because you knew that he could not suffer. That was one of the gleams that it is my business to find in assassins. And now come down into the village, and go your own way as free as the wind;

for I have said my last word."

They went down the winding stairs in utter silence, and came out into the sunlight by the smithy. Wilfred Bohun carefully unlatched the wooden gate of the yard, and going up to the inspector, said: "I wish to give myself up; I have killed my brother."

Review Questions
1. Who were the Bohun brothers? Compare and contrast their personalities.
2. Who did Wilfred meet as he entered the church?
3. How did the blacksmith explain Norman's death?
4. What force did Father Brown describe as, "One of the most frequently debated in the laws of nature"?
5. Who killed Norman Bohun? What did Father Brown do to the murderer? How did the murderer respond?

Thought Questions
1. Is it hard for you to watch people who seem to face no consequences for their actions? How do you respond? Why do you think people want life to be "fair"?
2. What do you think of the blacksmith's explanation? Was it consistent with the Bible? Is it different for God to use humans to deal out judgment and for men to play God? Discuss.
3. Who was the greater sinner, Norman or Wilfred? Explain.
4. Why did Father Brown let the murderer decide on his own fate? Did he know what choice the murderer would make? If so, how?
5. What is this story's point of view? How might the story be different, if, for example, it was narrated in first person?

"The Tell-Tale Heart"
Edgar Allan Poe

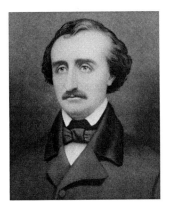

Edgar Allan Poe (1809-1849) was an American short story writer and literary critic. He is credited with perfecting and codifying the short story form. His specialty was mystery stories. Poe took a very dark view of human nature, and his writings reflect this. He was a master of looking inside the twisted and dark minds of criminals and victims alike. "The Tell-Tale Heart" is one of Poe's best-known works. This particular story is told from the perspective of a man who has committed murder, and who is soon to discover the terrible power of guilt.

True!—nervous—very, very dreadfully nervous I had been and am; but why will you say that I am mad? The disease had sharpened my senses—not destroyed—not dulled them. Above all was the sense of hearing acute. I heard all things in the heaven and in the earth. I heard many things in hell. How, then, am I mad? Hearken! and observe how healthily—how calmly I can tell you the whole story.

It is impossible to say how first the idea entered my brain; but once conceived, it haunted me day and night. Object there was none. Passion there was none. I loved the old man. He had never wronged me. He had never given me insult. For his gold I had no desire. I think it was his eye! yes, it was this! He had the eye of a vulture—a pale blue eye, with a film over it. Whenever it fell upon me, my blood ran cold; and so by degrees—very gradually—I made up my mind to take the life of the old man, and thus rid myself of the eye forever.

Now this is the point. You fancy me mad. Madmen know nothing. But you should have seen me. You should have seen how wisely I proceeded—with what caution—with what foresight—with what dissimulation I went to work! I was never kinder to the old man than during the whole week before I killed him. And every night, about midnight, I turned the latch of his door and opened it—oh so gently! And then, when I had made an opening sufficient for my head, I put in a dark lantern, all closed, closed, that no light shone out, and then I thrust in my head. Oh, you would have laughed to see how cunningly I thrust it in! I moved it slowly—very, very slowly, so that I might not disturb the old man's sleep. It took me an hour to place my whole head within the opening so far that I could see him as he lay upon his bed. Ha! Would a madman have been so wise as this? And then, when my head was well in the room, I undid the lantern cautiously—oh, so cautiously—cautiously (for the hinges creaked)—I undid it just so much that a single thin ray fell upon the vulture eye. And this I did for seven long nights—every night just at midnight—but I found the eye always closed; and so it was impossible to do the work; for it was not the old man who vexed me, but his Evil Eye.

And every morning, when the day broke, I went boldly into the chamber, and spoke courageously to him, calling him by name in a hearty tone, and inquiring how he had passed the night. So you see he would have been a very profound old man, indeed, to suspect that every night, just at twelve, I looked in upon him while he slept.

Upon the eighth night I was more than usually cautious in opening the door. A watch's minute hand moves more quickly than did mine. Never before that night had I felt the extent of my own powers—of my sagacity. I could scarcely contain my feelings of triumph. To think that there I was, opening the door, little by little, and he not even to dream of my secret deeds or thoughts. I fairly chuckled at the idea; and perhaps he heard me; for he moved on the bed suddenly, as if startled.

Now you may think that I drew back—but no. His room was as black as pitch with the thick darkness, (for the shutters were close fastened, through fear of robbers) and so I knew that he could not see the opening of the door, and I kept pushing it on steadily, steadily. I had my head in, and was about to open the lantern, when my thumb slipped upon the tin fastening, and the old man sprang up in bed, crying out—"Who's there?" I kept quite still and said nothing. For a whole hour I did not move a muscle, and in the meantime I did not hear him lie down. He was still sitting up in the bed listening;—just as I have done, night after night, hearkening to the death watches in the wall.

Presently I heard a slight groan, and I knew it was the groan of mortal terror. It was not a groan of pain or of grief—oh, no!—it was the low stifled sound that arises from the bottom of the soul when overcharged with awe. I knew the sound well. Many a night, just at midnight, when all the world slept, it has welled up from my own bosom, deepening, with its dreadful echo, the terrors that distracted me. I say I knew it well. I knew what the old man felt, and pitied him, although I chuckled at heart. I knew that he had been lying awake ever since the first slight noise, when he had turned in the bed. His fears had been ever since growing upon him. He had been trying to fancy them causeless, but could not. He had been saying to himself—"It is nothing but the wind in the chimney—it is only a mouse crossing the floor," or "It is merely a cricket which has made a single chirp." Yes, he had been trying to comfort himself with these suppositions: but he had found all in vain. All in vain; because Death, in approaching him had stalked with his black shadow before him, and enveloped the victim. And it was the mournful influence of the unperceived shadow that caused him to feel—although he neither saw nor heard—to feel the presence of my head within the room.

When I had waited a long time, very patiently, without hearing him lie down, I resolved to open a little—a very, very little crevice in the lantern. So I opened it—you cannot imagine how stealthily, stealthily—until, at length a simple dim ray, like the thread of the spider, shot from out the crevice and fell full upon the vulture eye.

It was open—wide, wide open—and I grew furious as I gazed upon it. I saw it with perfect distinctness—all a dull blue, with a hideous veil over it that chilled the very marrow in my bones; but I could see nothing else of the old man's face or person: for I had directed the ray as if by instinct, precisely upon the d— spot.

And have I not told you that what you mistake for madness is but over-acuteness of the sense?—now, I say, there came to my ears a low, dull, quick sound, such as a watch makes when enveloped in cotton. I knew that sound well, too. It was the beating of the old man's heart. It increased my fury, as the beating of a drum stimulates the soldier into courage.

But even yet I refrained and kept still. I scarcely breathed. I held the lantern motionless. I tried how steadily I could maintain the ray upon the eye. Meantime the hellish tattoo of the heart increased. It grew quicker and quicker, and louder and louder every instant. The old man's terror must have been extreme! It grew louder, I say, louder every moment!—do you mark me well I have told you that I am nervous: so I am. And now at the dead hour of the night, amid the dreadful silence of that old house, so strange a noise as this excited me to uncontrollable terror. Yet, for some minutes longer I refrained and stood still. But the beating grew louder, louder! I thought the heart must burst.

And now a new anxiety seized me—the sound would be heard by a neighbour! The old man's hour had come! With a loud yell, I threw open the lantern and leaped into the room. He shrieked once—once only. In an instant I dragged him to the floor, and pulled the heavy bed over him. I then smiled gaily, to find the deed so far done. But, for many minutes, the heart beat on with a muffled sound. This, however, did not vex me; it would not be heard through the wall. At length it ceased. The old man was dead. I removed the bed and examined the corpse. Yes, he was stone, stone dead. I placed my hand upon the heart and held it there many minutes. There was no pulsation.

He was stone dead. His eye would trouble me no more.

If still you think me mad, you will think so no longer when I describe the wise precautions I took for the concealment of the body. The night waned, and I worked hastily, but in silence. First of all I dismembered the corpse. I cut off the head and the arms and the legs.

I then took up three planks from the flooring of the chamber, and deposited all between the scantlings. I then replaced the boards so cleverly, so cunningly, that no human eye—not even his—could have detected any thing wrong. There was nothing to wash out—no stain of any kind—no blood-spot whatever. I had been too wary for that. A tub had caught all—ha! ha!

When I had made an end of these labors, it was four o'clock—still dark as midnight. As the bell sounded the hour, there came a knocking at the street door. I went down to open it with a light heart,—for what had I now to fear? There entered three men, who introduced themselves, with perfect suavity, as officers of the police. A shriek had been heard by a neighbour during the night; suspicion of foul play had been aroused; information had been lodged at the police office, and they (the officers) had been deputed to search the premises.

I smiled,—for what had I to fear? I bade the gentlemen welcome. The shriek, I said, was my own in a dream. The old man, I mentioned, was absent in the country. I took my visitors all over the house. I bade them search—search well. I led them, at length, to his chamber. I showed them his treasures, secure, undisturbed.

In the enthusiasm of my confidence, I brought chairs into the room, and desired them here to rest from their fatigues, while I myself, in the wild audacity of my perfect triumph, placed my own seat upon the very spot beneath which reposed the corpse of the victim.

The officers were satisfied. My manner had convinced them. I was singularly at ease. They sat, and while I answered cheerily, they chatted of familiar things.

But, ere long, I felt myself getting pale and wished them gone. My head ached, and I fancied a ringing in my ears: but still they sat and still chatted. The ringing became more distinct: — It continued and became more distinct: I talked more freely to get rid of the feeling: but it continued and gained definiteness — until, at length, I found that the noise was not within my ears.

No doubt I now grew very pale; — but I talked more fluently, and with a heightened voice. Yet the sound increased — and what could I do? It was a low, dull, quick sound — much such a sound as a watch makes when enveloped in cotton. I gasped for breath — and yet the officers heard it not. I talked more quickly — more vehemently; but the noise steadily increased. I arose and argued about trifles, in a high key and with violent gesticulations; but the noise steadily increased. Why would they not be gone? I paced the floor to and fro with heavy strides, as if excited to fury by the observations of the men — but the noise steadily increased. Oh God! what could I do? I foamed — I raved — I swore! I swung the chair upon which I had been sitting, and grated it upon the boards, but the noise arose over all and continually increased. It grew louder — louder — louder! And still the men chatted pleasantly, and smiled. Was it possible they heard not? Almighty God! — no, no! They heard! — they suspected! — they knew! — they were making a mockery of my horror! — this I thought, and this I think. But anything was better than this agony! Anything was more tolerable than this derision! I could bear those hypocritical smiles no longer! I felt that I must scream or die! and now — again! — hark! louder! louder! louder! louder!

"Villains!" I shrieked, "dissemble no more! I admit the deed! — tear up the planks! here, here! — It is the beating of his hideous heart!"

Review Questions
1. Why did the narrator want to kill the old man?
2. Why did the murderer hide the body? Where did he hide it?
3. How did he react to the arrival of the policemen? What was his explanation for the old man's dying shriek?
4. Did the policemen suspect him of the crime?
5. What convinced the murderer to confess?

Thought Questions
1. Why did the man want to convince readers of his sanity? Do you think he was sane?
2. How did the murderer hear a dead man's heartbeat? Was it real, or did he imagine it? Have you ever focused on something trivial that was irritating? Was it hard to stop?
3. Does everyone have a conscience? Do you think people are born with it, or is it learned?
4. Can guilt have a positive effect? Why does guilt become less powerful over time?
5. What is the effect of point of view in this story? Can you identify two places where point of view changes the impact of the story?

POINT OF VIEW

Writing Practice

Point of view is particularly important in mystery or suspense stories. A first person or single viewpoint story keeps the reader, as well as the character, in suspense about what is going to happen next. Third-person can imply that a story presents objective facts, when those "facts" are actually colored by the author's perspective. Alternately, a broader point of view may encourage the reader to identify with multiple characters and give a more complete picture of the situation.

Take a moment to compare the two stories you have just read. "The Tell-Tale Heart" is told in first person, allowing the narrator to personally make a case for his sanity. Would it be as effective if it were told in the third person? By contrast, "The Hammer of God" was written in third person. Would the solution to the mystery have been given away if it had been told in first person?

Take a look at the following paragraph. What point of view does it represent?

> Megan jogged down the stairs, her backpack thumping on her back. Boy will I be glad when school gets out, she thought. At the same time, she wouldn't see her friends very often during the summer. She frowned. They'd all be traveling, and she'd be stuck here. It's not fair, she thought grumpily. On another set of stairs at the other end of the building, her friend David was thinking the same thing. In fact, all over the school, her friends thought about the summer to come and wished things could be different. But Megan didn't know that, so she grumbled and scuffed her shoes on the cement as she went out to the car.

Now rewrite the paragraph in first person. What effect does the change have on the characters? What is the effect on the development of a plot? How might the rest of the story also change as a result?

What Does It Have To Do With Me?
MORAL APPLICATION

And the moral of the story is…

Using stories to make a point is an ancient device. Almost every story has some sort of moral lesson, whether it is obvious or subtle, and whether or not the author intended it to be there. The allegory, in which objects and characters stand in for something else (see "The Celestial Railroad" for an example of an allegory), is the most blatant use of stories for moral instruction. Other stories use this tool in subtler ways. Because very few people genuinely enjoy being "preached at," some of the most effective moral stories make their point clearly but allow the reader to make the final connection.

Remember when your parents wanted you to take piano or some other type of lessons? They pushed, cajoled, threatened, and bribed, so you sat at the piano and pressed the keys, but your heart wasn't in it. As a result, the tunes you played sounded flat and dull, and when your hour was up, you stopped, even in the middle of a song, and were out the door before the last note faded. Finally, your parents gave up, let you quit lessons, and closed the piano lid. Lo and behold, one day you had a sudden urge to play again. Of your own free will, you lifted the lid, sat down, and made music. And the music sounded ten times better than it had before.

The moral of this story is that when activities—and morals—are forced on you in a way that feels artificial and uncomfortable, your natural instinct is to push them away. Left to discover them on your own, you receive the training or message much more readily and to a much greater and longer-lasting effect. The same is true with respect to stories.

As you read the last few stories in this collection, think about their use of the story form for moral instruction. Pay particular attention to the following questions:

- What is the moral of the story?
- What is the author trying to reveal about human nature?
- What is the worldview of each of the characters?
- What do you think might be the author's worldview? What makes you think so?

Ask yourself what type of stories you enjoy reading, and which ones have taught you the most. When you write, keep these observations in mind.

"Stolen Fruit"
Saint Augustine

Artist's rendering of Augustine and Ethelbert as they meet under a tree at Canterbury Cathedral. Ethelbert reputedly later confessed Christ and was baptised.

Aurelius Augustine (354-430), later named Saint Augustine of Hippo, was a philosopher and bishop of the Catholic Church, as well as a respected writer and speaker. His philosophical works are notable because he made a great effort to integrate Christianity into the philosophical thought of his time. "Stolen Fruit" is an excerpt from Book 2, Chapters 4 and 6 of his master work *The Confessions of Saint Augustine*, a collection of personal reflections on his own sinful nature.

Chapter IV

Theft is punished by thy law, O Lord, and by the law written in men's hearts, which not even ingrained wickedness can erase. For what thief will tolerate another thief stealing from him? Even a rich thief will not tolerate a poor thief who is driven to theft by want. Yet I had a desire to commit robbery, and did so, compelled to it by neither hunger nor poverty, but through a contempt for well-doing and a strong impulse to iniquity. For I pilfered something which I already had in sufficient measure, and of much better quality. I did not desire to enjoy what I stole, but only the theft and the sin itself.

There was a pear tree close to our own vineyard, heavily laden with fruit, which was not tempting either for its color or for its flavor. Late one night—having prolonged our games in the streets until then, as our bad habit was—a group of young scoundrels, and I among them, went to shake and rob this tree. We carried off a huge load of pears, not to eat ourselves, but to dump out to the hogs, after barely tasting some of them ourselves. Doing this pleased us all the more because it was forbidden. Such was my heart, O God, such was my heart—which thou didst pity even in that bottomless pit. Behold, now let my heart confess to thee what it was seeking there, when I was being gratuitously wanton, having no inducement to evil but the evil itself. It was foul, and I loved it. I loved my own undoing. I loved my error—not that for which I erred but the error itself. A depraved soul, falling away from security in thee to destruction in itself, seeking nothing from the shameful deed but shame itself.

Chapter VI

What was it in you, O theft of mine, that I, poor wretch, doted on—you deed of darkness—in that sixteenth year of my age? Beautiful you were not, for you were a theft. But are you anything at all, so that I could analyze the case with you? Those pears that we stole were fair to the sight because they were thy creation, O Beauty beyond compare, O Creator of all, O thou good God—God the highest good and my true good. Those pears were truly pleasant to the sight, but it was not for them that my miserable soul lusted, for I had an abundance of better pears. I stole those simply that I might steal, for, having stolen them, I threw them away. My sole gratification in them was my own sin, which I was pleased to enjoy; for, if any one of these pears entered my mouth, the only good flavor it had was my sin in eating it. And now, O Lord my God, I ask what it was in that theft of mine that caused me such delight; for behold it had no beauty of its own—certainly not the sort of beauty that exists in justice and wisdom, nor such as is in the mind, memory senses, and the animal life of man; nor yet the kind that is the glory and beauty of the stars in their courses; nor the beauty of the earth, or the sea—teeming with spawning life, replacing in birth that which dies and decays. Indeed, it did not have that false and shadowy beauty which attends the deceptions of vice.

Thus the soul commits fornication when she is turned from thee, and seeks apart from thee what she cannot find pure and untainted until she returns to thee. All things thus imitate thee—but pervertedly—when they separate themselves far from thee and raise themselves up against thee. But, even in this act of perverse imitation, they acknowledge thee to be the Creator of all nature, and recognize that there is no place whither they can altogether separate themselves from thee. What was it, then, that I loved in that theft? And wherein was I imitating my Lord, even in a corrupted and perverted way? Did I wish, if only by gesture, to rebel against thy law, even though I had no power to do so actually—so that, even as a captive, I might produce a sort of counterfeit liberty, by doing with impunity deeds that were forbidden, in a deluded sense of omnipotence? Behold this servant of thine, fleeing from his Lord and following a shadow! O rottenness! O monstrousness of life and abyss of death! Could I find pleasure only in what was unlawful, and only because it was unlawful?

Review Questions
1. Why did Augustine steal the pears? Did he need them?
2. What did the boys do with the pears that they had stolen?
3. How old was Augustine when he committed this act?
4. What did Augustine call his "sole gratification"?
5. Augustine asked, "Could I find pleasure only in what was unlawful, and only because it was unlawful?" What does this comment mean?

Thought Questions
1. What motivates people to steal? If poverty is the reason, then why do people with plenty of money steal?
2. Augustine addresses his theft as if it were a person. Why do you think he uses this technique? What is the effect?
3. Do you ever have a desire to do wrong just because the opportunity arises? Why do you think humans enjoy sin? Is it possible to change that desire? If so, how?
4. What discourages you from acting on harmful desires? Threats of punishment? Your conscience? Does making something illegal make people more or less likely to do it? Explain.
5. What is the moral of this story? Does Augustine state it explicitly?

"Alypius and the Gladiators"
Saint Augustine

Another excerpt from Augustine's *Confessions*, "Alypius and the Gladiators" (from Book 6, Chapter 8) is about a young man who, in Rome with his friends, succumbed to peer pressure and the bloodlust of the Roman Circus.

He had gone on to Rome before me to study law—which was the worldly way which his parents were forever urging him to pursue—and there he was carried away again with an incredible passion for the gladiatorial shows. For, although he had been utterly opposed to such spectacles and detested them, one day he met by chance a company of his acquaintances and fellow students returning from dinner; and, with a friendly violence, they drew him, resisting and objecting vehemently, into the amphitheater, on a day of those cruel and murderous shows. He protested to them:

"Though you drag my body to that place and set me down there, you cannot force me to give my mind or lend my eyes to these shows. Thus I will be absent while present, and so overcome both you and them."

When they heard this, they dragged him on in, probably interested to see whether he could do as he said. When they got to the arena, and had taken what seats they could get, the whole place became a tumult of inhuman frenzy. But Alypius kept his eyes closed and forbade his mind to roam abroad after such wickedness. Would that he had shut his ears also! For when one of the combatants fell in the fight, a mighty cry from the whole audience stirred him so strongly that, overcome by curiosity and still prepared (as he thought) to despise and rise superior to it no matter what it was, he opened his eyes and was struck with a deeper wound in his soul than the victim whom he desired to see had been in his body. Thus he fell more miserably than the one whose fall had raised that mighty clamor which had entered through his ears and unlocked his eyes to make way for the wounding and beating down of his soul, which was more audacious than truly valiant—also it was weaker because it presumed on its own strength when it ought to have depended on Thee.

For, as soon as he saw the blood, he drank in with it a savage temper, and he did not turn away, but fixed his eyes on the bloody pastime, unwittingly drinking in the madness—delighted with the wicked contest and drunk with blood lust. He was now no longer the same man who came in, but was one of the mob he came into, a true companion of those who had brought him thither. Why need I say more? He looked, he shouted, he was excited, and he took away with him the madness that would stimulate him to come again: not only with those who first enticed him, but even without them; indeed, dragging in others besides. And yet from all this, with a most powerful and most merciful hand, thou didst pluck him and taught him not to rest his confidence in himself but in Thee—but not till long after.

Review Questions
1. Why did Alypius go to Rome? Under pressure from whom?
2. How did he end up at the gladiatorial contests?
3. Explain Alypius' statement: "Thus I will be absent while present, and so overcome both you and them."
4. What made him open his eyes at the Circus?
5. How was he changed after he saw the dying gladiator?

Thought Questions
1. Alypius was convinced to go to the gladiatorial contests by peer pressure—very literal pressure! Are you influenced by the choices of your peers? How much influence do you have over them? Do you use your influence wisely?
2. Think of the most violent movie, television program, or video game you have experienced. Do you remember how you reacted the first time you saw it? If you saw it a second time, was your reaction different?
3. Is it possible to expose yourself to violent media without becoming desensitized to it? How do you decide how much violence is too much?
4. Are people today any more civilized than men were during the time of the Roman Empire?
5. What is the moral of this story? How do you know? Is it subtle? Is it effective? Do you think morals have to be subtle to be effective?

MORAL APPLICATION

Writing Practice

Earlier in this collection, you read about finding the themes in literature; now you have added morals to that conversation. Although the two are closely linked, themes are the general topics that a story discusses, while morals, on the other hand, are the story's specific lessons or messages about that theme.

For example, revenge could be the general theme of a story, but the outcome of the story could suggest that revenge is noble and good or that it is cowardly and bad. Remember: not all morals are deliberately implanted by the author; it's a good reminder that your worldview almost always shows up in what you produce. To quote a 1940s book by American philosopher Richard Weaver, "Ideas have consequences."

Now it's your turn. Name a story from this collection or elsewhere that contains each of the morals listed below.

Pride goes before a fall.

Sin will always be discovered.

God is always with us.

It is better to give than to receive.

Don't judge based out outward appearances.

(Outside resources are optional for this exercise. At least one story in this anthology contains each of the morals listed.) If one of the stories you choose has a clearly stated moral, see if you can identify its other, unspoken morals.

Looking Back, Looking Forward

Congratulations! You have now worked your way through twenty-two classic short stories and selections of literature. Along the way, you've assembled a variety of reading and thinking tools that will be valuable in future reading and writing experiences. So, you may be thinking, what now?

The Next Step

Almost every author says the key to good writing is lots and lots of reading. If you can analyze the elements of a story and pay attention to the details of the writing, you will be better prepared to critique longer works of literature with insight and wisdom, and you will be well on your way to writing not only your own stories, but also excellent essays for high school and college.

For students in the sixth-to-ninth grade, or for learners of any age who are ready to ask questions and think analytically about literature, a great resource for general study is *Teaching the Classics*, from The Center for Literary Education. *Teaching the Classics* guides you through a list of questions in the Socratic style that can be applied to any story, as well as a basic five-part structure for understanding works of literature.

Another resource to consider is the next book in the *Words Aptly Spoken* series, *Words Aptly Spoken: American Literature*. In this guide, you will ask similar questions about the content and style of each novel. You will practice good reading habits, and then, taking what you've learned, practice explaining your ideas in essay form. Some people find creative writing to be natural and effortless, while writing in a formal, academic style is cause for panic. The step-by-step approach in this book will allow you to develop a new set of writing skills in an engaging, nonthreatening way.

Both of these books build on the skills you've begun to hone and will help you continue your journey through the world of literature.

Perspectives, Take Two

In today's society, mass media has an enormous impact on the way people view the world. Every day a million and one ideas compete for your attention. Most messages are designed to be absorbed passively and accepted without questioning. If nothing else, this book encourages you to practice reading (and, by default, listening and watching) with your brain fully engaged. If you can do this, you will be better prepared to distinguish between that which is merely enjoyable and that which is worthy of application to your own life.

In closing, as you continue this journey, it is worth repeating that participating in the great conversations of literature is an art that takes a lifetime to refine. However, it is an art that will yield a lifetime of fruit as you celebrate with family and friends the joy of laughing, crying, and simply bubbling over with excitement about the great stories which are now yours to share.

Best wishes on your journey!

Bibliography

Stories in order of appearance:

"A Man and the Snake," by Ambrose Bierce. First published in 1891 in the collection *Tales of Soldiers and Civilians*, also called *In the Midst of Life*.

"The Notorious Jumping Frog of Calaveras County," by Mark Twain. First published on November 18, 1865 in the *New York Saturday Press*, New York.

"The Cop and the Anthem," by O. Henry. First published on December 4, 1904 in *The World*, New York. Published in 1906 in the collection *The Four Million*.

"Little Girls Wiser than Men," by Leo Tolstoy. First published in 1885. First translated into English in 1907 by Louise and Aylmer Maude in the collection *Twenty-Three Tales by Tolstoy*.

"The Mansion," by Henry Van Dyke. First published in October 1911.

"The Hiltons' Holiday," by Sarah Orne Jewett. First published in September 1893 in *Century Magazine*, New York. Published in 1895 in the collection *The Life of Nancy*.

"The Schoolboy's Story," by Charles Dickens. First published in 1853 in "Another Round of Stories by the Christmas Fire," Household Words, London.

"The Celestial Railroad," by Nathaniel Hawthorne. First published in 1843 in the collection *Mosses from an Old Manse*.

"The Necklace," by Henri Guy de Maupassant. First published on February 17, 1884 as "La Parure" in *Le Gaulois*. Published in 1885 in the collection *Tales of Day and Night* (*Contes du jour et de la nuit*). First translated into English in 1888 by Jonathan Sturges in the collection *The Odd Number*.

"God Lives" (also translated "God Can Never Die"), by Hans Christian Andersen. First published in 1836 as *"Den gamle Gud lever endnu."* Translated into English in 1949 by Jean Hersholt.

"The Teapot," by Hans Christian Andersen. First published in December 1863 as "Theepotten" in *Folkekalender for Danmark*. Published on December 12, 1871 in the collection *Fairy Tales and Stories*. Fourth Volume (Eventyr og Historier. Fjerde Bind). First translated into English in 1872 by H.P. Paull.

"Father Zossima's brother," by Fyodor Dostoevsky. From *The Brothers Karamazov*. First published in 1880. First translated into English in 1912 by Constance Garnett.

"The Startling Painting," by Fyodor Dostoevsky. From *The Idiot*. First published in 1869. First translated into English in 1887 by Frederick Whishaw.

"The Casket Scenes," by William Shakespeare. From *The Merchant of Venice*. First performance recorded in 1605. First published in 1600 in quarto by Thomas Hayes.

"Iago's Intentions," by William Shakespeare. From *Othello*. First performance recorded on November 1, 1604 at Whitehall Palace, London. First published in 1622 in quarto by Thomas Walkly.

"The Pardoner's Tale," by Geoffrey Chaucer. From *The Canterbury Tales*. Manuscript finished in 1390s, incomplete. First printed in 1476 by William Caxton.

Paradise Lost, Book 1, by John Milton. First published in 1667 (10-book form). Published again in 1674 (12-book form).

"Christmas Bells," by Henry Wadsworth Longfellow. First published in 1864.

"The Hammer of God," by G.K. Chesterton. First published in 1911 in the collection *The Innocence of Father Brown*.

"The Tell-Tale Heart," by Edgar Allan Poe. First published in January 1843, in *The Pioneer*, Boston.

"Stolen Fruit" and "Alypius and the Gladiators," by Augustine. From *The Confessions of Saint Augustine*. First published circa 397-401. First translated into English in 1620 by Sir Tobie Matthew. Translated again in 1631 by William Watts.

Photo and Image Credits

All images in this book are reproduced with permission. The reproduction number is included in Library of Congress selections.

PAGE 15
Ambrose Bierce, Library of Congress, LC-USZ62-20182

PAGE 21
Mark Twain, Library of Congress, LC-USZ62-112065

PAGE 35
Count Leo Tolstoy, Library of Congress, LC-USZ62-128302

PAGE 41
Henry van Dyke, Library of Congress, LC-USZ62-128302

PAGE 73
Charles Dickens at his study at Gadshill, Library of Congress, LC-USZ62-117829

PAGE 85
Nathaniel Hawthorne, Library of Congress, LC-USZ62-2358

PAGE 107
Hans Christian Andersen, Library of Congress, LC-USZ62-43573

PAGE 121
William Shakespeare, Library of Congress, LC-USZ61-2145

PAGES 142-144
North Reading Room, west wall. Mural by Ezra Winter illustrating the characters in the Canterbury Tales by Geoffrey Chaucer. Library of Congress John Adams Building, Washington, D.C. LC-DIG-highsm-03162

PAGE 175
Longfellow, Library of Congress, LC-USZ62-15635

PAGE 193
Edgar Allen Poe, Library of Congress, LC-USZ62-136223

PAGE 203
Saint Augustine Statue, used under the Creative Commons Attribution 2.0 Generic license; author griannan. http://commons.wikimedia.org/wiki/File:Saint_Augustine_Statue.jpg

Additional products from  **Classical Conversations® MULTIMEDIA**

Words Aptly Spoken

Collect all five books in the *Words Aptly Spoken* series for a complete study complement to your literature library.

Classical Acts and Facts Science Cards

Classical Conversations' exclusive series of science acts and facts, arranged into four sets according to major science categories, will serve you and your family throughout your educational journey. These high-quality, laminated, 5″ x 8″ cards contain a comprehensive set of grammar pegs that relate to Foundations memory work all the way through our Challenge program's sciences. Over 120 unique acts and facts in all!

Please visit our online bookstore at www.ClassicalConversationsBooks.com to find these and other great homeschool resources.

Transcript Services

Beginning in the ninth grade, parents must keep a record of students' classes and grades in a permanent high school transcript. Transcripts are necessary for high school diploma, college entrance, and college scholarship applications.

Classical Conversations can help! For a modest annual fee, our transcript service, AcademicRecords.net, provides transcripts, medical records, and resume information in a professionally-formatted report that you can print for your records or e-mail to appropriate college admissions or scholarship providers.

Please visit www.AcademicRecords.net to sign up.

To help organize your records...

Student Planner

The student planner provides a system to help parents instill a sense of schedule and discipline in their student's coursework. Begin using this in Foundations, and by the time students are in the upper Challenge levels, they will already have a system in place to help them organize the fuller course load, as well as an easy tool to compile transcript information. $15.99

Visit www.ClassicalConversationsBooks.com to purchase.

Testing Services

We believe that standardized testing is an important part of preparing our children for college entrance exams, whether your state mandates testing or not.

We take a very pragmatic attitude toward testing: the actual test's content is not as important as the skill of test taking. We have chosen to offer the Stanford Achievement Test because it helps students prepare for the SAT I and the ACT tests. Stanford tests also provide parents with reliable data for evaluating progress in language and math skills. The Stanford Achievement Test is a nationally norm-referenced test.

Visit www.HomeschoolTestingServices.com for hosted testing sites near you.

3-Day Parent Practicums

Classical Conversations Parent Practicums — Improving your Vision

Each year, from May to July, Classical Conversations sponsors FREE one- and three-day Parent Practicums across the U.S. Because parents are a child's first and best teachers, they are key to their children's academic success. Only Classical Conversations provides parents with the tools to help.

Knowing a topic well and being able to teach it aren't always the same thing. Also, people who truly love learning enjoy digging deeper and finding ways to share what they know with others.

Our Practicum materials are fun, innovative, and thought-provoking.

Plan to use your brain and laugh a lot! This is for parents and teachers of all grade levels desiring to practice teaching from a classical, Christian perspective.

Practicums are FREE, but space is limited, so registration is required. For information about Parent Practicums, visit the Equipping Events section of our website at www.ClassicalConversations.com. For dates and locations of Parent Practicums in your area, go to www.ClassicalConversations.com and click on the Event Calendar.

CC Connected

Get connected with families across the nation and the world with CC Connected. CC Connected offers:
- Classical Conversations program and curriculum resources.
- Ad-free, secure forums for discussion and ideas.
- Classical Conversations articles and audio podcasts.
- Equipping academic resources for parents and educators.
- Special tools and resources updated throughout the year.

Please see www.ClassicalConversations.com for more information!

To find a Classical Conversations community near you...

Visit www.ClassicalConversations.com and click on your state on the map!